Paul

C000101229

The Earth and Us

Henry Haslam

www.the-earth-and-us.co.uk

Published in 2018 by FeedARead.com Publishing

A CIP catalogue record for this title is available from the British Library.

Cover design by Tina Bone. The globe image is used with the permission of the artist Chris Althen and the book *Painting for Peace in Ferguson* where the image was first published (paintingforpeacebook.com). The book tells the story of the hundreds of artists and volunteers who transformed boarded-up windows into works of art with messages of hope, healing and unity in Ferguson, Missouri, following protests and community upheaval in November 2014.

For Anna, Adam, Ben, Joe, Alice, Luke, Kathryn, Olivia,
Sam, Cara and Joshua

Acknowledgements

The idea for this book came from Professor Jane Plant CBE, environmental scientist and author of the best-selling *Your Life in Your Hands* and other books on diet, lifestyle and health, who proposed that we should collaborate in writing a book on the environment. She made valuable comments on an early, partial draft, but her untimely death in 2016 meant that she was not able to see it through. The present book remains true to the message she wished to convey: the human population has done and continues to do serious damage to the environment; this is because there are too many of us and we consume too much; and there are no simple technofixes – it is human behaviour that must change. The eventual form of the book, however, is mine, widened to include greater emphasis on the human dimension. This is not the book that Jane would have written – she would have agreed with some aspects of it, disagreed with others – but without her initiative it would not have been started.

I am most grateful to Chris Althen and Carol Klein for permission to use the globe image on the front cover, and to Tina Bone for turning the image into a cover design.

I thank Mark Anderson, Anthea Barran, David Constable, Mary Constable, Thirle Dale-Thomas, Mike Haslam, Sylvia Haslam, Roger Montague, Adrian Smith, Julia Tester and Brenda Watson for reading the book in draft and making numerous helpful comments. I am also grateful to Peter Simpson for his encouragement and support. The opinions and errors, of course, are my own.

CONTENTS

Part 1
Human Behaviour and the Natural World

This is a book about how we interact with the planet we live on: about the impact that our lives have on nature and the natural world, how we think about it, and the potential we have to do things differently in the future.

Part 1 looks at the way we behave towards our natural environment: the risks we take with the planet (chapter 1) and the irresponsible way we conduct debates about serious issues, taking carbon emissions and climate change as an example (chapter 2). The cause of much of the environmental damage lies in the consumer society (chapter 3), exacerbated by overpopulation (chapter 4).

It is incomprehensible to many of us today that in the not-so-distant past, decent, law-abiding people saw nothing wrong with the death penalty for sheep-stealing, or deporting criminals to Australia, or buying and selling slaves. Perhaps in 50 years time our present cavalier treatment of the environment will seem just as incomprehensible.

Chapter 1
The Risks we Take with Our Planet

The evil that men do lives after them.

William Shakespeare[1]

We are surrounded today, in our towns and cities, in our villages and in the countryside, by reminders of the work and achievements of past generations: buildings of great beauty, both small and large – the whole pattern of our townscapes and landscapes. For so much of this we are indebted to our ancestors. We have a great deal to thank them for.

We may then ask what contribution we, in our generation, are making to the future. There are not many buildings that will delight the eye in a hundred years' time. Worse than that, we are using up the Earth's supply of non-renewable resources, we are destroying rainforests and other natural habitats, and we are polluting soil, groundwater, rivers, oceans and atmosphere with man-made substances and waste.

Humans make great demands of the Earth's resources. In the past, the Earth was generally able to support our activities, but with nearly 7.5 billion of us and our ever-increasing demands, we are exceeding the Earth's capacity for self-renewal. Thoughtlessly, we have made, and we continue to make, many changes to our planet that are irreversible on the scale of a few human lifespans.

How has this come about? How is it that our species has come to treat our planet in such a way? We like to think of ourselves as intelligent. Carl Linnaeus in 1758 gave us the name *Homo sapiens* (wise human), and we have borne this accolade with pride ever since. We should be able to work out what is best for ourselves. We should be able to think about and care about future generations. Why do we appear not to care? That is what we shall try to understand in this book, but first I shall summarise briefly the present situation. A great deal has been written in recent years about the impact of human activities on the Earth, and this chapter only attempts a brief overview.

8

The Earth's resources

A Zambian, whose country has based its economy for more than a century on the mines of the copper belt, said to the economist Paul Collier, 'When the copper has run out, what will our children say about us?'.[2]

What, indeed, will future generations say about us all, if they inherit an Earth in which valuable resources have been used up? Known resources of most minerals could be made to last a very long time – but only if they are carefully managed to avoid waste. Metals in discarded products can be recovered for reuse (see chapter 13), but this may not be possible for other minerals, such as specialist clays, that are valued for their physical properties rather than for the chemical elements of which they are composed.

Nor is it possible for phosphorus. This element is essential to plant growth, and high crop yields depend on phosphate fertiliser. Some of the phosphate is taken up by the crop, some may remain in the soil, and the rest is washed away. Thus it is too widely dispersed to be easily recovered for reuse, so supplies of phosphorus may prove to be a problem in the future – perhaps in as little as 50 to 100 years.[3] Guano, a particularly good source of phosphorus since it contains nitrogen and potassium too, has been mined with no thought for the future: Peruvian resources of 23 million tons in the mid-nineteenth century had been reduced to 20,000 tons by 1911.[4]

We may, eventually, have to recover this element, and other chemical elements, from very low-grade deposits or from the sea. Ocean water is currently used as a source of salt (sodium chloride) and also for magnesium and potassium salts. In the future, sea water might be regarded as a source of as many as 40 other minerals and metals which are present in smaller quantities (ranging between 0.000008 parts per million (ppm) for gold and 65 ppm for bromine).[5]

Groundwater

About 70 per cent of the water we use, globally, is for agriculture, 20 per cent is for domestic use and 10 per cent is used in industry. Most of the world's fresh water (68.9 per cent) is in the form of ice. Only 0.3 per cent is in liquid form

9

on the surface, in rivers, lakes and wetlands. The remaining 30.8 per cent is groundwater.[6]

In much of the world, groundwater is being extracted for agriculture, at a faster rate than can be replenished through rainfall.[7] In fact, half the world's population live in countries that are draining their aquifers.[8] Sooner or later, this leads to serious water shortage. In land areas far from the sea, this may mean that water has to be pumped in for very long distances and that agricultural land is taken out of production because of the cost of irrigation. In coastal areas, different problems arise where groundwater has been extracted for irrigation or other purposes and salt water flows in to replace it – as in the Indus delta and in various coastal regions in the USA. Another consequence is the compaction of the aquifer rocks, leading to subsidence and consequent risk of flooding. Decades of groundwater extraction in Tokyo caused the city to subside by as much as two metres before extraction was stopped.[9] In Venice, too, subsidence due to groundwater extraction ceased when extraction ceased – but the compaction is permanent.[10]

Fossil fuels
Coal, petroleum and natural gas are non-renewable resources. Fossil fuels, once burnt, are gone for ever. Although known reserves are large, by today's standards, and there may be large quantities yet to be discovered, supplies are not limitless. It is irresponsible to destroy vast quantities of a non-renewable resource. There are other ways of generating energy that are cleaner, less polluting and sustainable (see chapter 13) – and this is before we consider the effect on the climate of releasing large quantities of carbon dioxide (CO_2), a greenhouse gas, when we burn fossil fuels; we shall consider this in the next chapter.

Peat
Peat is formed from decaying plant remains in acidic, boggy ground. It is a significant store for carbon and its loss releases CO_2 into the atmosphere. Peatlands cover about 3 per cent of the world's land area and contain 30 per cent of its soil carbon – about twice the quantity of carbon stored in all the world's forests. Peat can be lost by oxidation as a consequence of burning, draining, ploughing or extraction for use by local

people as a fuel or by gardeners as a growing medium – accounting for 8 per cent of all global anthropogenic carbon emissions.[11]

Exporting the problem

The UK imports large amounts of agricultural produce and manufactured goods. The environmental cost of producing these is met by the exporting country – enabling the UK to show a misleadingly favourable balance sheet. For example, the average UK resident uses 150 litres of water a day, which is comfortably supplied by our reasonably reliable rainfall. In addition, though, each of us consumes, on average, 30 times as much virtual water – water that has been used in the production of food and textiles that we import. Some of the big exporting countries, like Spain, Egypt, Morocco and Kenya, are facing acute water stress. We are importing water without paying for it – or, to put it another way exporting drought and water shortage.[12]

Natural habitats

Woodland and forest

Most of Britain's natural woodland, re-established after the glacial retreat of about ten thousand years ago, was cut down in the millennia that followed to make way for pasture and cultivation. Only 2 per cent of the land area of the UK is now covered by ancient woodland – and even this woodland, as we see it today, is the product of centuries of management. The survival of this small but valuable part of our heritage has constantly been under threat to make way for development. The idea that it could be replaced by planting trees elsewhere fails to take account of the time it takes for the full flora and fauna of a natural forest to develop; indeed, some of the organisms that make up the species balance in ancient woodland may never appear if the newly planted wood is isolated from old, established forest. For this reason the recent government proposal that this part of our heritage should enjoy a higher level of protection than hitherto is very much to be welcomed.[13]

In other countries, particularly in the tropics, vast areas of natural forest remain but are being destroyed to make land available for agriculture to feed the planet's burgeoning population and to satisfy world markets for timber, felled unsustainably from the forests.

Soil

Soil takes years to form: hundreds, thousands, maybe tens of thousands of years. It is formed by the physical and chemical breakdown of the underlying bedrock, aided by the action of plants and the decomposition of plant remains. Proportions vary hugely, but a typical soil might contain 45 per cent partially weathered rock, 25 per cent air, 25 per cent water and 5 per cent organic material; bacteria, earthworms and other organisms have a role in the decomposition of mineral and organic matter.[14] It is estimated that more carbon is stored in UK soils than in all the trees in the forests of Europe.[15]

Both our food supply and the natural fauna and flora of the earth depend on this valuable resource. We should care for it. When undisturbed by human intervention, plants and animals die where they have lived, returning organic matter, trace elements and nutrients to the soil. When they are taken away for human consumption or other use, the soil is depleted of carbon, trace elements and other nutrients. Moreover, deforestation, overgrazing, ploughing and other agricultural practices leave topsoils vulnerable to oxidation and erosion. In more than half the land area of the world, soils are a cause for concern.[16] The UK is losing 2.2 million tonnes of crucial topsoil each year, which costs the economy some £1.2 billion.[17] Globally, more than 25 billion tons are lost every year through the action of wind and rain.[18] The USA has lost about a third of its topsoil in the years since settled agriculture began. A Wisconsin farmer, expressing his satisfaction with the farm he had built up, was quoted seventy years ago: 'It's cost me seventeen years of sweat and hard work – and six inches of topsoil'.[19] In western Tennessee, six inches of topsoil loss has reduced maize yields by 42 per cent, and such relationships are not uncommon.[20]

The low rainfall and limited vegetation of semi-arid terrain allow only poor-quality soils to develop, low in water and organic matter. Undisturbed by human interference, these dry soils may be able to survive periods of drought, but they are particularly vulnerable to erosion and are readily lost when the plants that give them strength are destroyed by overgrazing or felling, or the soils themselves are disturbed by cultivation. Large areas of dry land that are suffering such degradation or are susceptible to it are seen today in the USA, Africa, Australia and much of Asia.[21]

Marine ecosystems
Large-scale commercial fishing has seriously depleted fish stocks, and modern industrial techniques cause lasting damage to the sea bed.

Biodiversity

There is nothing unusual about change. There has always been change in the natural world. We should be cautious in attributing a specific change to human influence, when there are natural changes taking place at at same time as human-induced changes.

Likewise, there is nothing unusual about extinction. It is thought that more than 99 per cent of all the species that have ever existed on Earth have become extinct. However, the rate of species loss has increased immensely since humans came to dominate so much of the planet. It is estimated that between 100 and 1000 species in every million are currently wiped out every year,[22] up to a thousand times faster than would be expected without human intervention. The International Union for the Conservation of Nature estimates that, as of 2013, 25 per cent of the Earth's mammals, 13 per cent of birds, 41 per cent of amphibians and 33 per cent of reef-building corals are at risk of extinction.[23] Insects and other inconspicuous species in complicated ecosystems may be lost or severely reduced in number without our even noticing – and with drastic consequences in a complicated ecosystem.

Sometimes the reasons behind population loss or extinction are well understood, sometimes not. Some examples of extinction or decline can be clearly correlated with human activity; others less obviously so. Some species we have hunted or eaten to extinction or scarcity. Many others have been lost through thoughtless destruction of their habitat, by the introduction of alien species that crowd out or attack native species, or by the pollution of rivers and lakes.[24] Often, it is a combination of these causes that leads to extinction. We may be destroying insect populations, for example, without knowing why – and perhaps without even realising what is happening. Insects can be important as pollinators, as food for vertebrates or as predators on other organisms; their loss from an ecosystem may have unforeseen consequences. It is sometimes suggested, for example, that the use of a class of insecticide known as neonicotinoids is responsible for a decline in honey-bee and bumblebee populations. Others say that the cause is a virus. Others that it is the disappearance of the diversity of plant life associated with natural ecosystems and small-scale traditional farming to make way for monoculture. About 75 per cent of native British plants require insects as pollinators, including some 60 per cent of our trees.[25] Wheat, barley and maize are pollinated by the wind, but animal-pollinated crops occupy about 20 per cent of the UK's cropland.[26]

Much of the killing was long ago. Large animals in Africa established a *modus vivendi* with early humans, but in every other continent the varied fauna of large animals was exterminated soon after the arrival of the first humans. In the seas, the worst of the slaughter of large vertebrates was in the eighteenth and nineteenth centuries, when the killing of whales and other animals vastly reduced their numbers.

The preservation of the great diversity of life forms is vital for its own sake, but there are financial implications as well. Some 27 per cent of the heads of global companies say that loss of natural diversity could adversely affect their businesses, and 25–30 per cent of the pharmaceutical market is based on natural genetic diversity.[27]

Today we keep lists of endangered species and monitor their well-being. Many species survive, and even flourish, as a result of conservation measures. Some have been taken off the endangered list.[28] Many are still threatened, however: it is still a battle to save elephants and rhinoceroses from being massacred by poachers for the value of their tusks and horns, and overfishing has severely reduced the stocks of blue-fin tuna. Both species of orang utan, Bornean and Sumatran, are classed as critically endangered because of the destruction of their habitat; the rainforests of these vast and underpopulated

14

islands are being felled to grow crops to satisfy world markets. These are just a few of the examples that we know about: how many more species, many of them small and inconspicuous, are being driven to extinction before we even learn of their existence?

Meanwhile, there has been a population explosion of humans and their domesticated animals. Ten thousand years ago, wild animals made up 99 per cent of the biomass of land and air vertebrates; now the equivalent figure is 4 per cent, the rest being humans and their animals.[29]

Most of the mammals and birds that we eat are farmed, but many of the fish are wild. Global capture today is nearly four times what it was in 1950, and many fish stocks are overexploited.[30]

Pollution

Our lives have been improved immeasurably by man-made chemicals developed, particularly, over the last hundred years, but there have been numerous occasions when their release into the environment has caused unforeseen damage to human health or to natural ecosystems. Human activity has also caused the release of natural materials, which have become a risk to human health. Substances, natural and man-made, that give cause for concern include trace elements (including radioactive elements), industrial chemicals, agricultural chemicals, pharmaceuticals, airborne particles and nanomaterials. An understanding of the sources, environmental pathways and hazards associated with such substances, as presented by Jane Plant and her colleagues in *Pollutants, Human Health and the Environment*,[31] can provide a scientific basis for regulating and controlling the manufacture and release of these and new materials in the future.

The atmosphere
The air doesn't respect political boundaries. Some pollutants might only disperse for short distances; others spread to neighbouring countries and all round the world.

Air pollution (including microscopic particles, nitrogen oxides, carbon monoxide and ozone) is a major cause of ill-health, increasing the risk of stroke, heart disease, lung cancer and respiratory diseases, including asthma, making it one of the world's biggest killers, accounting for one in ten deaths each year – 6.5 million people. The main sources of pollutants are forest fires, coal-fired power stations, factories, fuel burnt in homes for cooking and heating, vehicle exhausts, and gases released from fertilisers and animal waste.[32] Diesel engines have been used in road vehicles for many years, and their use was recently encouraged because their CO_2 emissions are lower than petrol engines. It is now realised, however, that the nitrogen oxides and particulates (microscopic particles) that they emit are a serious health hazard.

The ozone layer in the upper atmosphere has a vital function in protecting terrestrial life from ultraviolet radiation. From 1979 it became apparent that this layer was becoming depleted, particularly around the polar regions. This was attributed to the release of CFCs (chlorinated fluorocarbons), which were widely used in refrigerators and other equipment. The possible consequences were so great that the international community came together to agree the Montreal Protocol in 1987 – a remarkable example of international cooperation in the face of a global threat. The signatory states accepted a series of stepped limits on the production and use of CFCs, and the atmospheric levels of the most important chemicals have, since then, levelled off or decreased.

Carbon dioxide levels in the atmosphere during the last 200,000 years remained in the range 160–280 parts per million by volume until the industrial revolution. Since then, they have risen to 400 ppm, principally due to the burning of fossil fuels, and it is predicted that this may rise to 500 ppm by the end of the twenty-first century if recent trends continue. Increased levels of CO_2 in the atmosphere increase the retention of heat, bringing about changes in the Earth's climate (the so-called 'greenhouse effect'; see chapter 2).

Methane, which is 25 times as potent a greenhouse gas as CO_2 (although it breaks down much more rapidly in the atmosphere, with a half-life of 25 years), is responsible for 17 per cent of global warming. Concentrations in the atmosphere have risen from less than 800 ppb in pre-industrial times to nearly 1800 ppb today. It is estimated that nearly three quarters of emissions are from anthropogenic sources.[33]

The production of nitrogen fertilisers by the Haber-Bosch process emits millions of tons of CO_2, and their agricultural use releases nitrous oxide, a greenhouse gas 300 times more potent than CO_2, into the atmosphere:[34] levels have risen from 270 parts per billion in pre-industrial times to 319 ppb in 2005.[35]

Soil, groundwater, surface water, plants and animals
Persistent organic pollutants (POPs) are manufactured chemicals that do not break down readily. Some are used in industry or the household, after which they are released into the environment; others are used in agriculture, which means that they are introduced in larger quantities into the environment. Vast numbers of synthetic compounds have been released without a thought for what impact they may have.[36] In China, for example, a 2006–2011 soil survey found that 20 per cent of China's farmland contains pollutants in excess of permitted levels.[37] I shall just give a few examples of the consequences of pollution.

Populations of the bald eagle, the USA's national bird, were severely reduced during the twentieth century throughout much of North America by DDT, because of the way that such chemicals are concentrated up the food chain. DDT may be present at a concentration of 0.000003 ppm in rivers and lakes, but this becomes concentrated in plankton, which absorb the chemical with their food. It is further concentrated in small fish that feed off plankton, in large fish that eat the small fish and in fish-eating birds and other top predators, in which it may reach concentrations (25 ppm) sufficient to wipe out whole populations. In the case of the bald eagle, the bird's calcium metabolism was affected: their eggshells were too brittle to stand the weight of the adult bird and, as a consequence, no chicks hatched. Populations have recovered since the banning of DDT.

The cause of decline in vulture populations in India was different. This has been attributed to diclofenac, a non-steroidal anti-inflammatory drug (NSAID) administered to the livestock on which the vultures feed. The scarcity of vultures has led to the proliferation of other scavengers (dogs and rats) and the spread of disease.[38]

Nitrogen fertilisers increase crop yields enormously: world food production in 1990 was nearly three times that in 1950, whereas the area of farmland only increased by 10 per cent.[39] The amount of terrestrial nitrogen deposited by humans has more than doubled since pre-industrial times.[40] Fertilisers are applied in quantities that exceed what can be taken up by the crops, and the excess causes ecological changes over the land, river courses, groundwater and oceans. On land, fertilisers promote sturdy plants that flourish in nutrient-rich environments, leading to the loss of other, weaker species. In groundwater they contaminate drinking water; young infants are particularly susceptible to levels of nitrate in food and water above legally acceptable levels.[41] In watercourses they stimulate the growth of algae, leading to oxygen depletion and the loss of fish and other animals. Agricultural run-off is a major contributor to the eutrophication of fresh-water bodies.

Oceans

The oceans contain 1.338 billion cubic kilometres of water. We might think that that's enough water to be able to absorb all the rubbish we throw into it, but human activities have had a huge impact on these vast expanses. Rivers polluted with fertilisers and other chemicals, sewage and animal waste pour into the oceans, giving rise to large oxygen-depleted zones, inimical to animal life. There are said to be 405 dead zones in coastal waters.[42]

Plastics

A total of 8.3 billion tonnes of plastic has been manufactured worldwide since 1950, of which 6.3 billion tonnes is waste; 9 per cent of this waste has been recycled and 12 per cent incinerated; the rest is buried in landfill sites or finds its way into the oceans.[43] In Britain alone, more than 13 billion single-use plastic bottles are sold in a year – an average of 200 per person; only 57 per cent are recycled.[44] Most plastic products have a very short useful life – perhaps used just once as containers or packaging – but they take hundreds of years to degrade. Unless it is buried underground, much of this plastic will eventually find its way to the oceans, where it makes up 90 per cent of all floating litter and presents a hazard to wildlife. Some creatures mistake bits of plastic for food; others become entangled by discarded fishing nets. In parts of the North Pacific there are 1 million pieces of rubbish per square kilometre.[45] Just ten rivers are responsible for 90 per cent of the plastic that enters the sea: the Niger and Nile draining Africa; and the Amur, Ganges, Haihe, Indus, Mekong, Pearl, Yellow and Yangtze draining Asia.[46]

Microbeads have been in the news in recent years.[47] These tiny beads, made of plastics that take a long time to degrade, are contained in various personal-care products which are washed into the drainage system after use. Larger particles enter sewage sludge which is spread onto farmland, but the smaller beads are washed out to sea where they are ingested by wildlife. Similar problems arise with polyester fleeces and other synthetic clothes, which lose thousands of tiny fibres every time they are washed.

We have known for years about the damage done by plastics. At last, government and industry seem to be starting to do something about the problem, and the 2017 'Blue Planet II' BBC television series presented by David Attenborough has helped to increase public awareness – but why has it taken so long? Why did we introduce microbeads in the first place? Did we just close our minds to it? What other risks are we closing our minds to today?

Controlling the manufacture and release into the environment of new chemicals and materials

Much has been done at national and international levels to control and regulate the manufacture, use and disposal of chemicals. The EU's 2007 REACH (Registration, Evaluation, Authorisation and restriction of Chemicals) legislation places the burden of proof on manufacturers to provide evidence of the safety of their products before placing them on the market. Nevertheless, there are countless chemicals still being released into the environment that have never been properly assessed for their environmental impact. There are concerns, too, about the unknown effects of mixtures of chemicals, 'chemical cocktails'.[48]

The possible consequences of releasing man-made substances into the environment are so diverse that we cannot expect that they will all be foreseen and made the subject of appropriate regulation and legislation.

Ignorance

When Rudolf Diesel in the 1890s and others in the twentieth century developed the diesel engine and used it to power road vehicles, they had no idea of the health hazards from the exhaust fumes. These hazards were not even recognised when, for the past fifteen years, there have been tax incentives to encourage motorists to buy diesel vehicles, rather than petrol models, because of the lower CO_2 emissions.

When Paul Müller discovered the insecticidal properties of DDT in 1939, for which he was awarded the Nobel Prize in Physiology or Medicine, he had no idea of the harmful effect this chemical could have on birds of prey.

When, in the 1920s and 1930s, Thomas Midgley of General Motors Corporation developed a process to manufacture CFCs for use in refrigerators, he – and the corporation – had no idea of the damaging effect these chemicals could have in the upper atmosphere and thence on terrestrial life.[49]

When Alfred Sallmann and Rudolf Pfister synthesised diclofenac in 1973, it was no doubt tested on mammals before it was approved to be prescribed for humans, but it was not tested on Indian vultures.

When manufacturers introduced microbeads into personal care products, they did not think (though perhaps they should have done) of the consequences for wildlife.

It may be doubted whether even the most rigorous legislation and testing would have identified the threats to human and animal health of the release of these substances. We have no idea what damage is being done by the countless man-made substances that we continue to release, thoughtlessly, into the environment.

The one thing we do know is that we are conducting a gigantic experiment with this precious and fragile planet of ours, with little idea what the consequences will be.

Notes

1. Shakespeare, William, *Julius Caesar*, III, ii
2. Collier, Paul, *The Plundered Planet*, Penguin, 2011, 32
3. Cordell, D, Drangert, J-O, White, S, 2009. The story of phosphorus: Global food security and food for thought. *Global Environmental Change*, 19, 292–305
4. Vogt, William, *Road to Survival*, William Sloane Associates, 1948, 36

5. www.miningweekly.com/article/over-40-minerals-and-metals-contained-in-seawater-their-extraction-likely-to-increase-in-the-future-2016-04-01
6. Juniper, Tony, 2016, *What's really happening to our planet?*, Dorling Kindersley, 78
7. Juniper, 2016, 77,79
8. Wilson, Edward O, 2016, *Half-Earth: Our Planet's Fight for Life*, Liveright, 171
9. www.bbc.co.uk/news/science-environment-27202192
10. Montgomery, Carla W, 1997, *Environmental Geology*, McGraw-Hill, 5th edition, 231
11. Juniper, Tony, 2015, *What Nature Does for Britain*, Profile, 147,159
12. Porritt, Jonathon, 2009, Do the Maths, *Wem*, 14(3), March 2009, 5,6
13. *Fixing our broken housing market*, UK Government White Paper, February 2017
14. Juniper, Tony, 2013, *What has nature ever done for us?*, Profile, 30
15. Juniper 2013, 32
16. Montgomery, 1997
17. Pow, Rebecca, *Hansard*, 17 November 2016
18. Juniper, 2016, 74
19. Vogt, 1948
20. Montgomery, 1997
21. Juniper, 2016, 152; Montgomery, 1997, 205
22. Lynas, Brian, 2011, *The God Species*, Fourth Estate, 2011, 30
23. Emmott, Stephen, 2013, *10 Billion*, Penguin, 2013; and see http://www.wwf.org.uk/sites/default/files/2016-10/LPR_2016_summary_spread%20low%20res.pdf
24. Wilson, 2016
25. Juniper, 2015, 41
26. Juniper, 2015, 39
27. Juniper, 2013, 77
28. Wilson, 2016
29. Juniper, 2016, 149
30. Juniper, 2016, 156
31. Plant, Jane A, Voulvoulis, Nikolaus and Ragnasdottir, K Vala (editors), 2012, *Pollutants, Human Health and the Environment: a Risk Based Approach*, Wiley-Blackwell
32. www.chathamhouse.org/publications/twt/why-are-some-cities-more-polluted-others; Juniper, 2016, 144; according to the World Health Organisation (WHO), reported in *The Times*, 2 May 2018, air pollution causes 7 million deaths a year
33. Juniper, 2016, 119; Lynas, 2011; Wikipedia
34. Juniper, 2016, 119
35. Lynas, 2011
36. Eg Haslam, S M, 1990, *River Pollution*, Belhaven Press; Plant and others, 2012, 27,28; Juniper, 2016, 92,93
37. *The Economist*, 10 June 2017
38. Eg Tim Flannery, 2011, *Here on Earth*, Allen Lane; Juniper, 2013
39. Juniper, 2016
40. Lynas, 2011

41. McKinlay, Rebecca, Dassyne, Jason, Djamgoz, Mustafa B A, Plant, Jane A and Voulvoulis, Nikolaos, 2012, Agricultural pesticides and chemical fertilisers, in Plant and others, 2012, 197

42. Juniper, 2016, 162

43. *The Times*, 20 July 2017

44. *The Times*, 12 July 2017

45. Juniper, 2016, 164

46. *The Times*, 12 December 2017

47. Eg *Sunday Times*, 24 July 2016; Report by Environmental Audit Committee, 26 July 2016, https://publications.parliament.uk/pa/cm201617/cmselect/cmenvaud/179/17902.html]

48. Eg Selborne, Earl of, 2012, Foreword, in Plant and others, 2012; Juniper, 2016, 92; Lynas, 2011

49. Eg Lynas, 2011, Juniper, 2016

Chapter 2

Science and Society

We have also arranged things so that almost no one understands science and technology. This is a prescription for disaster. We might get away with it for a while, but sooner or later this combustible mixture of ignorance and power is going to blow up in our faces.

Carl Sagan[1]

The previous chapter is based on scientific research, and much of this book adopts a scientific approach. This chapter looks at the way science interacts with society and at some of the problems that arise when scientists try to communicate their findings to the public at large. We shall then see how this applies in the debate about anthropogenic global warming (AGW).

Let us start by asking what science is for. The first answer to this question is that it isn't *for* anything. Scientists study the Earth, the universe or the human body in order to satisfy their own curiosity. Science has no purpose except to increase our knowledge and understanding of the universe we live in.

The second answer is that the purpose of science (or, rather, the STEM subjects – science, technology, engineering and mathematics) is to improve the quality of our lives. Scientific discoveries are applied in the construction of computers, aircraft and bridges (for example), and in finding better ways of producing food and treating illness. Science feeds into business and industry, through technologists, engineers, inventors and entrepreneurs. We should remember that although the steady improvement in our material living standards in recent years tends to be linked, in public debate, to politics and economics, it wouldn't have happened without scientific and technological innovation. It is scientists and engineers, not politicians, who have brought us improvements in transport, communications, domestic appliances and medicine.

The third answer, and the one that we shall consider in this chapter, is that science can provide us with information that will help us to make better decisions, both in our personal lives and in the political arena. Many political decisions, as well as personal choices, can and should take account of the latest scientific understanding. Too often, however, we're let down by a failure to comprehend and take into account the contribution that scientific insights and evidence can provide.

Political issues and questions of personal lifestyle tend to be complex and controversial, and when scientists become involved in these areas they, too, may become involved in controversy.

Science, the public and the media

Scientific ideas that have social or political relevance should be made known to the public, and this requires communication skills as well as scientific skills. It is not enough to publish the results in a journal that will be read by just a few scientists working in the same field; they must be communicated through the media, and that means presenting them in a way that is attractive to the media. A media-friendly press-release summarising the significance of the work may be all that is required, but for more important scientific advances that may affect people's lives there may be a need for interviews, TV appearances or promotion through science journalists.

The only way that scientific information and ideas reach the general public is through the press and media, and they are likely to report controversy rather than agreement, definite answers (even if they are wrong) rather than honest uncertainty, breakthrough rather than work in progress,[2] human error rather than competence, and scare, sensation, disaster and tragedy rather than plodding on OK.

Many scientists have seen the need to relate to the public and to the political process, and they have learnt the language of the media and the language of public discourse. There has also been a change in the language used in scientific articles, as scientists become aware of the need to promote their work in order to get funding and get published. A 2015 study by scientists at the University of Utrecht found that the proportion of abstracts using adjectives like 'amazing', 'spectacular' and 'groundbreaking' had risen almost eightfold since the mid-1970s, and recent abstracts are nearly 40 times as likely to use the word 'novel'.[3]

Not everyone is comfortable with the image of the scientist as a good communicator. Frank Skinner probably speaks for many when he writes, 'I hate it when scientists try to be all populist and accessible. It's like politicians talking about football – it just doesn't ring true. Science isn't fun. It's just maths in fancy dress'.[4] I would dispute this, of course. I think it is important that scientists should make science accessible – but if they speak and write like tabloid journalists with an axe to grind they cannot be surprised if they find that they are viewed by the public with the same level of distrust.

An example of how the media can enable important scientific results to reach a wider public, while also leading to distortion of the findings, is provided by the story of Walter Mischel and his marshmallows. In the 1960s Mischel and his students started a series of tests with four-year-old children, to find out how much self-control they had in resisting the temptation to enjoy one treat (a marshmallow, for example, though this was not often used) when they knew that if they waited they would be able to enjoy two of the treats. Mischel found that the strength of self-control at this early age was a good indicator of success in school and in later life, and he published his results in the professional literature under titles such as 'The preschool self-imposed delay of immediate gratification for the sake of delayed but more valued rewards paradigm'. His work became more widely known in 2006, when the columnist David Brooks featured it in the *New York Times* under the title 'Marshmallows and Public Policy'. It was taken up by the media after that, dubbed 'the Marshmallow Test', and Brooks again discussed it in his 2011 best-seller *The Social Animal*.[5] Such publicity is to be welcomed, but Mischel came to realise that the media coverage gave the impression that we were stuck with whatever powers of self-control we possessed as a small child. This led him to write his 2014 book, *The Marshmallow Test*,[6] to emphasise the human capacity to develop our powers of self-control and to draw attention to the implications for public policy. We shall look at the relevance of this book to how we treat the environment in chapter 5.

Scientists and science writers thus have a difficult path to tread. If they are cautious and unemotional, what they have to say won't get through to the general public; if they are populist and speak with feeling about the social and political implications of science, they won't be trusted.

Communicating uncertainty

Writing in *The Times*, Ross Clark posed the question, 'Can we really trust chief scientific advisors any more?'[7] He started by referring to the spectacle of the Meteorological Office, in the midst of the coldest spell for years, trying to wriggle out of its prediction of a mild winter and, in the same week, the Government's admission that swine flu was not going to cause 65,000 deaths as predicted. He went on to recall the grim prophecies about bird flu in 2005, SARS in 2003, and the human form of mad-cow disease some years earlier. This led Clark, a journalist with no scientific qualifications, to be sceptical about the scientific advice on climate change.

How can a scientist respond to this? The first point to make is that scientists are well aware of the uncertainties of their predictions, but this does not always get through to the general public when their findings are reported by the media.

Scientists and politicians need to assess the risk attached to such low-probability high-consequence events: if we plan for a serious outbreak of swine flu and it turns out to be mild, we have wasted millions of pounds; but if there is a serious outbreak and we have not prepared for it, thousands of lives may be lost. In these circumstances, politicians may decide to be cautious and make plans for a serious outbreak.

Clark, in the article quoted above, accuses outwardly sober government scientists of spinning scares after the manner of the redtop journalist. This places scientists in a dilemma. If they present their findings in the measured language traditionally associated with scientists, placing emphasis on the uncertainties, they will not be reported and nobody will hear of their findings or their warnings. They rely on the media to get their message across, so they have to speak the language of the media – and the media like scare stories. David Spiegelhalter, Winton Professor of the Public Understanding of Risk at the University of Cambridge, has written of the need for scientists to be honest about risk.[8] His article is entitled 'Scientists need the guts to say: I don't know'. That is all very well, but what editor would allow column inches or air time to a scientist who wanted to say 'I don't know'?

If scientists acknowledge the areas in which some uncertainty remains, if they identify areas where further work needs to be done to increase our understanding, politically motivated opponents will cry 'not proven'. If, on the other hand, they simplify in order to get heard, leaving out the boring bits about uncertainty, they will again lay themselves open to criticism: this time, that they are biased, selective and therefore unreliable.

This dumbing down is quite unnecessary, of course. The public are very well able to deal with uncertainty and risk. People who bet on horses have quite a sophisticated understanding of uncertainty. In day-to-day life, we leave home when it's not raining, to take one simple example, and either the weather forecast or our own observation tells us that it might rain. We make our own assessment of the likelihood of rain and decide whether to take an umbrella. We also live with uncertainty about the moods and behaviour of our fellow human beings – and indeed uncertainty about our own future moods and behaviour. Uncertainty is part of everyday life.

The insurance industry, and all of us who take out insurance policies, know about the idea of risk: there is only a small risk that our house will burn down, but the consequences of a fire are so disastrous that we install smoke alarms and fire extinguishers and we take out insurance. We hope that this will be money wasted, and for most of us it is, but we don't cancel our home insurance just because the house didn't burn down last year. Ross Clark's examples need to be seen in this context. The flow of oil from the Deepwater Horizon rig in the Gulf of Mexico in 2010, described as the biggest environmental crisis in US history, is an example of a disaster which may have been assessed as unlikely to happen – but it did happen and the engineering solutions had not been prepared beforehand. Outside the scientific field, the banking crisis of 2008 is another example of a low-probability event with very serious consequences – and the seriousness of not preparing for it.

The problem is not that the public don't understand uncertainty. The problem is that many people, including many media people, have a one-sided understanding of science. With

27

memories, perhaps, of physics and chemistry at school, they know about the sort of science that can give precise answers to precise questions. They seem to forget that there are many other areas in which significant uncertainties remain in spite of huge advances in scientific understanding. We can recognise the contrast, for example, between the mathematical precision with which astronomers can predict, years ahead, exact details of an eclipse and the uncertainties, just days or hours ahead, in the meteorological prediction of the likelihood of clear skies to enable us to view it. This contrast applies particularly in the area of forecasting. Yesterday's rainfall is a matter of record, whereas tomorrow's is expressed as a percentage probability of precipitation; just as the result of yesterday's horse race is a matter of record, whereas tomorrow's result is expressed as betting odds.

Balance and imbalance

One of the problems with media coverage arises when there are two points of view, where each is advocated by well-qualified scientists but the evidence and support for one viewpoint is very much stronger than that for the other. I quote from evidence published in the Leveson Report:[9]

The media often has a tendency to pursue balance in its stories, by countering one claim with another, and allowing alternative viewpoints a right of reply. This is perfectly proper in, for example, political reporting. Yet in science, the practice can often lead to distortions of its own. In science, it is often the case that a mainstream opinion about the interpretation of known data is shared overwhelmingly by professionals in that field, for example with the safety of the MMR vaccine or the link between greenhouse gases and global warming. When this is the case, the effect of balancing opinion to stoke debate can be to create a misleading impression that dissent from the mainstream view is more widespread and serious than it actually is.

This habit of presenting two ill-balanced points of view as if they were equally well-founded is not confined to science. It applies in economics[10] – and no doubt other disciplines, too. Indeed, the problem of balance versus imbalance, accuracy versus distortion and spin, is widespread throughout the political scene, as recently documented by Mark Thompson.[11] When scientific findings have social or political implications, advocates of one particular point of view tend to treat them in the same way as any other political issue. A cleverly constructed phrase, like 'Frankenstein foods', may be misleading but that doesn't stop it being very powerful.

Science and politics

There is a serious lack of scientific expertise and understanding among our politicians and senior civil servants. Mark Henderson expands on this deficiency in some detail in *The Geek Manifesto*,[12] with examples to illustrate the need for a greater understanding of science, what it can do and the way it works.

To take one of his examples, when low levels of volcanic ash from the volcano Eyjafjallajökull in Iceland spread over Europe in 2010, airliners were grounded. It was known that thick clouds of ash caused engine failure, but nothing was known about the effects of lower concentrations – so zero tolerance was the only safe policy. Flights were restarted when tests had shown that ash posed no hazard at the low levels prevailing at that time. If tests to establish safety thresholds had been carried out earlier as a precaution, which is what scientists had advised, there would have been no need for airliners to be grounded.

Henderson distinguishes between evidence-based policies and policy-based evidence. In the former, policy-making follows the evidence. In the latter, policy comes first and evidence is selected to support it. Henderson gives the example of government policy in 2008 in relation to the classification of cannabis, when the government decided, for political reasons, not to implement the science-based advice of the Advisory Council on the Misuse of Drugs to downgrade certain recreational drugs from class A to class B.

That is not to say that scientific advice should always be followed slavishly. Science should sometimes be regarded as work in progress. If observation conflicts with current scientific theory, we should remain open to the possibility that the scientific theory is due for revision. Government policies may often take account of recent research in the social sciences, and this is a field in which there is always the possibility that the latest evidence-based opinions may subsequently be modified or even overturned.

Scientists also need to recognise that their evidence is just one aspect of a political issue. Politicians may need to take account of other factors such as public opinion, public perception, and the possible consequences and political practicability or desirability of implementing any policy based solely on certain specific scientific evidence. The decision of the government not to follow the advice of the Advisory Council on the Misuse of Drugs in 2008 was a case in point.

Another example of where political decisions may not follow where the science leads is the disposal of high-level radioactive waste. This waste will continue to present a hazard to human health and to animal and plant health for tens of thousands of years, so it is of the greatest importance that it should be disposed of in such a way that it does not escape into the environment. Nevertheless, there can be a great deal of public concern when it is thought that such waste may be buried nearby. When I worked in the British Geological Survey, research was carried out by colleagues of mine to determine the most suitable places for burial of this waste. At one stage of the work, certain localities were identified as deserving further investigation, but such was the local opposition that the work was cancelled. The strength of feeling in one area of the Scottish Highlands was so strong that when my own plans to work in the same area but on an unrelated research project were made known to the local press, it was mistakenly assumed that I was working on radioactive-waste disposal. My supposed activities were described as posing 'a threat worse than Hitler'[13] and local people were organised into a sort of neighbourhood watch to look out for me if I set foot on the hills. In recent years the only area in Britain considered for the storage or burial of high-level radioactive waste has been west Cumbria. This may not be the most suitable area from a scientific standpoint (the rock is fractured), but the local people have lived close to radioactive material for more than fifty years and understand the risks involved, and this is the only area to have come close to being acceptable, locally, as a storage site.[14]

That is why it is so important that government minsters and senior civil servants should be able to assess scientific evidence. Ministers need to have scientific advisors, but this is not enough. They need the expertise to be able to evaluate conflicting advice, understand the evidence and take it into account along with other political considerations. It was because Winston Churchill and his cabinet lacked the ability to evaluate conflicting scientific advice that they approved saturation bombing of German cities during the second world war, diverting air power that would have been better deployed elsewhere.[15] Ministers and civil servants should know how to incorporate science and a scientific way of thinking into the formation and implementation of policy. Science should not be written off as a specialist interest for the few: it is part of the world we live in, an integral part of current affairs. The same applies in local government, where local planning decisions, particularly, benefit from an understanding of environmental, land-management, flood-risk and nature-conservation issues.

I started this chapter by offering three answers to the question, 'What is science for?' If science is principally the pursuit of knowledge, then there may be little harm in scientists living in a different world from everyone else. That is not what we see today, however. Science has a huge influence on the way we live our lives, with the way we relate to each other and with how we relate to the natural world. It interacts with the political world and political decisions, and it is vitally important that scientists and politicians understand each other's disciplines and each other's language.

Margaret Thatcher was a politician who combined scientific and political expertise. Her scientific background enabled her to give legitimacy to environmental concerns. She took action against CFCs, in response to the threat to the ozone layer. She decided that Britain should support the formation of a European Environment Agency, which came into being in 1993. In a speech to the Royal Society in 1988 she said that 'we have unwittingly begun a massive experiment with the system of this planet itself'[16] and in 1990, speaking at the opening of the Hadley Centre for Climate Prediction and Research, she emphasised that we have 'a full repairing lease on this Earth'.[17] It was not only in scientific matters, however, that her scientific mind was an asset: her sharp questioning of lazy thinking on other issues, too, sometimes helped to bring clarity to policy making.[18]

The climate controversy

The debate

That is the background against which we should view public perception of the science of climate change. The scientific findings relating to climate change have strong political implications. Important political issues tend to become controversial, and anthropogenic global warming is just such an issue. Because both sides have a political message to get across and they use the media to communicate it, it is, perhaps, not surprising that it becomes like any other political message communicated via the media: contentious, opaque and muddled.

If the judgement of the overwhelming majority of climatologists and other scientists carried the day, it would not be necessary to write about the climate controversy, but their judgement is questioned by a significant minority of the population whose opinions are fuelled by some very articulate advocates. A poll in 2017 found that only 64 per cent of people in Britain thought that global warming was happening and was primarily caused by human activity such as burning fossil fuels.[19] Add to that the fact that in 2016 the USA elected a president who is not convinced by the conventional view and is dismantling some of the environmental policies put in place by his predecessor, and we are forced to recognise that climate change is a controversial issue.

There are two ways in which you can conduct a debate. If you want to score points off your opponents, you distract attention from their strongest arguments by concentrating on the weakest points, taking delight in exposing them to ridicule. You take every opportunity to impugn your opponents' motives, magnifying any financial or personal incentives they might have for arguing as they do. If, on the other hand, you are seeking to promote a deeper understanding of the issue, you address your opponents' strongest arguments; if you can, you demolish them and win your case; if not, you incorporate them in your own thinking. You are willing to assess the arguments against your own ideas and combine both sides of the debate into a new synthesis. Unfortunately, the climate controversy is a very good example of the former tactic, characterised by exaggerated claims, failure to address the valid arguments of the other side, accusation, counter-accusation, allegations of political bias, attacks on the personalities, qualifications and motives of the leading proponents (playing the man and not the ball) and so forth.

Some climate scientists seek publicity for their concerns by using scare tactics and making exaggerated claims without emphasising the uncertainties. Their critics accuse the climatologists and their supporters of being politically motivated; they focus on the scare tactics and exaggerated claims and use them to ridicule the conclusions. The debate becomes little more than a dialogue of the deaf.

Some of the advocates on both sides, however, argue their case convincingly. Whichever side your natural inclinations lead you to, you can find authoritative and well-presented arguments to support your views.[20] If it is in your nature to believe the experts, you will do so; if it is in your nature to distrust experts and anything that looks like a bandwagon, you will do so. If it comes naturally to you to believe that society's values and behaviour are in need of reform, you will find that the climatologists' argument supports your view; if it comes naturally to you to distrust scares, to oppose anything that threatens economic growth and to believe that it will all work out all right in the end, you will seek reasons to reject the climatologists' case. In America, there is a strong correlation with political alignment. More than 50 per cent of Democrats say that dealing with global warming is a priority, compared with about 15 per cent of Republicans.[21]

Concern about climate change is all about what might happen in the future. Established facts about historic increases in CO_2 levels in the atmosphere are only of concern because of the likely consequences if levels continue to rise. Predictions are, of their very nature, uncertain. If this year's predictions differ from those made five years ago, you don't have to know anything about climate science to guess that those in five years' time will be different again. It need have come as no surprise when predictions in 2017, taking account of the latest information, differed from earlier predictions; the next estimate will probably be different again – but we don't know in which direction. As it happened, the 2017 prediction indicated slower warming than previous forecasts. For some commentators, this proved that measures to reduce carbon emissions were unnecessary and indefensibly wasteful; other commentators welcomed the possibility that the measures already taken plus those planned for the near future might now be sufficient to prevent disaster, instead of merely too little, too late.

The arguments

On the one hand, it is claimed that there is a consensus among climate scientists, represented by the Intergovernmental Panel on Climate Change (IPCC), that continued increases in the levels of greenhouse gases in the atmosphere present a real threat to human life as we know it, with large changes in climate, extreme weather conditions, loss of ecosystems and biodiversity, acidification of the oceans, melting of the polar ice caps and rising sea levels threatening the many densely populated, low-lying land areas of the world.

Against them, there are a smaller number of people who maintain that the data do not justify the conclusions reached. They generally focus on the weak spots in the climatologists' argument. Christopher Booker, in *The Real Global Warming Disaster: Is the Obsession with 'Climate Change' Turning out to be the most Costly Scientific Blunder in History?*,[22] presents a devastating attack on the IPCC, Al Gore and the conventional view of climate change. He maintains that human activities have little influence on atmospheric levels of CO_2 and that our attempts to limit CO_2 emissions are unnecessary and costly. Such critics point out that throughout geological time there have been climate changes that were nothing to do with human activity. It is also argued that more CO_2 in the atmosphere boosts crop yields, and that more people die of cold than of heat, so global warming could be a good thing.

On the other side, Naomi Oreskes and Erik M Conway in *Merchants of Doubt: How a Handful of scientists obscured the Truth on Issues from Tobacco Smoke to Global Warming*,[23] accuse a few influential scientists in America of attempting to undermine the expertise and authority of mainstream scientific bodies on a succession of scientific issues including the link between smoking and cancer, the causes of acid rain, the ozone layer and global warming.

Critics focus on weaknesses in the climatologists' case. Here are two examples. They do not affect the real scientific argument, but they can be used to discredit climate scientists. The first was an obviously exaggerated and unfounded prediction that the Himalayan glaciers would disappear in 30 years, a claim that somehow found its way into the 2007 report of the IPCC. An inquiry into this 2007 report, commissioned jointly by UN Secretary General Ban Ki Moon and Dr Pachauri, head of the IPCC, said the IPCC should have been more rigorous in its assessments of climate change claims, paying more attention to alternative views. It recommended that literature that had not been peer reviewed (eg reports by environmental lobby groups) should be identified as such.[24] Commenting on this review, *The Times* concluded that the IPCC 'was so anxious that the fact of climate change should be accepted … that it deliberately overstated the more apocalyptic warnings in order to capture the headlines and make its voice heard. This advocacy, even in a good cause, was wholly unacceptable.'[25] In other words, the IPCC was adopting tactics that we might more commonly associate with politics and journalism than with science.

The second example was a series of emails emanating from the Climate Research Unit (CRU) of the University of East Anglia (UEA) and made public without authorisation in November 2009: the excerpts from these emails reproduced by James Delingpole in *Watermelons* do the scientists no credit.[26] The review of this incident, chaired by Sir Muir Russell, found (1) that the rigour and honesty of the CRU scientists were not in doubt and (2) that their behaviour had not prejudiced the balance of advice given to policy makers, but (3) that there had been a consistent pattern of failing to display the proper degree of openness, both on the part of the CRU scientists and on the part of the UEA, who failed to recognise not only the significance of statutory requirements but also the risk to the reputation of the University and, indeed, to the credibility of UK climate science.[27]

It is understandable, then, that this leaves many members of the public confused. Surveys show fluctuating levels of belief in man-made climate change and its threat to the way we live.

The science

So much for the controversy; what can we say about the science? It is worth noting where there is, and where there is not, scope for uncertainty, disagreement and controversy. Scientists tell us that the levels of CO_2 in the atmosphere are higher than they have been for at least 800,000 years,[28] having risen markedly since the industrial revolution as a consequence, principally, of the burning of fossil fuels and the production of cement. The record of past levels of atmospheric CO_2 is something that can be measured (by analysing air bubbles in ice cores taken from glaciers and ice fields) and can be tested by other scientists. Studies of the Vostok Antarctic ice core, for example, show that CO_2 levels over the last 200,000 years were in the range 160–280 parts per million by volume, very much lower than the 400 ppm of today and the 500 ppm predicted by the end of the twenty-first century if recent trends continue.[29] There is no reason to doubt this evidence. Similarly, it has been well understood for a long time that increased levels of CO_2 and other gases in the atmosphere increase the retention of heat from the sun's rays (the so-called 'greenhouse effect'): that is a physical property of the gases.

It is when we come to make predictions about changes in the climate that uncertainties arise. First, there are both the extent and the consequences of CO_2-induced global warming. The absorption of some of this heat in the upper and lower layers of the ocean offers one possible explanation for the levelling off of atmospheric temperatures during the early years of the twenty-first century: more than 90 per cent of the of the increase in energy during recent decades due to warming by greenhouse gases has gone towards increasing the ocean heat content.[30] Uncertainties also arise from the absorption of atmospheric CO_2 into the oceans, with unpredictable consequences for coral reefs and other life forms.

Other consequences of rising temperatures include (1) greater frequency and intensity of climatic extremes, such as heatwaves, droughts, floods and storms; (2) rising sea levels as a consequence of warming of the oceans and melting of the Antarctic and Greenland ice caps, eventually flooding low-lying areas of the globe; and (3) the breakdown of methane hydrates (crystalline solids consisting of gas and water molecules, present in vast quantities in permafrost regions, particularly in Siberia) to release methane, adding to the greenhouse effect. Rising levels of carbon-dioxide in the atmosphere lead to greening of much of the planet and increased crop yields.[31]

Second, there are other human activities, independent of carbon-dioxide emissions, that affect the climate. Emissions of some other gases (methane, for example) also increase the retention of heat in the atmosphere, while other gases and particulates (such as aerosols, particularly those derived from sulphates) have the opposite effect.[32] Replacing forest with crops and grassland makes the land paler and more reflective, thus absorbing less heat from the sun – just as the melting of ice in polar and mountain regions (which could eventually be irreversible) make it less reflective. Then there is the release into the atmosphere of carbon as a consequence of draining and ploughing in agricultural land: soil stores three times as much carbon as is held in the atmosphere, with peat being especially significant.

Third, there are many natural variables that affect the climate, independent of human activity. An important influence on climate change during the series of ice ages over the last million years has been the regular variations in the Earth's orbit around the sun; the next ice age is not expected for at least 30,000 years.[33] Other natural influences on the climate include changes in the sun's activity, the amount of greenhouse gases, dust and other particles introduced into the atmosphere by natural processes (such as volcanic activity), the geography of the oceans, continents and mountains, and the reflectivity of the Earth's surface.[34] There is also the long-term heating of the sun, which means that the Earth may not recover from a hot period as readily as it did hundreds of millions of years ago. We do not fully understand the different roles and the relative importance of all these factors.

Natural fluctuations in the climate are, generally, either relatively small (caused by fluctuations in sun-spot activity, for example) or, by human standards, very long term (the global temperature rise of 5–8 °C that characterised the Palaeocene–Eocene Thermal Maximum 55.5 million years ago, for example, 'resulted from a massive release of greenhouse gases into the atmosphere over a very short period of time in geological terms (about 10,000 years)'.[35] Abrupt events in the last 100,000 years (for example, those associated with the melting of the ice sheet over North America at the end of the last ice age) are attributed to changes in ocean circulation caused by input of very large quantities of fresh water from melting ice caps, followed by a return to the long-term trend.[36] What distinguishes anthropogenic global warming from these is the magnitude and irreversibility of the possible consequences on the scale of one to two hundred years. If we do nothing about the steady increase in CO_2 emissions we can expect many small, natural fluctuations in climate, but all against the possibility of a steady increase in global temperatures over the decades, accompanied by increasing frequency and severity of droughts, floods and storms, by a change in the temperature and acidity of the oceans and, eventually, by the melting of the Greenland and Antarctic ice caps, rising sea level and widespread flooding of low-lying areas.

The strongest argument in support of predictions of global warming is the rapid increase in carbon-dioxide levels in the atmosphere caused by human activity and the well-understood physics of the greenhouse effect. The strongest argument in the opponents' case is the uncertainty of all the other climatic and non-climatic variables.

Does it matter?

It can be argued that the climate debate is irrelevant, since we should be using clean, non-polluting, sustainable sources of energy and stop burning fossil fuels anyway. If we look at the other ways in which we damage the environment – principally pollution, habitat destruction leading to reduced biodiversity, and the depletion of non-renewable resources – and if we make the necessary changes to our way of life, we shall have reduced our CO_2 emissions anyway. You don't have to be convinced by the more pessimistic climate forecasts to see the need for action to preserve the environment by adopting sustainable lifestyles. Mining and burning fossil fuels is wasteful, dirty, polluting and, we are beginning to see, expensive. In fifty years' time we shall be amazed that we tolerated it for so long.

In his 2009 book *Sustainable Energy – without the hot air*, David MacKay wrote that his intention was to ignore climate change altogether because of all the controversies surrounding it.[37] His argument was to be: 'Never mind when fossil fuels are going to run out; never mind whether climate change is happening; *burning fossil fuels is not sustainable anyway*; let's imagine living sustainably, and figure out how much sustainable energy is available.' He did in fact mention climate change briefly, but his argument stands. We don't really need to spend time debating climate change: there are enough other reasons to phase out the use of fossil fuels for energy generation and to reduce our energy consumption. In the rest of this book I shall commend policies, technologies and lifestyles that aim to reduce the burning of fossil fuels and the release of CO_2 into the atmosphere.

Greenhouse gases are not the only important environmental issue. Indeed, it is most regrettable that the climate controversy, with all its uncertainties and the hype on both sides, has turned so many people away from taking environmental issues seriously and distracted attention from these other important issues. The most serious consequence of the climate controversy is that many of the tactics adopted by both sides have brought into disrepute environmental science and the noble ideal of caring for the Earth.

I end this chapter, as I ended the previous one, with the observation that we are conducting a gigantic experiment with this precious and fragile planet of ours, with little idea what the consequences will be.

Notes

1. Sagan, Carl, 1995/1997, *The Demon-Haunted World*, Random House
2. Leveson, Lord Justice, 2012, *Inquiry into the Culture, Practices and Ethics of the Press*, The Stationary Office, Vol II, 690–693
3. *The Times*, 17 December 2015
4. *The Times*, 30 April 2010
5. Brooks, David, 2011, *The Social Animal*, Short Books
6. Mischel, Walter, 2014, *The Marshmallow Test*, Bantam (Corgi, 2015)
7. *The Times*, 11 January 2010
8. *The Times*, 22 March 2010
9. Leveson, 2012, 690
10. Paul Johnson, *The Times*, 28 June 2016
11. Thompson, Mark, 2016, *Enough Said: What's Gone Wrong with the Language of Politics?*, The Bodley Head

12. Henderson, Mark, 2013, *The Geek Manifesto*, Corgi
13. *Lochaber Free Press*
14. *The Times*, 28 January 2017
15. C P Snow, quoted by Lisa Jardine, 'A point of view: Beware of experts', BBC Radio 4, 9 December 2011: www.bbc.co.uk/news/magazine-16110088
16. www.margaretthatcher.org/document/107346
17. www.margaretthatcher.org/document/108102
18. Charles Clover, *Sunday Times*, 21 April 2013
19. www.independent.co.uk/environment/scotland-climate-change-believers-more-england-wales-uk-global-warming-science-deniers-a7577881.html
20. Eg Houghton, John, 2015, *Global Warming: The Complete Briefing*, 5th edition, Cambridge University Press versus Marohasy, Jennifer (editor), 2017, *Climate Change: The Facts*, Connor Court Publishing
21. *The Economist*, 28 November 2015
22. Booker, Christopher, 2009, *The Real Global Warming Disaster: Is the Obsession with 'Climate Change' Turning out to be the most Costly Scientific Blunder in History?*, Continuum
23. Oreskes, Naomi and Conway, Erik M, 2011, *Merchants of Doubt: How a Handful of scientists obscured the Truth on Issues from Tobacco Smoke to Global Warming*, Bloomsbury
24. *The Times*, 31 August 2010
25. Leading article, *The Times*, 31 August 2010
26. Delingpole, James, 2012, *Watermelons*, revised edition, Biteback
27. www.cce-review.org/pdf/FINAL%20REPORT.pdf
28. Eg Juniper, Tony, 2016, *What's really happening to our planet?*, Dorling Kindersley, 118
29. Anderson, David E, Goudie, Andrew S and Parker, Adrian G, 2013, *Global Environments through the Quaternary: Exploring Environmental Change*, 2nd edition, Oxford University Press; Houghton, 2015
30. Houghton, 2015
31. Eg Idso, Craig D, 2017, Carbon Dioxide and Plant Growth, 189–200 in Marohasy, 2017; http://theconversation.com/rising-carbon-dioxide-is-greening-the-earth-but-its-not-all-good-news-58282
32. Houghton, 2015
33. Houghton, 2015
34. Anderson and others, 2013
35. Anderson and others, 2013
36. Houghton, 2015
37. www.withouthotair.com

Chapter 3
The Consumer Society

The great majority of people in English-speaking nations (Britain, America, Australia, Canada, Singapore) now define their lives through earnings, possessions, appearances and celebrity, and those things are making them miserable because they impede the meeting of fundamental needs.

Oliver James[1]

And it is precisely because material goods are flawed, but somehow plausible, proxies for our dreams and aspirations, that consumer culture seems on the surface to work so well. ... Consumer culture perpetuates itself here precisely because it succeeds so well at failure!

Tim Jackson[2]

The damage to the environment described in chapter 1 is the result of human activity. Much of it, notably pollution, depletion of non-renewable resources and waste creation, is done in order to fuel the high material standard of living in the richer countries. Average per-capita consumption over the world is increasing. The size of the world economy rose from $32 trillion in 2000 to $62 trillion when Lehmann brothers went bust in 2008 and $72 trillion at the end of 2012.[3] Total consumption will continue to rise as the population gets larger; more people means more mouths to feed and more goods to satisfy their aspirations.

People have always wanted to acquire things. We derive pleasure from our possessions. What makes today's consumer society different is the number of things we buy only to get rid of them or store them out of sight: the throwaway society.

The wealthy West

In Western countries, we live in an affluent society. We may not think so, with all the talk of 'credit crunch', 'broken Britain', 'austerity', the 'squeezed middle', the 'just-about managing' and so on, but we do. Compared with most of the peoples of the world, and with our own countries a mere 50 years ago, we are unimaginably wealthy, with a fantastically high material standard of living. (Some of us are not, and we shall look at the issues of poverty and inequality in chapter 14.)

Take a look at our roads. They are increasingly clogged up with vehicles. These vehicles are not all luxury cars for the very rich, nor are they all bottom-of-the-range cars for the poor.

Then look at the shops in any high street. Look at shopping centres and garden centres. Apart from supermarkets, there are very few retailers who offer the essentials of life at prices to suit people who are seriously short of money. Equally, there are very few who cater for the rich: for people who want the best and can afford to pay for it. Much of our economy is directed at people who have a bit of money to spare and can choose how to spend it.

Most of what is offered for sale is something we could do without – and that is why we have an advertising industry. Advertising starts from the premise that most people have no need of the product being advertised: their task is to persuade just a small number of people to buy something that they don't need. We are indoctrinated by advertisers and their clients to want their latest product.

As a consequence, much of what we buy is unnecessary. When we have bought it, we have to dispose of something else to make room for the new acquisition. Ten million pieces of furniture, for example, are thrown away in Britain every year. Or else we store it. Perhaps that is the real test of whether we bring too much into the house: how much of it do we soon want to dispose of or put out of sight into storage?

To Ikea last week to get a GÏZMØ. Nobody even knows what a GÏZMØ is for. You just know that you need one, especially as they are only £14. Then you get it home. You don't have the tool you need to build it, and you can't even remember where you were going to put it up. Eventually you dump it in the attic, alongside the CRÂPPÄCK and the FLÏMSZÏ you bought at Easter, and your long-forgotten sense of self-worth.

Hugo Rifkind[4]

The space occupied by our possessions doubled in the 30 years to 2010, and the value of our stuff more than doubled.[5]

All this provides little of what we really want. Studies have shown that we may think that buying more stuff will make us happier, but it doesn't. Below a certain living standard, of course, getting more does indeed bring happiness, but beyond that we become consumed with the desire for more; when we get it, we don't enjoy it; we just want more; and so it goes on;[6] there are other, less destructive, ways of achieving greater happiness (see chapter 5).

I have often heard elderly people look back on their childhood and say 'We were poor, but we were happy'. The combination of consumerist values and social inequality today leads many people to believe, mistakenly, that their happiness depends on possessing stuff that they can't afford. This leads to a sense of deprivation – and very often to debt as well.

There is a story about an interviewer who asked a Sri Lankan slum-dweller to rate her life satisfaction on a scale of one to ten. To the interviewer's surprise, the answer was ten: the woman had a son who respected her, a husband who loved her, and enough money to buy dye for her hair and to give to charity.[7]

The consumer society doesn't make us happier. It doesn't deliver. So how did we get here?

How we got here

Economic drivers

In the years after the first world war, manufacturers had to work out how to transform the wartime ethic of thrift and reuse – darning socks, keeping bits of string, sewing rags into rugs and so on – into a throwaway culture in which people replaced the old with the new. In America, the wartime 'Waste Not, Want Not' posters were replaced by 1917 by new signs reading 'Beware of Thrift and Unwise Economy'.[8]

In the United States in the 1920s, there was a problem with overproduction. Supply outstripped demand. Some public figures welcomed this. Farmers and factories could produce less. Workers could have more time off. Another view was voiced by Herbert Hoover (who was to be US President 1929–33) in an address to representatives of the advertising industry in 1925: 'You have taken over', he told them, 'the job of creating desire'.[9] The advertising industry has carried out this task very effectively all round the world.

The key to economic prosperity is the organised creation of dissatisfaction. … If everyone were satisfied no one would want to buy the new thing.

Charles Kettering [10]

J K Galbraith's widely acclaimed book, *The Affluent Society*, was first published in 1958.[11] The Modern Library rates it at No 46 in the top 100 non-fiction books of the twentieth century.[12] Galbraith starts this book by pointing out that for most of history poverty was an all-pervading fact of the world. 'Obviously', he wrote, 'it is not of ours.' More people in the United States at that time died of too much food than of too little.[13] He went on to say that our economic thinking had not adjusted to this new state of affairs but was still founded on the notion of 'consumer demand'.

A result of this affluence is that some of our wants are less 'urgent' (Galbraith's term) than others. He was at pains to argue that our needs for certain products couldn't be all that important if great efforts have to be made to persuade us that we have such needs: 'A man who is hungry need never be told of his need for food.'[14] This, however, does not lead us, as it should, to question our preoccupation with production: 'To cast doubt on the importance of production is thus to bring into question the foundation of the entire edifice'.[15] In pursuit of this end, he said, economics was divorced from any judgement about the goods that are produced. This is not quite true today, when strong moral judgements are expressed about certain economic activities, such as the production and trade in military weapons and recreational drugs. Smoking, alcohol and unhealthy foods are also frowned upon, and people are beginning – more and more – to question economic activities that damage the environment.

Galbraith goes on to say that the importance of the economy is not what it produces but the employment it provides. 'When men are unemployed, society does not miss the goods they do not produce. ... But the men who are without work *do* miss the income they no longer earn.'[16] We could add that they also miss the satisfaction that comes from the completion of a good day's work.

Another consequence of an economy based on the theory of consumer demand is consumer debt. We are persuaded to buy things we cannot afford, so, naturally, we have to borrow.[17] The habit of unsecured debt has increased a great deal since Galbraith's book, with 45 per cent of individuals in the UK having credit-card or store-card debt,[18] and with the introduction of student loans at a level that will land most students with many years of debt.

The amount of wasted effort that goes into producing stuff that is not needed led Galbraith to say: 'One could indeed argue that human happiness would be as effectively advanced by inefficiency in want creation as by efficiency in production.'[19]

The Affluent Society was widely read and widely praised – and just as widely ignored. Galbraith's lesson has not been learnt. We have gone on operating the economy as if the products are important, as if we really needed them, as if we still lived before the age of plenty, when the essentials of life were in short supply. We still believe that we need to produce more and more goods (we call it growth) to satisfy consumer demand.

It is therefore of prime importance, in this way of thinking, that we should maintain consumer demand. We have to keep persuading people who have everything they need that they want to buy more. One device that is commonly used to achieve this is the idea of fashion: our clothes, our cars and our household furnishings may have years of serviceable life in them, but we are told that we must discard them and buy new, so as to keep up with the latest fashion.

Another device is planned obsolescence. Goods are made so that they become obsolete. It would be possible to make things to last for a long time, but more things can be sold if they are designed and made in such a way that they have to be replaced, either because they decay or because spare parts cease to be available or because a subsequent model is more attractive in some way.

Over the last fifty years [in America], the lifespan of everyday 'durable' goods including refrigerators, toasters and washing machines has decreased anywhere between three and seven years.

Botsman and Rogers[20]

The whole edifice of our economic life is built on a falsehood; we are conned into thinking that life will be better for us if we get more stuff and throw away more stuff. Of course there are people and situations in real need, but most of the money, most of the stuff, is with people who have more than they need.

Galbraith expresses the problem in terms of 'consumer demand', but it is clear that this demand is artificial: the real driver is the wish to keep people in work. This, of course, is altogether estimable; nobody would quarrel with that. Two observations follow, however. The first is that in pre-industrial societies there was always work to be done. Why do we imagine that this is not true today? Unemployment will only become inevitable when all human needs that can be satisfied by human effort are being met – an unlikely situation. Unemployment arises not because there is no work to be done but because the worker or supplier and the customer cannot agree on payment (see further in chapter 14).

The second observation is that the economy we have described is driven to a considerable degree by the worker or supplier. The Universal Declaration of Human Rights, adopted by the General Assembly of the United nations in 1948, is a remarkable document, as relevant today as it was 70 years ago, but Article 23(1) seems hard to justify: 'Everyone has the right to work, to free choice of employment, to just and favourable conditions of work and to protection against unemployment.' The 'free choice of employment' conjures up a picture of a customer walking into a shop to buy food, only to be told by the shopkeeper that there isn't any food; nobody wants to produce it; everyone wants to write books, these days, so you can buy books instead.

Once we understand that so much human effort is devoted to making, advertising, selling, buying and throwing away things that that none of us really needs or wants, we can see that we have a huge opportunity to reshape the way our economy works.

An economy that is driven less by the supplier and more by the consumer might be able to concentrate resources (both workers and the money to pay for them) on what people actually want, what would actually increase their sense of well-being: at the time of writing, the areas in which we need more resources in Britain are medical and social care, education and security (police, justice, armed forces, diplomacy and other soft power). We should note, of course, that workers and consumers are not two separate groups of people: we are all consumers and nearly all of us are, have been or will be workers. We may also note that medical and social care, education and security do less damage to the environment than producing stuff. We shall return to this in Part 3.

Psychological drivers

We hear about the agricultural problem of soil erosion ... Surely no less serious is the matter of mind erosion; the dust storms of daily excitement and of continual triviality can easily blow away the sensitive topsoil of the spirit. The result is a barren and shallow nervous credulity.

Christopher Morley [21]

These economic drivers were conveniently reinforced by the twentieth-century assault on moral values (see chapter 6). We need some kind of values to guide us as we make decisions. In normal times, our motives of self-interest are moderated by moral values such as kindness, consideration, goodwill, honesty and integrity – to which may be added the wider issues of social and environmental awareness. When it became fashionable to question the validity of moral values, we were left with a void to be filled – and there was another set of values waiting to step in and take their place: monetary value. Money became the criterion by which many of our choices were made.

It is not so much that we have an ethic of consumption, but that – by default – it remains as one of the few meaningful experiences in our lives. There is a tangibility and satisfaction to buying – to picking out a new shirt or a new album and taking it home – that means that shopping remains for individuals a confirmation of their power to make things happen in the world.

Josie Appleton [22]

Money – how to acquire it and how to spend it – came to occupy a high place in the way we approached life's decisions. Money came to be the determining factor in decisions that might be better made by following moral principles or social norms. As Michael Sandel, Harvard political philosopher and 2009 Reith lecturer, has written,

Today, we often confuse market reasoning for moral reasoning. We fall into thinking that economic efficiency – getting goods to those with the greatest willingness and ability to pay for them – defines the common good. But this is a mistake ...

Michael Sandel [23]

He developed this point at length in *What Money Can't buy: The Moral Limits of Markets*.[24]

47

We are coming out of this now. People are once again willing to talk about right and wrong, to talk about morality, in human relationships, in business and in politics[25] (see chapter 6). More of us are realising that that there is more to life than consumption, more to life than possessions – not that we were ever really convinced but it seemed to be what everybody believed.

The desire to have money and to spend it, the desire to possess stuff, are part of human nature; they are always with us, but were normally held in check by the knowledge that there are other, more important and fundamental values. When these other values are lost, however, money and possessions readily occupy the vacuum.

In summary, mistaken economic and psychological ideas have led us to devote too much of our wealth and our energies to producing, advertising, purchasing and discarding unwanted goods, to the detriment of the planet and our own well-being.

Notes

1. James, Oliver, 2009, *Affluenza*, Vermillion, xvi
2. Jackson, Tim, 2009, *Prosperity without Growth*, Earthscan, 100
3. Lyons, Gerard, 2012, The Shift in the Balance of Economic and Financial Power, *Britain & Overseas*, Autumn 2012
4. Rifkind, Hugo, 2009, *The Times*, 4 December 2009
5. Lloyds TSB Insurance, quoted in *The Times*, 15 February 2010
6. Eg Haidt, Jonathan, 2007, *The Happiness Hypothesis*, Cornerstone; Layard, Richard, 2008, *Happiness: lessons from a new science*, Penguin; *The Times*, 28 April 2018
7. Esipova, Neli, quoted by Cristina Odone, *The Times*, 30 April 2016
8. Slade, Giles, 2006, *Made to Break: Technology and Obsolescence in America*, Harvard University Press, quoted in Botsman, Rachel and Rogers, Roo, 2011, *What's Mine is Yours: How Collaborative Consumption is Changing the Way We Live*, HarperCollins
9. Wallman, James, 2015, *Stuffocation*, Penguin, 2015
10. Kettering, Charles, 1929, Keep the Consumer Dissatisfied, *Nation's Business*, 17, no 1 (January 1929): 30–31,79, quoted in Botsman and Rogers, 2011
11. Galbraith, J K, 1958, *The Affluent Society*, Hamish Hamilton
12. www.modernlibrary.com/top-100/100-best-nonfiction
13. Galbraith, 1958, 97
14. Galbraith, 1958, 123
15. Galbraith, 1958, 111
16. Galbraith, 1958, 154
17. Galbraith, 1958, 156
18. *Household debt inequalities*, Office for National Statistics, 4 April 2016

19. Galbraith, 1958, 223
20. Botsman and Rogers, 2011
21. Morley, Christopher, 1936, *Streamlines*, Doubleday, quoted in Vogt, William, *Road to Survival*, William Sloane Associates, 1948
22. Appleton, Josie, review of Benjamin Barber, *Consumed*, www.spiked-online.com/index.php?/site/reviewofbooks_article/5026
23. Sandel, Michael, 2012, If I ruled the world, *Prospect*, October 2012
24. Sandel, Michael, 2012, *What Money Can't buy: The Moral Limits of Markets*, Allen Lane
25. EthicalSystems.org makes the world's best research available and accessible, for free, to anyone interested in improving the ethical culture and behaviour of an organisation

Chapter 4
The Growing Population

The more people, the harder it is to provide enough food, educate children and sustain the environment.

Bill Gates[1]

In every country where women have gained some degree of social and financial independence, their average fertility has dropped by a corresponding amount through individual personal choice.

Edward O Wilson[2]

Too many people

The more people there are in the world, the greater the damage they can do. The problems described in chapter 1 are aggravated by the size of the world's population. There is an interesting correlation, for example, between world population and carbon-dioxide concentrations in the atmosphere.[3]

If there were just 1 billion of us, as there were in 1800, the situation would be much less severe. The damage arising from deforestation, overgrazing and groundwater extraction would be more manageable, perhaps under the Earth's self-regulating powers, and greenhouse-gas emissions would be much lower. Edward O Wilson's dream of setting aside half the earth for nature (see page 161)[4] would be more readily achievable. Our environmental problems become more serious the more people there are.

Advances in medicine and hygiene, coinciding with the agricultural and industrial revolutions, have reduced childhood and infant mortality and extended the average adult life span. World population thus reached 3 billion in 1960 and 7 billion in 2011. United Nations projections in 2010 indicated that it would reach between 8 and 11 billion by 2050. Thereafter, projections range widely from, on the one hand, a continuing upward trend to 16 billion in 2100 and, on the other, a peak of 8 billion and falling back to 6 billion in 2100. These projections expect that fertility levels will fall; if they were to remain at present levels, world population would exceed 25 billion in

2100. The annual rate of increase peaked at 2 per cent in the 1960s and now stands at 1.1 per cent.[5]

The countries with highest population growth rate include Afghanistan and most of sub-Saharan Africa apart from South Africa. Countries with the lowest rate of growth include most of the Western world, Russia (where the population actually fell from 148.6 million in 1991 to 142.8 million in 2010 and there is now a generously funded scheme to boost the birthrate), China, Japan and most of Latin America.

If we are to see a sustainable future for the Earth, one of the first priorities must be to stabilise, and then reduce, the world's population. This message is not new. It was not even new when William Vogt wrote his widely read book *Road to Survival* in 1948,[6] warning that the dangers of soil erosion, groundwater depletion, deforestation and surface-water pollution are aggravated by population growth – and the global population then was less than 3 billion.

A reduction in the birth rate has socio-economic benefits. Living costs for smaller families are less than for large families, and it is easier for both parents to be wage-earners, so higher living standards follow smaller families, not the other way round. The Bill and Melinda Gates Foundation was established in 2000 to enhance healthcare and reduce extreme poverty across the world, and Melinda Gates has written that 'Contraceptives are also one of the greatest antipoverty innovations in history'.[7]

The well-known saying, 'If you educate a man, you educate an individual; but if you educate a woman, you educate a nation' recognises the important point that it is not only women who benefit from the education and general advancement of women: the whole community benefits. The evidence is clear, for example, that women's education and advancement is the key to reducing population growth. There is also plenty of evidence that when women get the opportunities that have traditionally been the preserve of men, they are no less successful than men.[8]

Control population growth: to do or taboo?

Like many of today's environmental concerns, population growth was widely discussed in the late 1960s: I remember a car sticker, 'Overpopulation is your baby'. Paul Ehrlich's *Population Bomb* was published in 1968; the Club of Rome was founded in that year and its *The Limits to Growth* was published in 1972.[9]

In the following decades the question of population growth was less discussed in Britain. A few years ago it was reported that David Attenborough, a powerful advocate of population control and a patron of the Optimum Population Trust, found there was 'some sort of bizarre taboo' about the issue that prevented population from being discussed.[10] It was thought that any suggestion that population should be controlled was an infringement on women's liberty to have children and therefore was unacceptable, with implications of government coercion and control. Any discussion of the population problem was thought of as coercive. This is to miss the point, however. There is no need to preach, telling people not to have more than a certain number of children. There is evidence from many countries that when certain conditions and opportunities are in place, women, on average, decide for themselves that they do not want large families. What is needed is some relatively simple actions that governments can facilitate: availability of contraceptive materials and information about birth control; education for girls; and opportunities for young women in the workplace. The idea is not to prevent women from having the children they want but to foster an environment in which, on average, they will want to have smaller families – and then to enable them to plan their families as they wish. Women who want large families will be offset by those who want one child or none at all.

In 1993, during this period when concern about population was out of fashion, a Population Summit of 60 national scientific academies, including the Royal Society, warned that, without a significant slowing of population growth, 'science and technology may not be able to prevent irreversible degradation and continued poverty for much of the world.' The Academies recommended 'zero population growth within the lifetime of our children.'[11]

The International Conference on Population and Development in Cairo in the following year ignored this advice, as well as the evidence of the success of family-planning programmes. Anything to do with population was deemed coercive, and even the word 'demographic' became politically incorrect. In Kenya, for example, following this conference, family-planning budgets dropped and the fall in fertility rates stalled.[12]

There are some who argue that population growth is confined to poor countries and it is the rich countries who are causing all the damage to the planet. We should concentrate on reducing consumption in the rich countries, so the argument runs, and not bother about population issues in poorer countries. This argument ignores the environmental damage in poor countries resulting from overgrazing, soil degradation and deforestation – all of which will be exacerbated by pressure on the land resulting from population growth. It also fails to take account of the natural and reasonable aspirations of poor people to adopt lifestyles that compare with those of the richer nations. Furthermore, each birth results in the environmental damage caused by all of that person's descendants. That is why population growth in the poorest countries is important: present-day individuals may have limited impact on the environment in the course of their short lives, but their descendants will hope for higher living standards and longer lives, with greater environmental impact. The more descendants they have, the greater the impact on the environment.

Another argument is that world poverty is a more important issue and we should be attending to that. Poverty is indeed an important issue – and it is closely tied in with population growth. To quote Melinda Gates again, 'No country in the last 50 years has emerged from poverty without expanding access to contraceptives.'[13]

Again, it can be argued that if we all lived sustainably the planet would hold many more people. The *Biosphere 2* experiment in Arizona, in which eight people lived sustainably for two years in an enclosed biosphere containing 2,000 square metres of farmland, some water and some atmosphere, showed that half an acre could support eight people.[14] Scaled up, this means that you could support 10,000 people per square mile. However, a two-year experiment with highly disciplined volunteers is not the same as everyday life. People need space.

They need space for living, working and recreation. They need contact with nature. They need solitude. There are few places on the planet, other than small, depopulated communities, where people believe that their quality of life would be enhanced if they had more people living nearby.

Fortunately, it is no longer taboo to talk about the desirability of limiting the world's population.[15] It is generally recognised that population growth represents a significant threat to the ability of our planet to remain a congenial and hospitable place for human habitation.

It is estimated that more than 220 million women who want to avoid a pregnancy are not using an effective contraceptive method, and that if all women who want to avoid a pregnancy used modern contraceptives, unintended pregnancies would fall by 70 per cent, from 74 million to 22 million a year.[16] That would mean a significant drop in the global birth rate.

One of the seven key responsibilities of the UK programme of aid to developing countries is 'improving the lives of girls and women through better education and a greater choice on family planning'.[17] In collaboration with the Bill and Melinda Gates Foundation, the UK programme prioritises women in Africa and the Indian subcontinent who want contraception but can't get it.[18]

Family Planning 2020, a global partnership that we're a part of, has set a goal of providing 120 million more women access to contraceptives by 2020. We're focusing on South Asia, where contraceptives are used by only a third of the women, and on Africa – where they're used by fewer than one in five.
Melinda Gates[19]

At the Family Planning Summit in London in July 2017, the Foundation announced an additional donation $375 million to family planning in poor countries.[20]

When fertility rates fall

It is instructive to look at the societies in which fertility rates have gone down in recent years. The first requirement is for birth-control advice and materials to be readily available and the second is that women should want to limit the size of their families.

The reduction in fertility rate from 6.1 to 3.4 in Bangladesh between 1980 and 1996, for example, has been attributed to the greater availability of knowledge and facilities.[21]

Iran adopted a national population policy in 1988. Fertility fell from six children per woman in 1974 to two in 2000. An education campaign was at the heart of this success story.[22] It is significant that Iran scores highly in education for women: for example, in 2012 women made up more than half of university students.

The causes of the huge fertility declines of the past 130 years are well established. Increased use of contraception is the major cause with important contributions from marriage postponement and abortion. Access to contraception and safe abortion are influenced by government policies and programmes. The broader drivers of fertility rate change include the empowerment of women, economic development, mortality decline, improved education, and the spread of new ideas and technologies.

The Royal Society[23]

There is abundant evidence that countries with lower birth rates are those in which girls and women have opportunities for schooling and for employment and self-employment: empowerment of young women. Of particular interest is the study of 296 districts in India by Murti, Guio and Drèze, who found that the only variables to have a statistically significant effect on fertility are female literacy and participation of women in the labour force.[24] It is these factors, rather than economic standard of living, that have the greatest effect on the birth rate.

Another factor influencing family size is falling child mortality. It might be thought that if more children survive to adulthood that would increase the population, but in fact the reverse is the case: women are more inclined to restrict the size of their family when they can be confident that their children will live.

A factor that seems to be less significant than might be supposed is religious teaching. Some Muslims are opposed to birth control but, with the exception of Afghanistan, Muslim countries are not among those with the highest birth rates. The campaign that led to the lowering of the birth rate in Iran had the full support of Islamic leaders.

In the Roman Catholic church, the papal encyclical 'Caritas in veritate' (July 2009) confirmed the traditional opposition to birth control. This document acknowledges the importance of environmental issues, but it fails to recognise the connection between an ever-increasing global population, a degraded environment, and poverty and suffering for billions of people. However, the evidence is that, even in countries where the Roman Catholic church is particularly strong, the other factors that we have considered – the availability of birth control methods and the empowerment of women – are more influential than papal teaching. In Italy, for example, the total fertility rate reached an all-time low of 1.18 children per woman in 1995; immigration since then has led to an increase in family size, but the total fertility rate remained very low, at 1.41 in 2008.[25]

The Chinese experience is instructive. When Mao Ze Dong came to power in 1949 he encouraged couples to have large families. The population rose from 540 million in 1950 to 850 million in 1970. Concerns about this rapid growth led to the introduction in 1970 of a voluntary policy to encourage late marriage, a long gap between children and fewer children – supported by ready availability of contraceptives. Fertility rates dropped from 5.8 in 1970 to 2.9 in 1979, though the population continued to grow because people born in the 1950s and 1960s were themselves now having children.

In 1978 the one-child policy was introduced: with various exceptions, couples living in towns were instructed by the government to restrict their families to one child. The result of this policy is that the average fertility rate fell to below replacement level, though the population continued to grow. It is claimed that the policy has prevented 300 million births, as well as helping 200 million people out of poverty.[26] The one-child policy also, however, gave rise to social and demographic problems (an ageing society with a shrinking workforce, for example, and a lack of extended family: not only would a child have no siblings, but there would be no uncles, aunts or cousins either) and to an excess of males – bald generalisations that conceal a multitude of personal tragedies.[27]

In late 2013 the one-child controls were relaxed, but by that time women had become accustomed to the financial, educational and other advantages of a one-child family: in Shanghai, 90 per cent of women of child-bearing age were eligible to have a second child, but only 5 per cent of them applied to do so.[28] The policy was replaced nationally by a two-child policy in January 2016. Early indications are that most couples appear to be content with just the one child.[29]

The consequences of this history of policy changes are that in 2016 the population grew by 8.1 million to 1.383 billion, as the long-term consequence of the growth policy of the 1950s and 1960s. The workforce fell by 3.49 million and the number of people aged 60 and above increased by 10.86 million.[30] This generational imbalance is set to get worse as all those born in the 1950s and 1960s leave the workforce.

Although it is true that the one-child policy reduced fertility, it was the voluntary policy of the 1970s that brought about the most dramatic falls in fertility.[31] It is also significant to compare with India. Kerala is in some ways similar to China, with high levels of basic education and health care, and it also has favourable features for women's empowerment. In the mid-1990s Kerala's fertility rate, achieved voluntarily, was 1.7 − lower than the 1.8 of China, achieved by the one-child policy.[32]

Other countries with low fertility rates, achieved without coercion, include Japan, Hong Kong, Singapore and Russia. In these countries, as in China, when populations are in steep decline fears are raised that the increasing numbers of older people, past working age, will put too much pressure on the declining numbers of working-age people who will have to support them. The governments in Japan and Singapore, for example, introduced financial incentives to persuade women to have more children.[33]

Government policies to encourage more births in order to solve the problem of generational imbalance ignore the pressing need to reduce the world's population. The imbalance can be solved, if their economies are thriving, by following the example of the United Kingdom and other European countries in allowing immigrants to join the workforce.

United Kingdom

The United Kingdom has been partially saved from the generational imbalance by immigration. The mid-2016 estimate of the UK population was about 65.65 million.[34] The population has been growing in recent years, partly because of immigration and partly because immigrant mothers tend to have larger families. In 2015, more than a third of babies born in England and Wales were to parents one or both of whom were born overseas. In some London boroughs more than 80 per cent of babies had a parent born abroad.[35] The fertility rate for UK-born women in 2015 was 1.76 children per woman, whereas that for foreign-born women was 2.08, close to the replacement rate of 2.1. Immigrants tend to be younger than the average population and have above-average family size, so they contribute to rising longevity and an increasing birth rate. In London, 73 per cent of residents were born overseas.[36]

The UK is a small country with limited space. For many years it has been unable to feed itself. Any development takes up land which can be, and probably has been, used to good purpose. A case can be made that we should aim for a steady decline in the total population. Against this however, there is a case for encouraging a limited amount of immigration, partly to prevent the development of too great a generation imbalance, partly to meet the needs of the economy, and partly to offer a home to refugees.

Notes

1. Gates, Bill, *The Times*, 23 October, 2010
2. Wilson, Edward O, 2016, *Half-Earth: Our Planet's Fight for Life*, Liveright, 190
3. Eg https://wattsupwiththat.com/2016/05/17/the-correlation-between-global-population-and-global-co2/
4. Wilson, 2016
5. *People and the planet*, 2012, The Royal Society Science Policy Centre Report 01/12
6. Vogt, William, *Road to Survival*, William Sloane Associates, 1948
7. www.gatesnotes.com/2017-Annual-Letter?WT.mc_id=02_14_2017_02_AL2017GFO_GF-GFO_&WT.tsrc=GFGFO
8. Eg Sen, Amartya, 1999, *Development as Freedom*, OUP paperback, 2001
9. Ehrlich, Paul, 1969, *Population Bomb*, Sierra Club – Ballantine Books; Meadows, Donella H, Meadows, Dennis L, Randers, Jørgen, and Behrens, William W III, 1972, *The Limits to Growth*, Potomac Associates
10. Rod Liddle, *Sunday Times*, 13 March 2011
11. Potts, Malcolm, 2008, Global Population growth – is it sustainable?, *Science in Parliament*, Spring 2008
12. Potts, 2008

13. www.gatesnotes.com/2017-Annual-Letter?
    WT.mc_id=02_14_2017_02_AL2017GFO_GF-
    GFO_&WT.tsrc=GFGFO
14. Juniper, Tony, 2013, *What has nature ever done for us?* Profile Books
15. Eg Bronwen Maddox, *The Times*, 1 January 2013
16. Singh, S, Darroch, J E and Ashford, L S, 2014, *Adding it up: The Costs and Benefits of Investing in Sexual and Reproductive Health 2014*, Guttmacher Institute
17. www.gov.uk/government/organisations/department-for-international-development/about
18. Eg www.gov.uk/government/news/justine-greening-and-melinda-gates-champion-the-rights-of-girls-and-women
19. www.gatesnotes.com/2017-Annual-Letter?
    WT.mc_id=02_14_2017_02_AL2017GFO_GF-
    GFO_&WT.tsrc=GFGFO
20. http://www.bbc.co.uk/programmes/p058d46z
21. Sen, 2001, 216
22. Porritt, Jonathan, 2009, Do the Maths, *WEM*, Vol 14(3), March 2009
23. *People and the planet*, 2012
24. Sen, 2001, 218
25. Wikipedia: Demographics of Italy
26. Hesketh, Therese, 2008, Global Population growth – is it sustainable? Lessons from China, *Science in Parliament*, Spring 2008, 20–21
27. Fong, Mei, 2016, *One Child*, Oneworld
28. Lewis, Leo, *The Times*, 2 February 2015
29. *The Times*, 23 January 2017
30. *The Times*, 23 January 2017
31. Hesketh, 2008
32. Sen, 2001, 221
33. *The Times*, 30 December 2009; 2 January 2010
34. www.ons.gov.uk/peoplepopulationandcommunity/
    populationandmigration/populationestimates/bulletins/
    annualmidyearpopulationestimates/latest
35. *The Times*, 1 December 2016
36. *The Times*, 26 August 2016

Part 2

The Human Mind and the Natural World

Caring about the environment is not a separate compartment of life. How we behave towards the nature and the natural world is an expression of human nature. Having looked at the impact of human behaviour on the environment, therefore, we now turn our attention to the creature responsible for the damage. What sort of creature are we? In chapter 5 we shall look at humans through the eyes of psychologists. In chapter 6 we see what the moral sense contributes to our thinking and our behaviour. In chapter 7 we look at humans as spiritual beings. Chapter 8 focuses on the enormous capacity of our species to change the way we think and the way we behave. Finally, chapter 9 offers responses to various objections that might be raised to the chapters so far. That's human nature: complex, moral, spiritual, adaptive and argumentative.

Chapter 5
How we Think and Decide

Know then thyself, presume not God to scan,
The proper study of mankind is man.
Placed on this isthmus of a middle state,
A being darkly wise, and rudely great:
With too much knowledge for the sceptic side,
With too much weakness for the stoic's pride,
He hangs between; in doubt to act or rest;
In doubt to deem himself a God, or beast;
In doubt his mind and body to prefer;
Born but to die, and reasoning but to err;
Alike in ignorance, his reason such,
Whether he thinks too little or too much;
Chaos of thought and passion, all confused;
Still by himself abused, or disabused;
Created half to rise, and half to fall;
Great lord of all things, yet a prey to all,
Sole judge of truth, in endless error hurled;
The glory, jest and riddle of the world!

Alexander Pope[1]

In previous chapters we have seen how human behaviour is increasingly damaging our planet as a place fit for human habitation. There are too many of us, and we deliberately choose lifestyles that damage our environment. In this chapter we shall look at some of the characteristics of our species, characteristics that give us such power to destroy our planet as a place fit for human life – and also, I believe, the ability to change the way we live and build a better future. It is by learning to live in harmony with our environment that we shall discover what it is to be truly human.

Homo semi-sapiens

The mind
The human species, it has been said, represents the crowning glory of life on Earth, the summit of the evolutionary tree. We have one thing that other creatures lack, a conscious, intelligent mind, a mind that can detach itself from the here and now (to

61

talk about yesterday's football, for example, or about famine in a distant country) and can form opinions, examine its own workings and make considered choices and decisions. The human brain is the most complex object in the known universe. This has given us a competitive advantage over other species.

Amazing though it is, however, somehow the human mind seems not to live up to its full potential. These advanced mental processes don't really work anything like as well as the highly developed instinctive and subconscious mental abilities that we share with other animals.

To take one example, when we are walking over rough ground, something that many other animals can do, our brain receives messages from the eyes, the feet and the sense of balance. It processes all this information and it controls and coordinates the numerous muscles that keep us walking and keep us upright, all without our having to think about it. Compared with the complexity of these mental tasks, a simple calculation of the kind that only humans can attempt (like multiplying 9876 by 5432) might seem easy – but most of us find it far more difficult than walking.

Recognition provides another example. Humans and other animals are able to recognise certain individuals of the same and different species. This works well as a subconscious process, but not if we rely on the conscious, intelligent, verbal part of our mind: try using words to describe some people who are well known to you, in such a way that someone else could use your description to identify those people in a crowd.

The animal mind can do amazing things – and do them well. The human mind can do many of the same things equally well. The uniquely human functions, in contrast, just don't work so well. The human mind has the ability to think clearly and rationally – yet so often our thoughts are confused and irrational, even to the point of stupidity. It provides us with the tools to communicate with one another in a very detailed and profound way – and yet so often our understanding of each other is terribly inadequate. We are able to appreciate beauty – and yet we are willing to destroy the beauty of nature and create ugliness in its place. We have a conscience and an ability to think about the consequences of our decisions (see chapter 6) – and yet we so often choose not to do the right thing.

Many people seem to hold the belief that humans are rational beings, and express surprise at what seems to them to be irrational or abnormal behaviour. This leads them to be uncomfortable when dealing with anyone whose mind is not working in a way that they would describe as normal or rational – as a result of overpowering emotion, for example, or severe anxiety or depression.

A moment's reflection, however, or a moment's self-examination, should tell us that humans are not rational beings. The human mind is inherently undisciplined. Time and again, it fails to concentrate on the matter in hand; it takes us off in directions we would rather not go; and it fails to provide us with the emotions, the will power and the rationality that we would like to have at our disposal.[2]

We really don't deserve to be called *Homo sapiens*. *Homo semi-sapiens*, perhaps. The human mind looks like work in progress, and the psychologist Steven Pinker provides evidence that progress has, indeed, been taking place.[3] Not only have humans become less violent: our mental powers have also been increasing.

The brain

The brain is the product of evolution, and evolution works by building on what is already there. It doesn't scrap what's there and start again a better way. The psychologist Gary Marcus shows how this 'kluge', as he calls it, can explain many of the ways the human mind works.[4] In particular, it can explain many of the ways in which the mind doesn't work as well as we might think it should.

The older parts of the brain have been refined over hundreds of millions of years. They are responsible for the mental functions that we share with many other species. Like other animals, we feed ourselves, we strive to keep alive, we produce offspring and we nurture our offspring until they are able to look after themselves. In order to achieve these objectives we have control over our body movements and we move around. These basic functions are controlled by the earlier regions of the brain. They also control the basic emotions (fear, pleasure, anger) and drives of the 'I want' variety (hunger, sex, dominance, care of offspring). All these functions are controlled from the brain – and they work really well.

The human brain is three times as large, in relation to body size, as the chimpanzee's. Much of the size comes from the cerebral cortex, especially the frontal lobes (the prefrontal cortex), which are associated with executive functions such as self-control, planning, reasoning and abstract thought. This part of the brain is also associated with the emotions that enable us to make decisions and set goals.[5] It is these parts of the brain and the associated mental functions that are the most recent add-ons, providing us with the mental powers that are unique to our species.

This new part of the brain acts slowly – and, as we have seen, it doesn't always work very well. The good news is that it is capable of self-improvement. We don't have to wait for the slow processes of natural selection. The architecture of our brain is more malleable than we realised, and we have the capacity to train and develop some of the functions of the prefrontal cortex – as we shall see later in this chapter.

In two minds

The elephant and the rider

Jonathan Haidt[6] advances the metaphor of the elephant and the rider for the working of the human mind: 'The mind is divided into parts that sometimes conflict.' Like a rider on the back of an elephant, the conscious, reasoning part of the mind has only limited control over what we actually think or do. The rider can control the elephant, 'but only when the elephant doesn't have desires of his own'.[7] The rider can see further into the future and can learn new skills and technologies, and so can help the elephant make better choices. Importantly, the rider acts as a spokesman, providing a (possibly spurious) reasoned defence of what the elephant has decided. However, the rider is an advisor or servant, not a king or president. It cannot order the elephant around against its will. It is the rider who has the power of language, and Haidt points out that we spend too much time concentrating on conscious, verbal thinking and don't make enough effort to understand the elephant and recognise what an important part of our nature it is.

How we make decisions

Other animals make decisions quickly, on the basis of information available to them. Natural selection has favoured individuals who lived in the moment and made decisions accordingly.[8] They are not able to think of different possible futures and take them into account when making decisions.

This is our inheritance. Some of the things humans do, similarly, are in response to very specific mental or physical circumstances. We are thirsty, so we drink. We have a craving for chocolate, so we eat some. We are too hot in front of the fire, so we move away. A car is about to hit us, so we move away. These actions are determined by the elephant, unless the rider intervenes. Other decisions are made by an interaction between the elephant and the rider.

Psychological investigations have demonstrated that humans, like other animals, tend to make decisions rapidly, without carefully thinking over the pros and cons; they tend to make them on the basis of known or supposed circumstances at the time of decision-making and influenced by their emotions or state of mind at the time. In one experiment, office workers were asked to select which snack they'd like to have in a week's time, in the late afternoon. Those that were hungry at the time of choosing were more likely to order unhealthy snacks, like crisps or sweets; those who were not hungry were more likely to choose healthy snacks – apples or bananas. How they felt at the time of choosing affected their decisions about something that would not happen until several days later.[9]

Unlike other animals, humans are able to consider different possible futures and take them into account. They are also able to take moral considerations into account. However, the decision-making process is not fully integrated with these new capacities; it fails to use the strengths of being fully human.

Daniel Kahneman describes in some detail in *Thinking, Fast and Slow* the 'systematic biases in our own decisions, intuitive preferences that consistently violate the rules of rational choice.'[10] He describes mental life in terms of two agents of thought, System 1 and System 2, which, respectively, produce fast and slow thinking. System 1 operates automatically and quickly, with little or no effort and no sense of voluntary control. It is basically intuitive and includes innate skills that we share with other animals, though it also includes acquired skills. System 2 is deliberative, allocating attention to mental activities that demand effort. Since the operation of System 2 requires mental effort (examples include mental arithmetic, and the self-control required to restrain our less attractive impulses) we are inclined to take the easy way out and avoid using it, following instead wherever System 1 might lead us: we use our intuitive judgement rather than trying to reason the issue out. We may like to believe that we are reasoning creatures, but we rely on our intuition far more than we recognise. Kahneman's book describes numerous ways in which System 1 (for all its undeniable strengths and value: what it does, it does well) gets it wrong and makes false judgements. System 2 can often do better, but it requires effort – and it is often too lazy to check the judgements and choices made by System 1.

Gary Marcus explains how the structure of the human brain can explain these aberrations of the mind: 'Rationality, pretty much by definition, demands a thorough and judicious balancing of evidence, but the circuitry of mammalian memory simply isn't attuned to that purpose. The speed and context-sensitivity of memory no doubt helped our ancestors, who had to make snap decisions in a challenging environment. But in modern times, this former asset has become a liability. When context tells us one thing, but rationality another, rationality often loses.'[11]

What is important for our purposes is that when we make decisions, our feelings, our desires at the time of choosing, tend to weigh much more heavily than any consideration of the future. We have the ability to think of possible futures and sometimes we take these considerations into account, but all too often the present situation and our present state of mind are the dominant influences. However, we can learn to give greater weight to long-term considerations.

Motivation and goal-setting: the pursuit of happiness

Evolution didn't evolve us to be happy, it evolved us to pursue happiness.
Gary Marcus[12]

Why do people behave as they do? Can we understand what it is that makes us damage our environment? Can we go on from there to understand what might motivate us to behave in less damaging ways? Is it possible for us to change? If so, what would make us change? Is it possible for the creative energies that humans possess to be harnessed in a more constructive way? Is there anything that politicians and other leaders can do to help this? There are many possible answers to these questions.

It is easy to say that all we want for ourselves, and for our families and friends, is to be happy. We want to be happy, or avoid unhappiness and pain. We make decisions because we think they will make us feel good; because we think they will be in our best interests in one way or another. Happiness, at one level or another, is what we strive for. We may know well enough what we mean, but happiness, in this sense, is very hard to define. We may think that other words, like pleasure, joy, contentment, flourishing or well-being, may better express what we mean. For simplicity, I shall use the term happiness in the text that follows, though I recognise the inadequacy of the word.

The human personality is full of contradictions and paradoxes.[13] In trying to find happiness, we may seek risk, excitement and danger, or we may seek peace, tranquility and security; we may seek happiness through competition with other people, or through cooperation; through conflict or through mutual esteem; through conformity (influenced by authority or by peer approval) or by challenging or rebelling against accepted norms of thought or behaviour. At a deeper level, we may seek happiness through immediate gratification of the senses, or through setting aside these senses and looking to the long term (see below); from immediate gratification by giving way to temptation, or through resisting temptation and trying to do the right thing (see below). This saying of Mark Twain is an example of the difficulty in pinning down just what we mean by seeking happiness: 'Do something every day that you don't want to do; this is the golden rule for acquiring the habit of doing your duty without pain.'

Although it is possible to make generalisations, and many aspects of the human personality are indeed common to almost all humans, we also need to remember that each of us is unique. Choices and activities that bring happiness and fulfilment to one will not do so for another: 'A musician must make music, an artist must paint, a poet must write, if he is to be ultimately at peace with himself. What a man can be, he must be. He must be true to his own nature. This need we may call self-actualisation.'[14]

Haidt discusses the pursuit of happiness at some length in *The Happiness Hypothesis*. One commonly held view is that happiness comes from getting what we want; the resulting happiness from this tends to be short-lived. Another view is that happiness comes from within, from breaking emotional attachments and cultivating an attitude of acceptance. We could say that the first of these views is a victory for the elephant, the second a defeat. In fact, happiness comes from within and from without. Some of our efforts to achieve happiness are more likely to be successful than others. This is where the rider needs to influence the elephant, steering it in directions that are more likely to lead to happiness. The influence of the rider is even greater if the goal is human flourishing – which is probably too sophisticated a concept for the elephant to appreciate.

It has been found that there are some things that we seek because we believe they will make us happy, but they fail.[15] Chasing after wealth and prestige, for example, will usually backfire. The acquisition of luxury goods often fails to make us happy – particularly important and relevant to the theme of this book. More generally, wealth, above a certain level, fails to make us any happier.[16] Greater happiness is found in people who pursue less materialistic goals.

David Brooks, in *The Social Animal*,[17] also points out that people are not good at judging what will make them happy. As well as overvaluing money and possessions, they undervalue the bonds with family and friends and the importance of tough challenges. Mihaly Csikszentmihalyi describes how, for many people, the most satisfying state of all is that of total immersion in a task that is challenging yet closely matched to their abilities.[18] This state, which he calls 'flow', includes a vast range of activities: physical activities, including sport; artistic creativity; any kind of mental or physical skill, including going for a run or doing a crossword puzzle.

Martin Seligman drew on this work to propose a fundamental distinction between pleasures and gratifications.[19] Pleasures, such as food and sex, are 'delights that have clear sensory and strong emotional components'. Gratifications are activities that engage you fully, draw on your strengths and allow you to lose self-consciousness. The elephant is liable to overindulge in pleasures, but gratifications, identified by the rider, provide more lasting happiness.

Eric Lambin's list of five categories of factors that determine a happy life (drawn from many studies in the literature)[20] includes:

- Personal situation: health, affective life, leisure, work, mobility
- A feeling of security: the fear of criminality, conflicts, wars
- The social environment: belonging to a network of relationships, feeling of confidence, availability in case of need
- The institutional environment: freedom, political involvement, the proper functioning of the justice system
- The natural environment: freedom from noise and pollution, access to preserved natural spaces, the feeling of being connected to nature.

Note the last of these. Many studies have shown the beneficial effects of contact with nature.

Seligman is a leading proponent of positive psychology: the exploration of 'what makes life worth living and building the enabling conditions of a life worth living'. In *Flourish: a new understanding of happiness and well-being – and how to achieve them*,[21] he discusses the ingredients of such a life. They include:

- Meaning (belonging to and serving something that you believe is bigger than the self)
- Gratitude
- Counting blessings
- Performing acts of kindness
- Good relationships with other people

These characteristics are associated with the prefrontal cortex.

We may note from the above that the kind of activities that bring us the greatest happiness and satisfaction often have a low environmental impact. Activities with a high environmental impact fail to deliver the happiness that they promise.

There is another important motivator for human behaviour, which forms a significant part of human thinking, and that is the wish to do as we ought, the wish to be good. This has received very little attention from psychologists, with notable exceptions like Jonathan Haidt, but it is an important part of the human make-up, as discussed in the next chapter.

Self-control

The very term 'self-control' speaks of the duality of human nature: one part of us wishes to control another part. It is an ancient term, but it recognises the conflict within us, as illustrated by Haidt's elephant-and-rider metaphor.

The marshmallow test has become widely known since it was brought to the attention of a general readership by the *New York Times* columnist David Brooks in 2006. Devised in the 1960s by the pioneering psychologist Walter Mischel, the test involved sitting a four-year-old (pre-school) child alone in a room with a treat (a marshmallow, say) and a bell. The child was told that if they rang the bell the experimenter would return at once and they could eat the marshmallow. Alternatively, if they waited till the experimenter returned (15 or 20 minutes, perhaps) they could have two marshmallows. Naturally, the child would prefer the second option, but this required a degree of self-control which is unusual in a four-year-old. Mischel recorded the length of time that each child could wait before ringing the bell or tasting the marshmallow. In following up the child in school and in later life, he found that the amount of self-control exhibited at the age of four was a remarkably good guide to success in later life.[22]

Recounted like this, it would seem that our destiny was settled by the age of four, but Mischel went on to show that this is not so. We have seen how Jonathan Haidt used the metaphor of the elephant and the rider to illustrate the thinking associated with the older (limbic system) and newer (pre-frontal cortex) parts of the brain, and Daniel Kahneman used the terms 'thinking fast' and 'thinking slow'. Mischel uses the terms 'hot emotional system' and 'cool cognitive system'.

70

He describes plans and strategies that can be used successfully to learn, develop and strengthen our self-control and enable the cool aspect of our nature to master the hot aspect. This enables him to paint a positive picture of the human potential for self-generated change. He shows how the development of self-control can enable youngsters from the most disadvantaged backgrounds in New York to develop their potential far beyond what might be expected from their background.

In Britain, John Bird, who has done so much to help people to lift themselves out of homelessness and poverty, writes of the importance of delayed gratification in enabling people to escape from poverty: 'Delayed gratification is what we need to inspire in people in desperate circumstances that they wish to end. And don't patronise the homeless by saying they are not capable of delayed gratification'.[23]

One of the outstanding features of the human mind is its capacity for self-improvement. We have the capacity to change the way we think, to learn new ways of operating. Mischel presents evidence that the human mind is much more flexible and malleable than has often been supposed. Self-control can be nurtured. Training can yield not just improvements in self-control but also changes in the neural functions of the brain.[24] Self-control can be strengthened over an individual's lifetime and it can 'vary in strength across societies and historical periods'.[25]

Self-control does not provide us with goals. It gives us the freedom to identify our goals and has an important role in helping us to achieve them.

Applications to sustainable living

… the real question, which is that of human motivation. What leads people to spoil their environment, and what leads them to protect it?

Roger Scruton[26]

What leads us to care for those who are not yet born?

Roger Scruton[27]

As we have seen, part of the human brain – and therefore part of our thinking and behaviour – closely resembles that of our pre-human ancestors and part is unique to humans. A great deal of human behaviour, both good and bad, can thus be understood in terms of our pre-human animal ancestry. It is motivated by our instincts and emotions, and we can see similar behaviour in other animals, most notably in chimpanzees, our closest relatives.[28]

A study of our inheritance can thus help us to understand what leads us to be so destructive of our environment. A modern understanding of how the two parts of our mind relate to one another can help us to train ourselves to care for the environment.

One characteristic that we inherit from our pre-human ancestors is a sense of **ownership**. In other species, this applies particularly to food and territory; animals try to take from others, and to defend what is their own. We do the same. We also like to get hold of more than enough to satisfy present needs, and even here we recognise our similarity to other animals when we talk of squirrelling things away.

For other species and for pre-modern humans, it makes sense to be acquisitive, to get and keep what we can. Archaeological studies show that a love of artefacts goes back a long time. Today's affluent society, however, gives us the opportunity to acquire so much more than we need. This leads to the consumer society that we discussed in Chapter 3.

Another inherited characteristic is a hunger for **power**. Other species have social structures based on power, as exemplified by terms like 'pecking order' and 'alpha male', and humans are the same. Power over others gives us status and security (or that's what we like to think), as well as raising our self-esteem (so important in today's thinking).

In the modern world we try to reduce the power of the powerful, but this is never more than partially successful, partly because power-hunger is ingrained in our nature and partly because the only way power can be reined in is by the power of another.

Possessions, skill and power are attractive for themselves, but in many species they have a specially important role in **creating a favourable impression**, particularly in attracting a mate. This provides a very powerful motive in other species and in ourselves. The attraction of a mate is one of the most powerful of life forces. This may encourage ostentatious extravagance, as in the peacock's tail, or displays of power, as in the alpha male.

In humans, the desire to impress someone of the opposite sex is extended to a desire to impress people we like – and even people we don't like: 'Too many people spend money they haven't earned to buy things they don't want to impress people they don't like.'[29]

A third characteristic that we share with other species is **self-centredness**. We automatically put our own interests, or our perceived interests first. This is tempered, in mammals and birds, by the instinct to care for our own offspring, and this caring instinct may be extended to caring for others (especially in humans),[30] but in most circumstances priority goes to the self. Again, this makes sense for pre-modern humans and other species, but it does not make sense for modern humans if it means depriving future generations of the opportunities that we ourselves are enjoying.

A fourth characteristic is that, like other animals, we are creatures of **habit**. When we have got used to a certain way of thinking or behaving, we tend to stick to it. We are capable of change, but change requires strong incentive and/or mental effort and, as Daniel Kahneman points out, when it comes to mental effort we tend to be lazy.

An understanding of these inherited and ingrained human characteristics can help us to see how it is that we have wrought such damage on our environment. In the metaphor of the rider and the elephant, the elephant seeks possessions, power and a rich, powerful and attractive mate; it thinks only of self and the present, and has no desire – nor, indeed, the ability – to weigh up the arguments for or against change or to consider the future. The lazy rider is happy enough to travel along with the elephant. If it makes any contribution at all, it is to work out ways of satisfying the elephant's demands and devising clever arguments to justify whatever it is that the elephant wants to do. Applied to environmental damage, we can see the lethal power of the elephant's narrow-visioned motives supported by the rider's intelligence.

If the rider sets aside his laziness – if the human applies that greatest of human attributes, the mind – he can train himself, and the elephant, to live an environment-friendly lifestyle. The desire for possessions and power can be directed away from destructive actions. We can train ourselves not to be impressed by an environmentally destructive lifestyle and, instead, to admire the people we know who find ways to live sustainably. Other species can be trained to change their habitual ways, but we humans can train ourselves.

We can conclude, therefore, that many of the behavioural characteristics that lead us to damage our environment have their roots in ways of thinking inherited from our prehuman ancestors and that the way to adopt lives that are more in harmony with the Earth and with each other is through seeking to develop the uniquely human attributes that are centred in the later, human part of the brain. It is by this training that *Homo semi-sapiens* might be able to evolve into a creature that deserves the title *Homo sapiens*.

Notes

1. Pope, Alexander, 1734, *An Essay on Man*
2. Gary Marcus, in *Kluge*, gives numerous examples, as does Daniel Kahneman in *Thinking, Fast and Slow* – and we can easily think of more from our own experience
3. Pinker, Steven, 2011, *The Better Angels of Our Nature*, Allen Lane
4. Marcus, Gary, 2008, *Kluge: The Haphazard Evolution of the Human Mind*, Faber and Faber
5. Haidt, Jonathan 2007, *The Happiness Hypothesis: Finding Modern Truth in Ancient Wisdom*, Cornerstone (first published by Basic Books, 2006)
6. Haidt, 2007; Haidt, Jonathan, 2012, *The Righteous Mind: Why Good People are Divided by Politics and Religion*, Pantheon Books, 2012
7. Haidt, 2007, 4
8. Marcus, 2008, 84
9. Marcus, 2008, 83; other examples in Kahneman, 2011
10. Kahneman, Daniel, 2011, *Thinking, Fast and Slow*, Allen Lane
11. Marcus, 2008
12. Marcus, 2008, 139
13. Eg Talbot, Colin, 2005, *The Paradoxical Primate*, Imprint Academic
14. Maslow, Abraham, 1954, *Motivation and Personality*, Harper and Row
15. Haidt, 2007
16. Eg Layard, Richard, 2008, *Happiness: lessons from a new science*, Penguin; Kahneman, Daniel and others, 2006, Would you be happier if you were richer?: A focusing illusion, *Science*, 312(5782), 1908–1910 (quoted in Marcus, 2008); Lambin, Eric, 2012, *An ecology of happiness*, University of Chicago Press; Belton, Teresa, 2014, *Happier People Healthier Planet*, Silverwood Books; *The Times*, 28 April 2018
17. Brooks, David, 2011, *The Social Animal*, Short Books

18. Csikszentmihalyi, Mihaly, 1990, *Flow: The Psychology of Optimal Experience*, Harper Collins
19. Quoted by Haidt, 2007
20. Lambin, 2012
21. Seligman, Martin, 2011, *Flourish: a new understanding of happiness and well-being – and how to achieve them*, Nicholas Brealey
22. Mischel, Walter, 2015, *The Marshmallow Test*, Corgi (first published by Bantam Press, 2014)
23. Bird, John, 2016, Be patient, we'll end poverty with delayed gratification, *The Big Issue*, May 30 – June 5, 2016, p11
24. Mischel, 2015, 235
25. Pinker, 2011, 738
26. Scruton, Roger, 2012, *Green Philosophy: How to Think Seriously About the Planet*, Atlantic Books, 137
27. Scruton, 2012, 208
28. Eg de Waal, Frans, 1982, *Chimpanzee Politics*, Harper & Row; Goodall, Jane, 1990, *Through a Window*, George Weidenfeld & Nicholson; de Waal, Frans, 1996, *Good Natured: The Origins of Right and Wrong in Humans and other Animals*, Harvard University Press
29. Will Smith
30. Haslam, Henry, 2005, *The Moral Mind*, Imprint Academic, and references therein

Chapter 6
Ethics and the Environment

I fully subscribe to the judgement of those writers who maintain that of all the differences between man and the lower animals, the moral sense or conscience is by far the most important.

Charles Darwin[1]

Self-control, as we have seen in the last chapter, can help us to achieve our goals. But how do we set our goals? One of the features of the human mind is the moral sense or conscience, the sense that there are morally right and wrong ways to behave. There is general agreement about some moral issues, whereas in other issues there is room for disagreement. We can debate whether certain actions are good or bad – but one thing we can agree on is that the debate is about something real, something that matters. In an earlier book, *The Moral Mind*,[2] I surveyed our moral thinking as an important aspect of the human personality, drawing attention, particularly, to the way it engages with patterns of behaviour that we have inherited from our pre-human primate ancestors. Three main conclusions can be drawn from this study.

The first conclusion is that the moral sense is an important part of the human personality, part of what makes us human. It comes naturally to us to consider that we, or other people, ought or ought not to have acted in a certain way. We apply words like good, bad, right and wrong to human behaviour, and we think that these words mean something, and something that matters. 'Distinguishing between right and wrong' is a human universal.[3]

David Brooks puts it like this. 'We do have a strong impulse to be as moral as possible, or to justify ourselves when our morality is in question. Having a universal moral sense does not mean that people always or even often act in good and virtuous ways. It's more about what we admire than what we do, more about the judgements we make than our ability to live up to them. But we are possessed by a deep motivation to be and be seen as a moral person.'[4]

The second conclusion is that, as Brooks points out, this moral sense doesn't, in practice, seem to make a lot of difference to the way we behave. Other species manage very well without a moral sense.[5] If an alien observer were asked to identify the only moral animal on Earth it is unlikely that they would automatically point at the human species.[6] When we say that humans are moral beings, we mean that they are capable of making moral judgements, not that their behaviour is morally superior to that of other creatures.

How we actually behave is not influenced particularly by our moral sense. We are driven, much more, by our instincts (the elephant – see chapter 5), inherited from our pre-human ancestors, and by what we perceive to be in our interests or to bring us happiness, in the short term or the long term (the rider).

The third conclusion is that our moral feelings cannot be explained, or explained away, in terms of anything else. They are not all a matter of upbringing or culture; it is true that we obtain many of our moral values from our parents and from the community in which we live, but our own moral sense may well lead us to reject some of these values as we seek to establish our own personal moral framework.

Nor can our moral sense be explained by current evolutionary theory. Several authors have suggested that it can be accounted for by the Darwinian theory of natural selection, but this hypothesis does not stand up to scrutiny. T H Huxley expressed it succinctly: 'Cosmic evolution may teach us how the good and evil tendencies of man may have come about; but, in itself, it is incompetent to furnish any better reason why what we call good is preferable to what we call evil than we had before.'[7] The argument is spelt out in detail in *The Moral Mind*.[8]

Finally, there is no simple correlation between the moral sense and religion. People with no religious belief can have just as strong a moral sense as religious believers, and believers often find that there is a conflict between the moral teaching of their religion and their own innate sense of right and wrong.

We are so used to living with this sense that some behaviours are right and others are wrong that we take it for granted. We do not realise what an extraordinary phenomenon it is: powerful enough to triumph over every theory that we can put forward in our attempts to pin it down or constrain it, and yet pitifully weak in its ability to make us live virtuous lives. Perhaps that is why the subject has always had a fascination for philosophers but, with very few exceptions,[9] it has been largely ignored by psychologists and sociologists.

Looked at in the context of *Homo semi-sapiens* as described in the previous chapter:

- The moral sense is a uniquely human attribute, associated with the human, frontal lobes of the brain. Some primates show early signs of moral awareness,[10] but it is much more developed in humans.

- Like other uniquely human attributes, it doesn't work very well. In one sense, our moral convictions are our own, but to regard them as entirely subjective doesn't seem quite good enough. As Bertrand Russell put it, 'I cannot see how to refute arguments for the subjectivity of moral values, but I find myself incapable of believing that all that is wrong with wanton cruelty is that I don't like it'.[11] We feel that our moral convictions are more than just a personal emotion. We feel that we are reaching out and trying to express something outside and beyond ourselves – but we can't quite grasp what that something is. Also, as we have noted, whatever we might mean by good behaviour, humans are not notably better behaved than other species.

- The elephant (in Haidt's metaphor) has no understanding of morality. As the rider seeks to control the elephant, he may (or may not) try to make it behave in a morally right way.

The twentieth-century assault on moral values

There is overwhelming evidence that the moral sense is an important part of the human personality (see above). For most of history, it has been taken for granted that moral values were real. Great thinkers have considered what was good and bad behaviour, and many volumes have been written on the subject. However, for a large part of the twentieth century, much of what had previously been taken for granted was questioned. The weakening of respect for authority and the decline of religious belief, left many people confused about the value and validity of moral sentiments, feeling that these scruples may not be intellectually defensible. This trend was led – or at least encouraged – by philosophers such as A J Ayer, who claimed that statements like 'Stealing money is wrong' have no factual meaning, being simply expressions of moral sentiment or emotion.[12]

In a world of liberal values and expanding horizons, and in learning to appreciate and understand other people and societies, we were no longer satisfied with a traditional system of clear-cut values. There was a general feeling that tolerance, understanding and compassion were more important than strict adherence to traditional moral codes. These new virtues are, of course, also moral values, but the word 'morality' was apt to be associated with rigid codes of the past. It became smart to be cynical, to deride moral sentiments and assume that all human behaviour was influenced by base motives. Simon Blackburn, in *Being Good*, wrote, 'What bothers [people], I believe, are the many causes we have to fear that ethical claims are a kind of sham'.[13]

We are coming out of this phase now. Once again, most people take for granted the existence and importance of moral values. Writers and politicians readily talk about 'the right thing to do'. Business people have seen the consequences that followed from the loss of their former reputation for probity. Business leaders and their professional bodies are emphasising the importance of ethical values.

The environment: a moral issue

The message of this book is that we should treat the environment better. This is a moral message. It is about how we ought to live our lives. Traditionally, moral thinking and teaching have been associated mainly with our personal lives, how we behave towards one another. Since the middle of the twentieth century, many people have become uncomfortable with this emphasis on personal behaviour, with the consequence that discussion and writing have tended to concentrate more on political and social issues, but the question 'What should I do in these circumstances?' is one that arises in every area of life.

In the distant past, the issues of overpopulation and environmental damage scarcely arose, but they have become increasingly important in recent years. Today, many of the decisions we take have some impact on the environment, and this applies both to the choices we make in our personal lives and to political decisions.

There is no escaping it: the way we treat our environment is a moral issue. A J McMichael, for example, in summing up the problem in his classic book *Planetary Overload*, writes about 'the general moral problem ... of bequeathing to future generations a negative legacy, an ecologically damaged world.'[14] Paul Collier in *The Plundered Planet* writes 'We have an ethical responsibility to bequeath to unborn generations either the natural assets bequeathed to us, or other assets of equivalent value'.[15] Nicholas Stern in *A Blueprint for a safer planet* writes 'There is no getting away from the fact that making policy towards climate change unavoidably requires one to take a stance on ethical questions'.[16] Roger Scruton in *Green Philosophy* writes, 'Environmental problems are problems of *morality*, not economics.'[17] I could have quoted in similar vein from other writers.

Concern for the environment is not a minor, peripheral matter, with but a small part to play on the ethical stage. Environmental issues are central to the choices we make. The book entitled *Teach Yourself Ethical Living* in the highly regarded Teach Yourself series places care for the environment at the heart of ethical living.[18] For the author, Peter MacBride, 'Ethical living is about sustainability, about not using up irreplaceable resources, about keeping our environment healthy, about dealing fairly with other people.'

From a philosophical standpoint, there are several different reasons why we should value the environment.[19] Broadly, they fall into two categories, those that value the Earth and nature because of their value to humanity and those that value the non-human world for its own sake. Over the centuries, and particularly since the early nineteenth century, there has been a growing sense that our concern for the well-being of others should be extended beyond humans to other species, starting with those most similar to ourselves, chimpanzees and the other great apes, and extending to all sentient creatures.[20]

How we make moral decisions

Emotion and reason

Reasoning can play an important part in helping us to reach a moral decision (especially when we are weighing up the possible consequences of a proposed course of action), but the starting point and driving force lie in the emotions, as pointed out by the philosopher David Hume: 'Morality is more properly felt than judg'd of'; and 'Reason is, and ought only to be the slave of the passions, and can never pretend to any other office than to serve and obey them.'[21] The psychologist Jonathan Haidt agrees: 'Morality is driven by emotions and intuitions, not reasoning.'[22]

The reasoning mind, however, can support our moral emotions, helping us to work out how to apply those moral feelings in specific circumstances. We must remember, though, that it can also provide invaluable service to our other emotions, likes and dislikes, which may have nothing to do with moral thinking. Benjamin Franklin expressed this pithily: 'So convenient a thing it is to be a reasonable creature, since it enables one to find or make a reason for everything one has a mind to do'.[23]

Three ways of thinking about moral issues

There are three main approaches to moral decision-making. The first is **moral principle**. It is wrong to steal or murder, for example. Kindness and generosity are good. Applied to the environment, there are two obvious moral principles: that we should pass this planet on to future generations in as good a condition as we inherited it, and, more fundamentally, that we should regard waste and destruction as morally wrong. Looking after the Earth may not have been a moral principle in the past, but looking after our houses, our fields, our woodlands and our water supply has long been something we have taken for granted, just as it is part of our nature to care about the future well-being of our children and their children. Parents make sacrifices for the sake of their children and take a pride in what they can leave behind for them. Members of the armed forces risk their lives, and some lose their lives, for the sake of the future. There is a stark contrast between the sacrifice expressed in J M Edmonds' first-world-war epitaph,

'When you go home, tell them of us and say, "For your tomorrows these gave their today"'[24] and the short-sighted, uncaring selfishness that we described in the first part of this book.

We traditionally disapprove of extravagance and waste ('Waste not, want not'; 'Make do and mend'). Wanton destruction is widely regarded as a moral issue. Mary Midgley illustrates this in an article entitled 'Duties concerning Islands', in which she asks her readers to imagine that, before leaving his island, Robinson Crusoe had decided to set fire to it and devastate it; it is clearly her intention that her readers should feel a moral abhorrence at such senseless destruction.[25]

The second approach is to judge an action by its consequences (**consequentialist ethics**). What are the likely consequences? What other consequences are unlikely but possible? What would be the benefits? What would be the losses? This kind of thinking is very important in environmental issues. As we have seen, there can be no doubt that if we continue as we are we run a serious risk of destroying the Earth as a place congenial for human life. It is difficult to imagine a moral code that would approve of this. Much of our Earth-damaging behaviour may seem to be entirely innocent in principle – unlike Mary Midgley's imagined island arsonist – but is seen to be morally wrong because of its consequences. We are considering making a purchase: what is the environmental impact of the various products we are considering? We want to make a journey: what is the environmental impact of the various possible ways of reaching our destination? These questions underlie much of the discussion in the third part of this book, where we shall consider how our lifestyle and the economy might look if we attached more importance to caring for the environment.

The third approach, **virtue ethics**, focuses on the character of the person, rather than on the deed itself or its consequences. It is a question of self-image, the kind of person that we want to be; it's about our own integrity. Do I want to be the kind of person who cares about the Earth and about the future? Or do I see myself as the kind of person who lives a life of self-indulgence, not caring that I leave behind me a damaged planet?

Virtue ethics would lead us to be the kind of people who don't leave litter around, who are scrupulous about recycling, who don't ask questions like 'What's the point? Look at the way other people are behaving – they don't care'.

Whatever our approach, the desire to lead a good life should lead us to want to live in a planet-friendly way.

Notes

1. Darwin, Charles, 1871, *The Descent of Man*
2. Haslam, Henry, 2005, *The Moral Mind*, Imprint Academic
3. Brown, Donald E, 1991, *Human Universals*, McGraw-Hill; list reproduced in Pinker, Steven, 2002, *The Blank Slate: The Modern Denial of Human Nature*, Penguin
4. Brooks, David, 2011, *The Social Animal*, Short Books, p288
5. Eg Lorenz, Konrad, 1952, *King Solomon's Ring*, Methuen; Goodall, Jane, 1990, *Through a Window*, George Weidenfeld & Nicholson; de Waal, Frans, 1996, *Good Natured: The Origins of Right and Wrong in Humans and other Animals*, Harvard University Press
6. Flack, Jessica and de Waal, Frans, 2000, 'Any Animal Whatever': Darwinian Building Blocks of Morality in Monkeys and Apes, 1–29 in Katz, Leonard (editor), *Evolutionary Origins of Morality*, Imprint Academic
7. Huxley, T H, 1895, *Evolution & Ethics and other Essays*, Macmillan
8. Haslam, 2005, 81–88
9. Eg Wright, Derek, 1971, *The Psychology of Moral Behaviour*, Penguin; Haidt, Jonathan, 2012, *The Righteous Mind*, Pantheon Books and references therein; and see Haslam, 2005, 18–21
10. Eg Lorenz, Konrad, 1954, *Man Meets Dog*, Methuen; Goodall, 1990; de Waal, 1996; Haslam, 2005; Frans de Waal, Frans, 2013, *The Bonobo and the Atheist*, W W Norton
11. Russell, Bertrand, 1960, Notes on PHILOSOPHY, January 1960, *Philosophy*, 35, 146–147
12. Ayer, A J, 1936, *Language, Truth and Logic*, Victor Gollancz
13. Blackburn, Simon, 2001, *Being Good*, Oxford University Press
14. McMichael, A J, 1993, *Planetary Overload*, Cambridge University Press
15. Collier, Paul, *The Plundered Planet*, Penguin, 2011, 32
16. Stern, Nicholas, 2009, *A Blueprint for a Safer Planet: How to Manage Climate Change and Create a New Era of Progress and Prosperity*, Bodley Head, 77
17. Scruton, Roger, 2012, *Green Philosophy: How to Think Seriously About the Planet*, Atlantic Books, 185
18. MacBride, Peter, 2008, *Teach Yourself Ethical Living*, Hodder Education
19. Armstrong, Adrian C, 2009, *Here for our Children's Children: Why we should Care for the Earth*, Imprint Academic
20. Eg Darwin, 1871; Singer, Peter, 1983, *The Expanding Circle*, Oxford University Press; Haslam, 2005; Ryder, Richard D, 2011, *Speciesism, Painism and Happiness: A Morality for the Twenty-first Century*, Imprint Academic, 2011
21. Hume, David, 1790, *A Treatise on Human Nature*

22. Haidt, Jonathan 2007, *The Happiness Hypothesis: Finding Modern Truth in Ancient Wisdom*, Cornerstone (first published by Basic Books, 2006)
23. Franklin, Benjamin, 1791, quoted by Haidt, 2007
24. Edmonds, John Maxwell, 1919, *Inscriptions suggested for War Memorials*. Better known is the modified version inscribed on the war memorial at Kohima in north-east India
25. Midgley, Mary, 1983, Duties concerning Islands, *Encounter*, 60/2, 36–44

Chapter 7

Roots of Modern Thinking about the Environment: Religion, Spirituality and the Environmental Movement

What people do about their ecology depends on what they think about themselves in relation to things around them. Human ecology is deeply conditioned by beliefs about our nature and destiny – that is, by religion.

Lynn White, Jr[1]

If the environmental crisis was a matter of data and information it would be over now. We know what the problems are. The trouble is we're not touching anybody's hearts or minds, and the only forces that have ever done that in history are the arts and religion, and very often they're one and the same thing. So I think we should invite key religious leaders to come together with all the major conservation groups to see how we can save the planet.

HRH Prince Philip, Duke of Edinburgh[2]

For most peoples in most of history, how they look after their environment is closely bound up with how they see their place in the world and thus with their religious beliefs: 'Ideas about land and nature are central to every culture'.[3] Only in the West and in recent times have religion and nature been seen as separate entities.[4]

The modern Western world, with its burgeoning population and technological inventions, has far greater power for the destruction of nature – and Western power and lifestyles are spreading round the globe. That is not to say, though, that non-Western cultures are not destructive. People in every culture transform their surroundings in order to live and feed themselves, but the modern world has more power; some of the new, man-made ecosystems are sustainable, others damage the land in ways that may or may not be reversible in a human timescale. Moreover, it is human nature not to live up to our ideals, so although non-Western cultures may hold to ideals of living in harmony with nature we must not be surprised if their practice is different: 'Discrepancies between theory and practice should not surprise us'.[5]

85

We shall consider the more secular, modern Western approach to environmental issues later in the chapter, but first we shall look at how religious beliefs and teaching relate to how we look after our environment.

Religion and the environment

There is a sense, present in most humans and most societies, that there is something greater, more important or more powerful than ourselves; the sense that if our lives are directed entirely to serving human ends we are missing out on something important. Some kind of religion, or belief in the supernatural is found in all known human societies.[6] We have 'intimations of a level of reality beyond the narrowly material or the purely biological'.[7]

The most influential religions have roots going back many centuries. They originated long before the industrial era, long before humans developed their present destructive power. Human influence on the environment was not the important issue that it is today, and yet these religions contain, in their early teachings, the message that we should care for the Earth.

It was his recognition of the crucial role of religion in inspiring us to care about the environment that led HRH Prince Philip to found the Alliance of Religions and Conservation (ARC)[8] in 1995. ARC is a secular body that helps the world's major faiths to develop environmental programmes based on their own core teachings, beliefs and practices.

A similar recognition of the importance of religion in the way we treat the environment led to the establishment of the Forum on Religion and Ecology at Yale: 'The Forum arose from a series of ten conferences on the world's religions and ecology held at Harvard from 1996 to 1998'; it explores 'religious worldviews, texts, and ethics in order to broaden understanding of the complex nature of current environmental concerns'.[9] Mary Evelyn Tucker, one of the Forum's founders, has written of the 'growing alliance of religion and ecology within the academic world and within religious communities ... As key repositories of enduring civilisational values and as indispensable motivators in moral transformation, religions have an important role to play in projecting persuasive visions of a more sustainable future.'[10]

Twelve religions

There are twelve faiths represented in ARC. The eleven founder members (Bahá'í, Buddhism, Christianity, Daoism, Hinduism, Islam, Jainism, Judaism, Shintoism, Sikhism and Zoroastrianism) were joined in 2013 by Confucianism. Together, these faiths own seven per cent of the habitable surface of the planet, and if they invested together, would be the world's third largest identifiable block of holders of stocks and shares. Between them the faiths reach out to every village and town, they have the trust of more people than any other national or international group, and their followers number at least two-thirds of the world's population.

These twelve faiths all originated between the Mediterranean Sea and the Pacific Ocean: five in the Near and Middle East, four in the Indian subcontinent, and three in the Far East. The following summaries are taken mostly from the ARC website.[11]

Bahá'í

The Bahá'í faith dates from 1844, making it the most recent of the world's monotheistic religions. It was founded by an Iranian nobleman, Bahá'u'lláh, and it now has about 5 million followers worldwide.

Central to the Bahá'í faith is the belief that humanity is a single race with a common destiny. The words of Bahá'u'lláh, 'The earth is but one country, and mankind its citizens', summarise the Bahá'í sense of world citizenship and their commitment to stewardship of the earth. Bahá'í Scriptures describe nature as an emanation of God's will. Bahá'u'lláh's promise that civilisation will exist on this planet for a minimum of 5,000 centuries compels his followers to consider the long-term impact of decisions made today. Science and technology should help humanity to live in harmony with nature. Science should be guided by spiritual principles, to preserve as much as possible the earth's biodiversity and natural order, in a way that ensures long-term sustainability.

Buddhism

Buddhism was founded around 550 BC by Siddhartha Gautama, who was born in north India as a Hindu prince. He left his palace as a young man and spent six years in the forest seeking an end to suffering, eventually achieving enlightenment under a Bodhi tree. The Buddha, or Enlightened One, as he came to be known, dedicated the rest of his life to teaching the path to enlightenment. There are about 500 million Buddhists today.

Buddha taught people to live simply and appreciate the natural cycle of life. Craving and greed only bring unhappiness, since demands for material possessions can never be satisfied. The solution to the environmental crisis begins with the individual.

Christianity

Jesus was born into a Jewish family near Jerusalem and put to death in about AD 33. Christians believe that he was uniquely the Son of God – God living in human form – and that his teachings tell us of the nature of God as creator, redeemer and sustainer. Christians recognise the imperfections at the heart of the human condition and believe that, through Jesus, all can be reconciled to the loving God. Repentance is thus a central theme in Christian belief. Today there are three main traditions: the Roman Catholic, Protestant and Orthodox churches. It is estimated that there are about 2000 million Christians in the world today.

Christians, in common with Jews and Muslims, believe that the Earth is God's creation. The three religions agree in placing humans at the apex of creation, so they value human life more than animal life. It should follow from this that humans have special responsibilities for looking after the Earth.[12] Christianity recognises the tension that exists between this responsibility and the human tendency to rebel against God. The main Christian churches have recently been re-examining their teaching and practice in the light of current environmental concerns. They see the need to repent for the harm that has been done to the Earth, and to seek new ways of living that restore balance and hope of life to our endangered planet.

Confucianism

Confucianism is the earliest of the three main religious traditions in China (the others being Daoism and Buddhism). It is based on the teachings of Kong Zi (579–551 BC), Master

Kong (better known in English as Confucius), who is revered in Chinese history for the moral code he taught, based on ethics, humanity and love.

Confucius taught a holistic understanding of the universe, emphasising the responsibility of every person to behave respectfully and with care to contribute to the general well-being of creation. The interests of humanity are served by looking after the interests of all of nature.

In Japan, it was Confucian and Neo-Confucian scholars who, since the seventeenth century, have sought to understand the natural world so as to be able to conserve it for future generations.[13]

Daoism

Daoism can be traced back to Shamanism, which spread into Mongolia and China at least ten thousand years ago. Daoism was formally established as a religion about two thousand years ago. It has had a powerful influence on Chinese thought and behaviour. Dao means 'the way', and the 'three jewels of the Dao' are compassion, moderation and humility. It is estimated that there are between 20 and 50 million Daoists in the world.

Four main principles of Daoism guide the relationship between humanity and nature: humans should obey the Earth and help everything to grow in its own way; they should maintain the balance between the opposing forces of Yin and Yang, so as to be in harmony with nature; they should hold back from development that runs counter to the harmony and balance of nature; and Daoism judges affluence by the number of different species. If all things in the universe grow well, a society is a community of affluence. If not, it is in decline.

Hinduism

Hinduism has evolved over thousands of years, growing out of the rich cultures of ancient India. For Hindus, the purpose of life is to understand spiritual truth. They believe that the soul is eternal and lives many lives, born sometimes in a human body, sometimes in another animal and sometimes in a plant. Karma, meaning action, is important because actions bring reactions. Every experience is linked to past actions, but by practising yoga, or spiritual discipline, one can change one's actions and so change one's future. There are about 1000 million Hindus in the world, most of whom live in India.

Hindus believe that all living beings are sacred because they are parts of God, and should be treated with respect and compassion. They like to live close to nature. Simple living is seen as a virtue, and true happiness comes from within, not from possessions. This philosophy seems at odds with the massive industrialisation and pollution that characterise much of modern India, though the traditional approaches to nature may still be seen in rural villages.

Islam

The Prophet Muhammad, the founder of Islam, was born in 570 in Arabia and died in 632. Muslims believe that Muhammad received messages from God, which, after his death, were written down by his followers in the Qur'an. The sayings and deeds of Muhammad were recorded in the Hadith. These writings are the source of guidance for all Muslims. There are about 1300 million Muslims in the world.

Muslims believe that God created humans to be guardians of his creation. They are to avoid wastefulness. The Qur'an says: 'The servants of the Merciful God are those who walk gently upon the earth.'[14] The laws of Islam protect animals from cruelty, conserve forests and limit the growth of cities.

Jainism

Most of the founders of the ancient Jain religion, the 24 Tirthankaras, lived before recorded history. The last, Mahavira, was born about 540 BC and gathered many followers. The Jain religion became influential in northern India, but by the twelfth century it was in decline, as Hinduism and Islam spread through India. The goal of the Jain religion is to achieve liberation from the cycle of birth and death, but there are few who achieve this. For most Jains, the ideal is to live a good life by practice of the Three Jewels: right knowledge, right faith and right conduct. There are more than 7 million Jains today. Jainism was a strong influence on Mahatma Gandhi.

The five vows of Jainism are: non-violence (not harming any creature; Jains are vegetarians); truthfulness (including not saying hurtful things); non-stealing (this includes avoiding greed and exploitation); chastity (respect is given to celibate monks and nuns); and detachment from the pleasures of this world, which are viewed as illusion.

Judaism

Abraham is regarded as the father of the Jewish people. He is thought to have lived around 1900 BC. The Jewish religion centres on the story of the Jews, as the people of God. It is the story of how God guided them and cared for them, how they sometimes obeyed him and sometimes rebelled against him. There are about 13 million Jews in the world today, mostly in America and Israel.

The Jewish attitude to nature is based on the belief that the universe is the work of the creator, and we should care for it. Love of God includes love of all creation, living and inanimate. Jewish teaching is that agricultural land should be rested for one year in seven, to improve and strengthen it.

Shintoism

Shinto is the natural spirituality of Japan. It is essentially a body of rituals, having no fundamental creeds or written teachings. It did not become a formal religious institution till the sixth century, but it incorporates spiritual practices dating from much earlier. It is estimated that there are about 120 million adherents in Japan, but such estimates are uncertain since most Japanese incorporate features of Shinto and Buddhism in their lives without a specific attachment to either.

The Japanese people felt the divine within nature, so they came to hold the ideal of a life that was in harmony with and united with nature. Pollution was considered anathema.[15]

Sikhism

The word Sikh means student of the Truth. The Sikh faith began in India in the fifteenth century, at a time of tension between the Muslim religion of the ruling Mughal Empire and the Hindu faith of the majority of the population. There were ten Sikh gurus, starting with Guru Nanak (1469–1539). Sikhs believe in one God. They emphasise service to the community and devotion to God. To Sikhs, all people are equal, regardless of caste, creed, race or sex. There are about 19 million Sikhs, 18 million of whom are in India.

Sikhs cultivate awareness and respect for the dignity of all life, human or otherwise. Many Sikhs are vegetarian. The ideal life is simple, and free from conspicuous waste – a life that stresses mastery over the self rather than mastery over nature.

Zoroastrianism

Zoroastrianism was founded by the prophet Zarathustra, who lived about 1200 BC (or possibly later, around 600 BC). The religion became the state religion of the Persian Empire (550–330 BC) and later of the Sassanian Empire (AD 224–651). Zoroastrians believe that a spirit of evil is in perpetual conflict with the creator God, who is wise, good and just – but vulnerable. The role of humans is to serve the creator and to be his assistants in a world broken by evil. There are now about 150,000 Zoroastrians worldwide, mostly in Mumbai.

Zoroastrianism claims to be the world's oldest revealed religion and also the world's first proponent of ecology, through caring for the earth. It is humanity's task to care for the universe.

Today

These twelve religions differ widely in their ideas about the nature of God, the purpose and function of religion, and in what are the most important things in life. They are all agreed, however, in the importance of the natural world and humanity's responsibility for caring for it.

We need to remember that a religion's teaching gives its adherents ideals to aim for. It is not a statement of how religious people actually live. As we noted in chapters 5 and 6, human nature is complex, and people do not live up to their ideals. Moreover, in many nations and communities religious teaching has lost influence in recent years, to be replaced by economic prosperity as the foremost goal in life – and concern for the environment gets forgotten.

The ARC website shows how faith communities all over the world are trying to take a lead in initiating and promoting good practice in sustainable living. In Britain, Christian churches are prominent among those drawing attention to environmental issues and promoting good practice.

Folk religion

I use the term folk religion, or indigenous religion, for the unstructured sense of the sacred that appears to have been present in most cultures before the arrival of more formal religion some two thousand or more years ago. In some cultures it remains the predominant belief, while in others, such as Western Christendom, it survives in the form of ancient rituals and customs.

In her Introduction to *Nature Across Cultures: Views of Nature and the Environment in Non-Western Cultures*, Helaine Selin writes that a theme throughout the book is the interconnectedness between religion and nature.[16] Some chapters of the book are devoted to the main non-Western religions (Buddhism, Confucianism, Daoism, Hinduism, Islam and Judaism), but the greater part is devoted to other peoples, whose spirituality and sense of the sacred is less organised and defined. We should avoid over-romanticising these cultures, since one can find tales of wilful destruction as well as careful husbandry, but it is possible to discern a sense that humans living in harmony with nature is how things ought to be.[17]

As an example of this harmony, pre-industrial peoples have been able to combine a respect for animals with an unquestioning acceptance of the need to kill them for food. J G Frazer gives examples from all over the world and points out that 'savages' considered that animals possessed intelligence, feelings and souls, like humans: they did not make sharp distinctions between humans and other animals.[18] Recent examples of this kind of kinship between a man and the animal he kills have been described in the Bushmen of southern Africa and the reindeer people of Siberia.[19] Modern urbanised humans no longer live close to animals that are reared for slaughter. This may be one of the reasons that more people have become vegetarians and vegans.

Examples of how non-Western cultures relate to nature

'We are the land' is how many **Native Americans** sum up their relationship with the natural world. 'The relationship between human life and non-human life is at the heart of Native American spirituality … This is one reason why the displacement of Native Americans from their lands, and the subsequent damage to the land, was and is so socially and psychologically devastating.'[20] In different parts of North America there is evidence both of careful stewardship of the land and of ecological damage – and also of significant modification to create a new, but sustainable, ecosystem.

In the **Arctic** of North America (the Dene and the Inuit) and Siberia, understanding of nature is bound up with an understanding of the spirit world. People are part of nature. In the Dene worldview, people should strive for respect and humility. For the Inuit, nature is one realm, equal with the human realm and the spiritual realm.[21] In Siberia, the reindeer, both wild and domesticated, has retained its central place in the practical and spiritual life of the people. The vast Arctic wilderness is filled with animals, humans and spirits – and memories of their interactions down the ages.[22]

In **Oceania** (comprising New Zealand, Papua New Guinea and the Pacific Islands as far as Hawai'i and Easter Island) there are historical examples of resource depletion and environmental degradation, as well as examples of resource management and environmental protection. Resource management may involve replacing the original forest with secondary forest, comprising plants that are useful for food or other purposes. Resource management is often connected with religious observances and taboos, and reflects an awareness that resources are finite and depletable. The land and sea are more than material resources: they yield spiritual sustenance as well, with markers of identity, history and belonging.[23]

Pacific islanders take a sufficiently integrated view of land and sea resources to realise that pollution from modern industrial mining and logging enterprises is liable to affect nearby marine environments.[24]

The **Aboriginals of Australia** have a strong sense of being part of the land. Their lives as hunter-gatherers depended on understanding the land with its flora and fauna, working with them, ensuring that these valuable resources were not over-exploited. Their land-management practices were sustained by their system of cultural traditions and religious beliefs. They probably had a greater impact on their environment than most non-Western peoples because of the role of fire in their land-management practices. The effect of burning, however, was to create a productive environment, not a degraded one, by replacing mature forests with open woodland and grassland for game. Some native plants need fire in order to germinate. Fire also facilitated travel and hunting.

Like other world cultures, the Aboriginal way of life was disrupted by European settlement – perhaps more than most because their way of life depended on having control over very large areas. European settlement put an end to traditional burning, by restricting the areas over which the Aboriginals had control. They continued to use fire, but with a different regime, leading to changes in the flora and fauna. Without the regular, controlled burning, the forests became vulnerable to fires initiated by lightning strikes – which, being large and uncontrolled, can be more damaging.[25]

All these peoples live close to the land and understand it at a level of detail that might surprise many office-working Westerners.[26] Stories abound of disastrous mistakes made by incomers who lack this understanding. The consequences of mining and logging in the Pacific islands quoted above are but one example. Another is the celebrated Tanganyika Groundnut Scheme. In 1946 the British Government initiated a scheme to grow groundnuts, for vegetable oil, in 600 km^2 of central Tanganyika (now mainland Tanzania). They chose an area which, though superficially similar to the surrounding country, had few human inhabitants, as they did not want to have to displace too many people. Had they enquired, the planners would have learnt that the reason for the low population density was that the rainfall was known to be particularly unreliable. The land was unsuitable. The scheme failed – at huge expense – and was eventually cancelled in 1951.[27]

Religion, secularism and the modern world

Economic development and religion

The industrial revolution grew out of Western Christendom. Recent Chinese scholars, asked to account for the pre-eminence of the West, concluded that it was not their guns or their political or economic systems but their religion – Christianity.[28]

Christianity is about the relationship between God and each individual person. Humans are the peak of God's creation. Nature is God's creation: it is not, of itself, sacred (as it is in Daoism, Hinduism, Shinto and many folk religions). The interests of humans are important – more important than nature. The last 300 years have brought wealth, health, longer life, education and greater choice for most people in the West and many people in the rest of the world. All of these changes would have been thought of as beneficial by most Christians. Poverty, ill-health and lack of education were regarded as evils that should be eradicated. This was an assumption that few religious leaders would challenge. In 1967, Lynn White could write 'Our science and technology have grown out of Christian attitudes towards man's relation to nature which are almost universally held not only by Christians and neo-Christians but also by those who fondly regard themselves as post-Christians. … We are superior to nature, contemptuous of it, willing to use it for our slightest whim'.[29] Some religious and moral leaders criticised specific harmful trends, such as excessive greed or destructiveness or the misuse of power, but there was no reason to challenge the underlying belief that scientific and technological advances were making life better for most people and were therefore to be welcomed. As time went on, Christians and others became aware of the fundamental flaws in the route we were taking and the serious consequences for the future. This has re-awakened the realisation that humans have a responsibility, under God, to care for the Earth.

Buddhism is another person-centred religion. In Thailand, Buddhism, which there incorporates both spirit and Brahmanic (early Hindu) beliefs and practices, can be interpreted to support either development or conservation.[30] The Thai government has used them in support of a policy of economic growth – while some Buddhist monks use them to promote an environmental ethic.

Japan in the seventeenth century was becoming densely populated and much of it was suffering deforestation. It was saved from total loss of its forest by religious leaders – Shinto, Buddhist and, particularly, Confucian and Neo-Confucian. Following the Meiji Restoration of 1868, Japan embarked on a course of Westernisation, at the price of river pollution and environmental degradation. Environmental pressure groups have had some success in recent decades, leading, for example, to the establishment of the Environment Agency in 1971.[31]

Modern Western secularism

In Britain today, and in much of the West, formal religious observance is much less than it used to be. That is not to say, however, that religion is a declining force in world affairs. Worldwide, religious adherence is growing in numbers and influence, as discussed by John Micklethwait and Adrian Wooldridge in *God is Back: How the Global Rise of Faith is Changing the World*.[32]

There are many shades of opinion among non-believers, of which the most clearly defined and organised is atheistic humanism. This, as its name implies, focuses particularly on humans and how we relate to one another. Some of its principles, such as its emphasis on the scientific method, human welfare, equal human dignity and equal justice under the law, rest on Christian foundations.[33] The philosopher John Gray is scathing about this relationship, describing humanism as 'a secular religion thrown together from decaying scraps of Christian myth'.[34] His *Straw Dogs* is an attack on the humanist belief in progress and on the notion that humans are different from other animals. He commends Daoist, Shinto, Hindu and animist cultures for their willingness to recognise that humans are kin to all other animals.

Humanists UK (formerly the British Humanist Association) is less concerned with personal morality than with philosophy (atheism) and social and political issues. Environmental issues do not come high in their priorities.[35]

Such humanists are in a minority, however. Although formal religious observance in Britain is much less than it used to be, there is a great deal of interest in spirituality. Many people who find that the dogmas and rituals of organised religion have little to offer them are nonetheless aware of a spiritual side to their existence. Many such people value the role of Christianity in our culture and tradition. They are glad that the church is there, and would be sorry to see it go. There is a 'silent majority who consider themselves in some sense "spiritual" without quite knowing what that means', in the words of Jonathan Rowson.[36] In his 2014 report for the Royal Society for the Encouragement of Arts, Manufactures and Commerce, Rowson writes 'It feels implausible to imagine we will return to religion in its current form en masse, so we are in this curious post-secular state where socially and politically we need the emphasis on solidarity, practice and experience previously found in religion to defend the integrity of the public realm, but culturally and intellectually we can't go back if the condition of entry is adhering to beliefs that we don't identify with.'[37]

Colin Tudge probably speaks for many when he writes that in the 1960s 'we tended to pursue the ludicrous idea that all life could be reduced to physics, and physics to maths, and that was the end of it. Yet I never quite felt that that was the end of it. I always had an ill-informed but nonetheless powerful feeling that there is a great deal more to life and the universe than meets the eye – or ever can meet the eye ... I always felt too – in fact I think I took it to be self-evident – that St Francis was right: that other creatures are truly our fellows'.[38] He goes on to make the case that we should take seriously the idea of the transcendent.

Mastery or humility

Christianity and humanism both place emphasis on human well-being. Too easily, this can turn into the pursuit of more possessions, more comfort, more consumerism, more economic growth, more self-indulgence.

It can also, in the modern world, lead to the false belief that humans are masters of the universe. The successes of the nineteenth century encouraged a Victorian understanding of humans as both a product of nature and also subduers of it.[39] By the mid-twentieth century, the latter view was prevailing: 'Modern man', wrote E F Schumacher, 'does not experience himself as a part of nature but as an outside force destined to dominate and conquer it.'[40]

There may have been a time when to see ourselves as masters of the world may have been a harmless fantasy, but at the beginning of the twenty-first century it has become horribly half-true: we now have the power to destroy our world as a hospitable and congenial place for humans to live (and I haven't even mentioned nuclear, chemical and biological weapons). In the Western world the historic Christian values of self-denial have been replaced by the consumerist values of self-indulgence. Our affluent lifestyle is viewed with envy by people living in the other countries of the world, and many of them now find it in their power to enjoy a similar lifestyle. In the past, the reliance on nature and its self-correcting powers was sufficient to restore a great deal of what we had damaged, but many people now realise that this is no longer so.

Most religions, if not all, teach people a spirit of humility before the power and mystery of God and nature (including the weather). Humility is not much commended these days, when people prefer to promote self-esteem instead. Humility is not necessarily at odds with self-esteem (they can both mean to have a realistic assessment of oneself, with one's strengths and weaknesses), but the difference in emphasis can easily lead people to believe in and follow a me-first approach to life, a sense that we are in control. A sense of entitlement.

Two philosophers, Michael Sandel and Michael Hauskeller, draw a contrast between a life motivated by this 'drive to mastery' and one lived with a sense of giftedness.[41] The sense of giftedness can help us to cultivate the qualities of gratitude and humility, valuable guides through the vicissitudes of life.

Religious people and non-believers can share this sense of life as gift. We can come together in the belief that it is worth putting our greatest efforts into something that is greater, more magnificent and more lasting than our day-to-day lives. All of us can wonder at the grandeur and beauty of the Earth; at its complexity and its simplicity; at its power and its frailty. All of us can seek to live our lives in harmony with the Earth, respecting both its immensity and its fragility, with a sense of giftedness that leads us to believe that we ourselves should be givers in our turn.

Roger Scruton points out that governments tend to look at environmental problems in economic terms, 'a triumph of instrumental reasoning, which describes things with a value as things with a price.'[42] This may be inevitable to some degree (and the last chapter of this book is devoted to economics), but Scruton is surely right that this is 'one of the features of the modern world against which the environmentalists are, or ought to be, in rebellion. The environmental problem arises because we have treated the earth as an object and an instrument.'

99

Finally

We have seen how, in non-Western cultures, looking after the land is bound up with the way people see themselves and thus with their religious beliefs. In other words, how people relate to the land and to nature is of the first importance.

Western societies, led perhaps by Western Christendom and its atheistic spin-off, humanism, have lost sight of this with their focus on people and their material well-being. We must return to our roots: thankful for the bounty of nature and for the human ability to harness it and at the same time conscious of our obligation to care for the natural world and pass it on to the future.

HRH The Prince of Wales, has long been a passionate advocate for environmental causes. In *Harmony*, he appeals to us to question the current mechanistic way of looking at the world and to appreciate again that humans are part of nature, part of the natural order: 'Essentially it is the spiritual dimension to our existence that has been dangerously neglected during the modern era – the dimension that is related to our intuitive feelings about things'.[43]

The modern environmental movement

It is the West that has given birth to our present environmental problems – the unintended consequences of the innovations in industry, agriculture, medicine and hygiene that have enabled us to live longer, healthier and more prosperous lives. It is in the West, too, that the recent environmental movement has grown – a disenchantment with modern Western lifestyles, a sense that we are in danger of losing something important and, increasingly, an awareness of the irreversible damage we are doing to our planet. The leading thinkers of this movement may or may not have been religious believers, but their ideals are generally expressed in non-religious language.

Our present concern for the Earth has many strands. The first is represented by two mid-nineteenth-century writers whose appreciation of nature and recognition of the way that the modern world was separating us from it influenced many subsequent writers and anticipated much present-day environmentalist thinking. Henry David Thoreau (1817–62), an American naturalist and author, is best known for his book

Walden, or life in the Woods, describing the time he spent living simply in a self-made shanty.[44] John Muir (1838–1914) was born in Scotland, but spent most of his life in America. His evocative writings about the call of the wild still resonate today: 'Thousands of tired, nerve-shaken, over-civilised people are beginning to find out that going to the mountains is going home; that wildness is a necessity.' 'Everybody needs beauty as well as bread, places to play in and pray in, where nature may heal and give strength to body and soul.' 'The mountains are calling and I must go.' He founded the Sierra Club, now the largest environmental organisation in the United States, to 'do something for wildness and make the mountains glad' and he was influential in the establishment of national parks in America. The Scottish charity founded in 1983 to conserve and protect wild places was named after him – the John Muir Trust.

Another strand was concern about the use of agricultural chemicals. Robert McCarrison, Albert Howard and Rudolf Steiner, in the 1920s, were early pioneers of what came to be known as organic agriculture – farming with naturally occurring fertilisers and pesticides rather than manufactured chemicals. Another pioneer was Eve Balfour, who helped to found the Soil Association in 1946.

In the broader cultural sense, Clough Williams-Ellis was another pioneer. 'In giving voice in the 1920s to the growing consciousness of the harmful effects of a developed industrial economy, in campaigning for legislation and an outlook of planning ahead, and embodying an alternative vision in the Morris tradition in all that he did, he could be claimed as the first environmentalist in the modern sense.'[45] In *England and the Octopus*[46] he deplored the urbanisation of the countryside – and, as if to make his point by way of contrast, the village he designed and built at Portmeirion in North Wales displays a joie-de-vivre that is rare in twentieth-century British architecture. He was a founder of the Council for the Preservation of Rural Wales (now the Campaign for the Protection of Rural Wales) in 1928 and played a leading role in advising on the establishment of National Parks in England and Wales.

William Vogt's *Road to Survival* (1948) mounted a sustained attack on the consumer society, population pressures and the degradation of the land. Much of what I have written in the early chapters of this book was aptly summarised by Vogt seventy years ago: 'Despoiled forests, wildlife extermination, overgrazing, and the dropping of water tables are unforeseen and unwanted byblows of a vigorous and adolescent culture on the loose'.[47] He focused mainly on America but included the rest of the world too. He strongly criticised Britain and other European countries for allowing their populations to grow beyond the numbers that they could feed and their consequent dependence on the New World for food.

Vogt recorded that biologists throughout the world were alarmed by the widespread and unselective use of DDT, because it destroyed insects that are valuable to humans (pollinators, for example, and species that parasitise destructive insects). He also pointed out that insects inimical to humans could have a valuable function: by keeping people away, they helped to preserve natural habitats (the tsetse fly in parts of Africa, for example).

The turning point for DDT and for public awareness of environmental issues, however, came with the publication in 1962 of Rachel Carson's *Silent Spring*, one of the most influential books of the twentieth century.[48] This book documented in detail the harmful effects of pesticides, particularly the widely used DDT. Carson also accused the chemical industry of spreading disinformation and public officials of accepting industry claims uncritically. The concerns raised in *Silent Spring* led to DDT being banned in the USA and its use being greatly restricted worldwide, and to the establishment in 1970 of the US Environmental Protection Agency.

From this time, environmental issues became topics of general public interest, with numerous books and articles. Charities and pressure groups were established, and Green parties appeared on the political scene. Earth Summits became a feature of the political calendar, and in 2008 the UK passed its Climate Change Act.

Notes

1. White, Lynn Jr, 1967, The historical roots of our ecologic crisis, *Science*, 155 (10 March 1967), 1203–1207
2. HRH Prince Philip, Duke of Edinburgh, 1986, quoted by Martin Palmer, Radio 4 Sunday Programme, 30 October 2011. Thus was formed the WWF network of

religions and conservation in 1986, and, subsequently, the Alliance of Religions and Conservation in 1995

3. Selin, Helaine, 2003, Introduction, in Selin, Helaine (editor), 2003, *Nature across Cultures: Views of Nature and the Environment in Non-Western Cultures*, Springer

4. Selin, 2003, Introduction

5. Kalland, Arne, 2003, Environmentalism and images of the other, 1–17 in Selin (editor), 2003

6. Brown, Donald E, 1991, *Human Universals*, McGraw-Hill; list reproduced in Pinker, Steven, 2002, *The Blank Slate: The Modern Denial of Human Nature*, Penguin

7. O'Hear, Anthony, 1999, *After Progress*, Bloomsbury

8. www.arcworld.org

9. http://fore.yale.edu/files/Forum_Overview.pdf

10. Tucker, Mary Evelyn, 2003, Worldviews and Ecology: the interaction of cosmology and cultivation, 115–127 in Selin (editor), 2003

11. www.arcworld.org

12. Soloman, Norman, Harries, Richard and Winter, Tim (editors), 2005, *Abraham's Children: Jews, Christians and Muslims in conversation*, T&T Clark

13. Tucker, John A, 2003, Japanese views of Nature and the Environment', 161–163 in Selin (editor) 2003

14. Murad, Abdal Hakim, 2009, 'Thought for the Day', BBC Radio 4, 18 December 2009

15. Tucker, John A, 2003

16. Selin, 2003, Introduction

17. Selin (editor), 2003; eg Kalland, 2003, 8–9

18. Frazer, J G, 1890 (and subsequent editions), *The Golden Bough*, Macmillan

19. King, Simon, 'My Life with Animals', BBC2, 23 March 2008; Vitebski, Piers, 2011, *Reindeer People: Living with Animals and Spirits in Siberia*, Harper Perennial

20. Booth, Annie L, 2003, We are the Land: Native American Views of Nature, 329–349 in Selin (editor), 2003

21. Bielawski, Ellen, 2003, Nature doesn't come as clean as we can think it: Dene, Inuit, Scientists, Nature and Environment in the Canadian North, 311–327 in Selin (editor), 2003

22. Vitebski, 2011

23. Hviding, Edvard, 2003, Both Sides of the Beach: Knowledges of Nature and Oceania, 245–275 in Selin (editor), 2003

24. Hviding, 2003

25. Kohen, J L, 2003, Knowing Country: Indigenous Australians and the Land, 229–243 in Selin (editor), 2003

26. Chapters in Selin (editor), 2003

27. Eg Kesby, John D, 2003, The Perception of Nature and the Environment in Sub-Saharan Africa, 211–228 in Selin (editor), 2003

28. Ferguson, Niall, 2011, *Civilization*, Allen Lane, 287

29. White, 1967

30. Darlington, Susan M, 2003, The Spirit(s) of Conservation in Buddhist Thailand, 129–145 in Selin (editor), 2003

31. Tucker, John A, 2003

32. Micklethwait, John and Wooldridge, Adrian, 2009, *God is Back: How the Global Rise of Faith is Changing the World*, Penguin

33. Spencer, Nick, 2017, Review (in *Church Times*, 10 March 2017) of Hobson, Theo, 2017, *God created humanism: The Christian basis of secular values*, SPCK

34. Gray, John, 2003, *Straw Dogs*, Granta Books

35. https://humanism.org.uk

36. Rowson, Jonathan, *RSA Journal* Summer 2013, 40–43

37. See Rowson's 2014 RSA report: *Spiritualise; Revitalising spirituality to address 21st century challenges*

38. Tudge, Colin, 2013, *Why Genes are not Selfish and People are Nice: A Challenge to the Dangerous Ideas that Dominate Our Lives*, Floris Books

39. Demant, V A, 1949, Man and Nature, 236–240 in *The Ideas and Beliefs of the Victorians*, Sylvan Press

40. Schumacher, E F, 1973, *Small is Beautiful: A Study of Economics as if People Mattered*

41. Sandel, Michael, 2007, *The Case Against Perfection*, The Belknap Press of Harvard University Press; discussed by Hauskeller, Michael, 2011, Human Enhancement and the Giftedness of Life, *Philosophical Papers*, 40:1, 55–79

42. Scruton, Roger, 2012, *The Face of God: The Gifford Lectures 2010*, Continuum

43. HRH The Prince of Wales, Juniper, Tony and Skelly, Ian, 2010, *Harmony: A New Way of Looking at our World*, Blue Door, 9

44. Thoreau, David, 1854, *Walden, or life in the Woods*

45. Haslam, Richard, 1983, Wales's Universal Architect: Sir Clough Williams-Ellis (1883–1978), *Country Life*, 21 July 1983, 130–132

46. Williams-Ellis, Clough, 1928, *England and the Octopus*, Geoffrey Bles

47. Vogt, William, *Road to Survival*, William Sloane Associates, 1948, 33

48. Carson, Rachel, 1962, *Silent Spring*, Houghton Mifflin

Chapter 8
The Capacity to Adapt and Change

Change is not merely necessary to life – it is life.

Alvin Toffler[1]

One of the great strengths of our species is our ability to innovate and adapt. It was this ability that enabled us to survive when Neanderthals died out.[2] Our adaptability has enabled us to colonise and flourish in many different environments. Today, we find humans in cold climates (Inuit in the American Arctic, reindeer people in the Siberian tundra) and hot climates; in dry climates (the Sahara) and wet climates. Humans live off diets that are almost entirely animal (Inuit, Maasai) and entirely vegetable (the Jain in India). This ability may give us hope that we can make the necessary changes to our lifestyles to enable human life to flourish on earth for many years into the future.

The problems described in the early chapters of this book can be addressed only if the human species as a whole changes its behaviour to give greater priority to caring for the environment. This is a huge challenge, but is not impossible.

There is an old saying that 'You can't change human nature'. However, as the economic historian R H Tawney wrote, 'The conventional statement that human nature does not change is plausible only so long as attention is focussed on those aspects of it which are least distinctively human'.[3] We can now interpret this statement in terms of modern understanding of the way the mind works (chapter 5): behaviours that are determined by the part of the brain that we inherited from our pre-human ancestors are hard to change, but thoughts and behaviour that use the human, logical brain can be changed more easily.

However, if we divide our mental processes into the rational and the emotional, it is clear that rational thinking is not enough to change our behaviour. Information and argument are insufficient. We have known for years about the damage we are doing to the planet and the risks for the future. We are also bombarded with good advice about things we can do to live in a more sustainable way. Change happens only when our emotions are engaged.

If we think in terms of Jonathan Haidt's metaphor (page 64), the rider can, with skill and patience, retrain the elephant. The intention comes from the rider, but change will happen only when the elephant has been retrained.

In terms of Daniel Kahneman's metaphor (page 65), behavioural change requires the engagement of the rational, but inherently lazy, System 2 – which can then retrain the fast-thinking System 1.

In the world of the twenty-first century, our lives are changing rapidly anyway – that much is clear. Where we have a choice is in deciding which route to take. Collectively and individually, we can decide whether to pursue ways of living that have a high and damaging impact on our planet and our futures or whether to take advantage of the opportunities outlined in the third part of this book to lead fulfilled lives that are in harmony with the Earth.

How change happens: some examples

The reasons why societies change their behaviour, their way of thinking and their ideas are many and various, as the following examples show.

Fashion

Some of the commonest examples of changes of behaviour relate to fashion. A new fashion in clothes, hairstyle, popular music, interior decoration, architecture, possessions or behaviour can be copied all over the world within a very short time of its introduction. Why? Partly because people like novelty (as long as they believe that they are in control: we don't like change being imposed on us); partly because they like to be like everyone else. This process has nothing to do with government action. Industry, the media, celebrities, marketing and peer pressure all play a part in disseminating and popularising the latest fashion.

Can we come to see the adoption of sustainable lifestyles (chapter 10) as fashionable? There is no good reason why we shouldn't. Indeed, there are encouraging indications that this is happening.

Public opinion

Then there are changes of opinion, changes in what we approve of or disapprove of. In the last seventy years there has been a change in public attitudes to race, smoking, sexual relationships and drink driving, for example. These changes of opinion may have been in part influenced by the government through leadership and legislation, but the result has been a considerable change in the way people think about such issues.

There have been significant changes in Britain in attitudes towards animal welfare. The first legislation against cruelty to animals was in 1822, and the SPCA (later to become the RSPCA) was founded two years later. Bear-baiting and cock-fighting were outlawed in 1835 and 1849 respectively. This trend has continued up to the present time. The public mood in Britain has been to impose ever-stricter controls on the way we treat animals. The numbers of people following vegetarian and vegan diets has increased over the years.

Some changes are associated with particular people (William Wilberforce for slavery; Emmeline Pankhurst and the suffragettes with votes for women; Rosa Parks and Martin Luther King for African-American civil rights in America) but many changes in moral values and social attitudes have no such focus. It's just that, to many people, they seem right. Their time has come.

The herd instinct

An important factor in any change of opinion or behaviour is the herd instinct, the importance of the peer group. We all like to assert our individuality and to buck the trend from time to time, but most of us most of the time like to behave like other people in our circle and hold similar opinions on important matters. The driving force for this may be external (pressure from some authority figure or from our peers) or it may be internal (from our own wish to follow a leader or friends we admire; or, if not to follow them, to behave in ways that will win their admiration and enhance our reputation). 'What matters to us most is our relationships with fellow humans – the most commanding force for change'.[4] Even leaving aside the question of peer pressure, we are more likely to make a change in our lifestyle (give up smoking, for example) if someone we know or admire has led the way.

The first years of the twenty-first century have seen a significant increase in the number of people who are active in small, mostly local, associations.[5]

The British Social Attitudes survey found a steady increase (comparing 1993, 2000 and 2010) in environmentally friendly behaviours, such as making an effort to recycle and cutting back on driving the car. There is still a long way to go, but there is progress.

Self-interest

Then, it helps if people can see that a change delivers a real benefit for themselves. That is why it is important to get across the message that caring for the environment is not the path to misery. Spending more on experiences and services and less on stuff, travelling by less damaging means of transport and using less energy will come naturally to us as we learn more about what it is that truly brings us satisfying, fulfilled lives. Eating less meat is not only good for the environment; it also greatly improves our health and saves us money (see pages 164–167). Smaller families are what women want (on average) when they have opportunities for education and employment (see chapter 4).

As well as developing the kind of technologies that will enable us to buy and travel without damaging the environment, therefore, we also need to learn about human nature, learn about ourselves. We need to learn that humans derive more happiness from building up relationships than they do from buying stuff that they don't need. We need to learn the satisfaction that comes from working together for a good cause. There may be sacrifices involved in adopting an environment-friendly lifestyle, but they can be more than balanced by the benefits that it brings.

Some examples

The few examples below illustrate how change can be initiated by various influences.

Change spreading from neighbour to neighbour, with no outside leadership or influence: maize in Africa

Peasant farmers the world over are known to be resistant to change, and yet, when maize was first introduced into Sub-Saharan Africa from the New World, brought by traders in about the year 1500, it spread throughout the continent, becoming a major food source during the eighteenth and nineteenth centuries, and reaching Ethiopia in the twentieth and twenty-first centuries. People saw its advantages, and they changed their behaviour. James McCann celebrates the ingenuity of African farmers as they adapted the crop to local customs and climatic conditions.[6] It was not that maize was a particularly good food – indeed, in some places it replaced sorghum, which is a more nutritious food – nor is it particularly well suited to local climatic conditions (sorghum and millets are more resistant to drought), but it was easy to grow and easy to prepare as food.

This was a change of behaviour and lifestyle that swept across a continent. In these early years there was no advertising, no aggressive marketing, no government agricultural policy, no media, no agricultural officers with their good advice, no celebrities. Just simple people recognising that their neighbours had a good idea and adopting it.

Private enterprise and local initiative, aided by government at arm's length: the industrial revolution

The industrial revolution in England brought huge changes. Large numbers of people moved from the land to the towns during the nineteenth century: 'Although political decisions helped the process of adaptation, they did not initiate it, and were themselves the result of campaigns and movements that originated in civil society. British society adapted to the industrial revolution in the same way as it had set the revolution in motion: by private enterprise and civil association.'[7]

Suppliers of goods and services: advertising

Successful advertising makes good use of a knowledge of human nature. Edward Bernays, a nephew of Sigmund Freud, recognised that his uncle's psychological insights had real value in advertising. He reasoned that if he could tap into peoples' desire to feel good, powerful and sexy, he could sell them just about anything. After the success of his 1929 advertising campaign to persuade women to smoke cigarettes (appealing to their wish to be free to behave the same as men), he wrote, 'It was on this day that I learnt that age-old customs could be broken down by a dramatic appeal, disseminated by the network of media.'[8]

However, if we can be brainwashed into believing that we have to keep acquiring more stuff, then we can also learn to see this for the fraud that it is.

A mass movement, led and inspired by government: Dig for Victory
'Rarely – perhaps never – has an attempt by a British Government to substantially influence the behaviour of the British public been so warmly received or so fondly remembered as Dig for Victory.' So writes Dan Smith in his account of the 'Dig for Victory' campaign in the second world war.[9] In 1939, three quarters of the nation's food came from overseas. With the outbreak of war that year, it was clear that food supplies were at risk from enemy action – a lesson learned from the first world war. The government had provided incentives for farmers to plough up grassland and put it to crops, but this was not enough: it initiated a campaign to encourage as many people as possible to use their gardens or apply for allotments to grow food. The slogan 'Dig for Victory' first appeared in a leader in the *Evening Standard*, written, it is thought, by the young Michael Foot, who was leader writer for the paper at the time and went on to become leader of the Labour party from 1980 to 1983.

It took a while for the campaign to get going, but by 1942 there had been a fundamental change in behaviour. The number of allotments rose from about 835,000 in 1939 to 1,400,000 in 1943. Between 55 and 60 per cent of families were growing their own vegetables, totalling more than one million tons.

Inter-governmental agreement: Montreal Protocol
The 1987 Montreal Protocol on substances that deplete the ozone layer was an international treaty to protect the ozone layer by phasing out the production of substances thought to be responsible for ozone depletion. Such was its success that it has been held up as an exceptional example of international co-operation. Kofi Annan, UN Secretary General 1997–2006, claimed that it is 'perhaps the single most successful international agreement to date'.[10]

The agents for change were not so much the general public as the scientists who identified the need for change and advised accordingly, the manufacturers who developed the technologies so that the agreement could be implemented, and the governments, who understood the issues, could see that there was a short-term benefit with no significant costs to their own citizens, and got together, decided on change and then enforced it in their own countries.[11]

The role of government in social change

Traditionally, there have been three ways in which governments have tried to change social behaviour. The first is legislation: what activities should be legally enforced or made illegal. The second is financial: what activities should be taxed or subsidised. The third is providing information and advice, trying to persuade people to act in one way rather than another. All of these can be effective, and they all have a part to play in environmental protection, but other, subtler, strategies may sometimes be successful.

Nudge

In their influential book *Nudge*, Richard Thaler (recipient of the 2017 Nobel Memorial Prize in Economic Sciences for his contributions to behavioural economics) and Cass Sunstein point out how readily people are influenced in their behaviour and decisions by what they call 'choice architecture'.[12] Our choice of food in a cafeteria is influenced by the way the food is arranged, for example. Our choice of medical treatment is influenced by the way the doctor tells us about the options. We are influenced by the design and layout of forms that require us to make a decision: an on-line form can offer us a default option that involves spending or borrowing more money, for example. It is important to realise that these choice architects may influence our decision but they do not determine it: they can nudge us, but the actual decision rests with us. In a given population, they may be able to influence outcomes by a few percentage points.

Thaler and Sunstein remind us that we are influenced by factors such as past experience, natural optimism, inertia (tendency to chose the status quo or the default option), temptation (which leads us to develop self-control strategies), and following the herd (we make choices that conform to what we think other people are choosing). Nudging takes account of these and other human characteristics.

Taking up the argument of *Nudge*, the British government in 2010 set up a Behavioural Insights Team (now Behavioural Insights Ltd) to investigate ways in which behavioural insights can be used to reduce fraud, error and debt.[13] Its successes include improvements to road safety, reduction in household gas consumption, earlier payment of taxes, better attendance at job fairs, expanded educational opportunity, and improved school attendance and exam results.

Thaler and Sunstein suggest that nudges and improved choice architecture could be applied to environmental issues. Many environmental problems are on a scale where mere nudges are quite inadequate and legislation is called for, supported where appropriate by international treaties. There are many lifestyle issues, though, for which legislation would impose too great a restriction on personal liberty (how many miles we travel in a year, for example, and how), and a combination of financial incentives and nudges may be the best approach. Governments and others who seek to influence the way people behave should base their efforts on an understanding of human behaviour and how it can be influenced.

Thaler and Sunstein quote the control of acid deposition ('acid rain') in the USA as an example of the successful use of incentives – in this instance, financial incentives in the form of an emission trading system. They consider this to be among the most spectacular success stories in US environmental regulation, with near-perfect compliance, low compliance costs and huge annual benefits.

Another nudging technique that they commend is disclosure. The US Toxic Release Inventory is available on the EPA (Environmental Protection Agency) website, where the media and environmental groups can see it and give publicity to the worst offenders. Customers who are environmentally aware will be inclined to patronise shops and other businesses with a good environmental record if this record is readily available.

Reasons for optimism

Zac Goldsmith wrote in 2009 that almost everything that needs to be done in terms of environmental policy was already being done somewhere in the world. Many of these ideas are discussed in his book *The Constant Economy*.[14] Writing several years later, I also have found that many of the changes and new initiatives that I hope to see in the future (Part 3 of this book) are already taking place. Here is a selection of recent news items:

- China added 1.6 per cent to its forest cover each year from 2000 to 2010.[15]
- Deforestation in the Brazilian Amazon region fell by 70 per cent between 2005 and 2013.[16]
- It was noted in the USA in 2015 that consumers were buying less stuff and spending more on gym membership, dining out etc.[17] A year later there was a suggestion of 'peak shop' in the UK, as consumers spent less on stuff and more on experiences. Steve Howard of Ikea suggested in a speech in January 2016 that 'we've hit peak red meat, peak sugar, peak stuff, peak home furnishings'.[18]
- British solar panels generated more energy than coal-fired power stations in May 2016.[19]
- The Scottish government set a target of reducing emissions by 43 per cent by 2020. It achieved this reduction six years early.[20]
- In 2015, UK greenhouse-gas emissions fell 3.3 per cent to 497 million tonnes CO_2 equivalent, the lowest in at least 65 years.[21]
- A consumer survey found that one third of US consumers would pay a premium of at least 10 per cent for a craft product rather than a big-name brand.[22]
- In one of his last actions as US President, Barack Obama underlined his determination to put conservation and climate change at the heart of his legacy by creating the largest wildlife reserve on the planet, 1.5 million km^2 off the coast of Hawaii.[23]
- Younger people in the UK are consuming less milk and dairy products than older people.[24]

113

- Battery-powered cars and plug-in hybrids together accounted for 29 per cent of new car sales in Norway in 2016.[25]
- According to a 2015 report by the international company PwC, young people, particularly, believe that access to material things is more important than ownership. Owning a car is seen as particularly wasteful.[26]
- People are spending less on stuff and more on experiences: recreation, culture, hotels and restaurants.[27] These all give employment to people, not robots, and, apart from the cost of travel, their environmental impact is generally low.
- Twelve of the biggest chocolate companies made a commitment to end the deforestation caused by their industry.[28]
- There was a a 62 per cent drop in the number of new coal-fired power plants started worldwide in 2016 and a 48 per cent reduction in pre-construction activity, bringing climate goals within feasible reach.[29]
- Bill Gates is heading up a group of 20 investors who have put together a $1 billion fund to discover a means of delivering 'cheap and reliable clean energy to the world'.[30]
- Globally, renewable energy has increased by 14 per cent a year over the past five years, and 22 countries managed to grow their economies while reducing emissions.[31]
- In the UK, the period between June and September 2017 was the cleanest on record, with more than half the electricity coming from low-carbon sources. Carbon emissions in the electricity sector were half the level in 2012.[32]

Notes

1. Toffler, Alvin, 1970, *Future Shock*
2. Wynn, Thomas and Coolidge, Frederick L, 2012, *How to think like a Neandertal*, Oxford University Press; Wynn, Thomas and Coolidge, Frederick L, 2012, The Inner Neanderthal, *New Scientist*, 14 January 2012, 26–27; Marr, Andrew, 2012, *A History of the World*, Macmillan
3. Tawney, R H, 1926, *Religion and the rise of Capitalism*
4. Rosenberg, Tina, 2011, *Join the Club*, WW Norton
5. Hemming, Henry, 2011, *Together: How Small Groups Achieve Big Things*. John Murray

6. McCann, James C, 2006. *Maize and Grace: Africa's encounter with a New World crop, 1500–2000*, Harvard University Press
7. Scruton, Roger, 2012, *Green Philosophy: How to Think Seriously About the Planet*, Atlantic Books, 54
8. Quoted in Botsman, Rachel and Rogers, Roo, 2011, *What's Mine is Yours: How Collaborative Consumption is Changing the Way We Live*, HarperCollins, 22–23
9. Smith, Dan, 2011, *The Spade as Mighty as the Sword: The Story of Second World War's 'Dig for Victory' Campaign*, Aurum
10. Wikipedia
11. Eg Scruton, 2012, 305
12. Thaler, Rchard and Sunstein, Cass, 2009, *Nudge*, Penguin
13. www.behaviouralinsights.co.uk; *Sunday Times*, 15 October 2017
14. Goldsmith, Zac, 2009, *The Constant Economy*, Atlantic Books, 7
15. *New Scientist*, 16 June 2012
16. Pearce, Fred, *New Scientist*, 9 November 2013
17. Stelzer, Irwin, *Sunday Times*, 23 August 2015
18. *The Times*, 18 January 2016
19. *The Times*, 12 July 2016
20. *The Times*, 15 June 2016, Scottish edition
21. *The Times*, 12 July 2016
22. Stelzer, Irwin, *Sunday Times*, 24 July 2016
23. *The Times*, 27 August 2016
24. *The Times*, 7 September, 2016
25. *The Economist*, 18 February 2017
26. *The Times*, 21 April 2015
27. *The Times*, 21 April 2015; 9 January 2017
28. *The Times*, 17 March 2017
29. http://content.sierraclub.org/press-releases/2017/03/new-report-global-coal-plant-development-freefall-sparks-renewed-hope-climate
30. Stelzer, Irwin, *Sunday Times*, 26 March 2017; www.forbes.com/sites/kerryadolan/2016/12/12/bill-gates-launches-1-billion-breakthrough-energy-investment-fund/#1771ef2b5b7d
31. *The Times*, 14 November 2017
32. *The Times*, 28 December 2017

Chapter 9
A Robust and Healthy Debate

It is better to debate a question without settling it than to settle a question without debating it.

Joseph Joubert

What I have said so far may all seem rather obvious: I hope so. However, to some people it may seem controversial, and many readers may have found queries arising in their mind, so here I shall try to address some of the more obvious objections that may be raised. I shall discuss first some objections that focus on the reality of the threats to the environment, followed by others that focus on the ability of humans to meet those challenges, and lastly two more general points.

'Should I really be bothered about the environment?'

'There is no need at all to bother about the environment'

There are some Christians, a small minority, who see no need to care for the environment. They are expecting God to return soon to destroy the Earth, and therefore there is no point in being concerned about the more distant future. There is also a strand in Buddhist thinking that believes that the world will inevitably disintegrate and then begin anew.[1] This, too, could lead to a sense that there is no need to care for the long-term health of the Earth.

Apart from these, I do not know of any religious teaching that would disagree with the proposition that we have an obligation to consider the future and take care of the environment. Nor do I know of any non-religious philosophy that openly advocates or tolerates massive destruction of living matter on our planet.

Nevertheless, there are a large number of people who just don't want to be bothered. Perhaps they are naturally sceptical about anything that politicians have to say, or anything that scientists have to say. Perhaps they don't like being harangued and lectured to. Perhaps they are just put off by the fervour or the hectoring tone of some eco-enthusiasts. Perhaps they don't care to think long-term. Perhaps they think why bother when one person can make so little difference (see below). Perhaps they don't want to hear a message that would interfere with the way they live their lives (and that is why I try to paint a happier picture, rather than a grim one, when I discuss, in the rest of this book, how we might live more planet-friendly lives).

Such people will look for arguments to back up their feelings. They could find their sentiments validated by the sort of writers who lambast the environmental movement.[2] These writers don't actually say that it's fine if we trash the planet, and I don't expect that they actually believe that it is fine. However, by pouring scorn on environmentalists and all their works and encouraging their readers to distrust those who speak up for the environment, they give the OK to anyone who does want to keep on trashing the planet just as surely as if they did believe it (see further below).

I hope that readers of this book will by now be convinced that there really is a need for us to bother about the environment. Trashing the planet is not such a good idea.

'I know the environment is important, but there are other, more important, things to bother about'

More widespread is the feeling that, although looking after the environment is a good idea, other considerations are more important. These considerations may be purely selfish (driving the car when I could just as well walk), or they may be good in themselves (driving someone else to hospital) and I have to make a judgement as which of two conflicting moral principles carries the most weight.

We are all aware that our lifestyles inflict some damage on the environment. We cannot reduce our footprint to zero, but we all have daily choices: circumstances where we can decide to take the planet-friendly option or the planet-harming option.

'There is so much poverty and deprivation in the world; looking after nature and the environment is a luxury that we cannot afford'

Global poverty is indeed a serious issue in a world of plenty – but it can best be addressed by addressing environmental issues as well. When something goes wrong, it is often the poor who get hit the hardest, and this is true of environmental degradation.

Jeffrey Sachs is a development economist. In 2005 he published *The End of Poverty: How We Can Make it Happen in Our Lifetime*. However, poverty cannot be tackled in isolation: environmental problems had to be tackled at the same time. His next book, published in 2009, was *Common Wealth: Economics for a Crowded Planet*.[3] Another economist, Paul Collier, followed a similar road: his book on world poverty, *The Bottom Billion: Why the Poorest Countries are Failing and What Can Be Done About It* (2008) was followed by a book on the environment, *The Plundered Planet: How to Reconcile Prosperity With Nature* (2010).[4] The Bill and Melinda Gates foundation was founded twenty years ago, with the object of reducing poverty and improving healthcare throughout the world. In order to achieve this, the foundation has taken a leading role in promoting population control (see page 54) and Bill Gates has taken a lead in promoting clean energy for the world (page 114).

It is the poorest countries and the poorest people that are suffering and will suffer most from environmental degradation and climate change. Pollution alone is held responsible for 9 million premature deaths in 2015 – 16 per cent of all global deaths; 92 per cent of these were in low-income and middle-income countries.[5] It is the poorest countries that are the most vulnerable to rising sea level and extreme weather events. It is in their interests that we should all change our ways. Likewise, we in rich countries cannot expect the poorer countries to join us in promoting planet-friendly economies and sustainable lifestyles if we do not also support them when they want to join us in enjoying more comfortable lifestyles.

'Global warming would be a good thing: bring it on!'

More people die of cold than of heat. Melting of sea ice will open up more routes for shipping. Melting of the Greenland and Antarctic ice caps will open up more land for agriculture. More CO_2 in the atmosphere is leading to faster crop growth and higher crop yields. England is becoming more suitable for the cultivation of such warm-climate crops as vines, tea and watermelons.[6]

This argument has to be set against sea-level rise, flooding densely populated and fertile areas of the world – a huge loss – and the unpredictable consequences of rapid climate change on natural ecosystems that lack the capacity for equally rapid adaptation.

'There's no need to bother about population. The countries with growing populations are poor countries and all the damage is done by rich countries. Anyway, if we all lived sustainably the Earth could hold lots more people'

Population is discussed in detail in chapter 4.

'Don't worry: human ingenuity will sort it'

Matt Ridley's *The Rational Optimist: how prosperity evolves* is an anti-doom book.[7] Its main thesis is a good one: that division of labour, the market in goods and services, the inventive power of the human mind and our ability to use new discoveries to build on the experience of the past enable us to become ever more prosperous and to tackle problems of increasing complexity. Ridley recognises the force of arguments like 'if we carry on as we are we shall end up in a mess' – and then points out, rightly, that we won't carry on as we are. The thing about humans, and most especially since the industrial revolution, is that we invent, adapt and change, and we do this in ways that cannot be predicted.

Thus far I can share his optimism. When it comes to climate change, however, his view is that 'the probability of rapid and severe climate change is small; the probability of net harm from the likely change is small …' – and he is optimistic that we shall adapt to climate change and develop suitable low-carbon technologies. I think that he underestimates the severity of the risk, but more importantly he fails to address the other environmental issues. He recognises the dangers of pollution and habitat destruction, but he does not discuss them in any detail and therefore does not give them a chance to dent his optimism, and he dismisses the question of depletion of non-renewable resources with the argument that previous predictions that world supplies will be exhausted have proved false, so all predictions that we shall run out will also prove false (see below).

119

It is true that we can learn from the past, but this should not blind us to the possibility that the future may be different. In the past, human ingenuity has kept up with, and often run ahead of, the development of new problems, but we are in a new era. Our destructive power is immeasurably greater than ever before, and it seems that human ingenuity in recent decades has been directed more at promoting and enhancing this destruction for short-term gain, real or imagined, than at mitigating it or halting it. It is true that, in words of Sheikh Yamani, 'the Stone Age did not come to an end because we had a lack of stones',[8] but the age of affluence may well come to an end because we have ruined the environment on which that affluence rests and depends.

Ridley may well be right – and I hope he is – that human ingenuity can enable us to meet the environmental challenges that confront us, but it was human ingenuity that gave us the power to inflict such damage in the first place. Human ingenuity and technological innovation can achieve a great deal, for good or ill. Which is it to be?

'You can't trust anything environmental activists say, can you?'

Several writers seek to undermine the case put forward by environmentalists (see above).[9] I wonder what they are aiming to achieve. If their aim is to get their readers to ignore everybody who says it is a good idea to care for the environment, they are probably being very successful; invective is an effective weapon. I am reluctant to attribute such malign motives to them, but if that is not their aim, I wonder why they do it.

Environmental issues can be very complicated, and there is plenty of scope for healthy debate about what we want to achieve and how we should set about trying to achieve it. As with any political debate, you would not be surprised to find that ideas range from the inspirational, through the sensible, the might-work-or-might-not, the unlikely-but-give-it-a-go and the well-intentioned-but-misguided, all the way to the downright dotty.

The success of such a debate depends upon a common starting point and a common objective: that there is cause for concern in the way we are looking after the environment and that we need to work together to explore ways of looking after it better.

That is not where these writers start from, nor is it how they operate. They concentrate their spleen on the green activists themselves: 'The people who tell you that AGW [anthropogenic global warming] is a near certainty are a bunch of liars, cheats and frauds'.[10] They suggest that they are politically or financially motivated: Owen Paterson writes of 'the highly paid globe-trotters of the Green Blob who besieged me with their self-serving demands'.[11] They draw attention to any bad practice in the way environmentalists seek to promote their views (eg the infamous Norwich emails). Insofar as they address the scientific evidence at all, they point at any weaknesses in the argument (like the plainly indefensible notion that the Himalayan glaciers would melt within 30 years) to distract attention from the strong evidence.

The use of these tactics instead of serious scientific or political argument may be a lot of fun, but it brings into disrepute the idea that we should look after the environment. By concentrating too much on what is controversial we can be in danger of missing the bits that are not.

These writers give us food for thought. They do indeed make a strong case that we should not be too confident in our predictions, but by the same token some of their own assertions and predictions look a bit out of date after a few years.

'Other doomsayers have been proved wrong'

This argument carries some weight, but not as much as we might think. It is a bit like saying that your friends keep warning you not to ignore the stop sign at your favourite blind crossroads but they've always been wrong so far.

There is, indeed, a long history of prophets of environmental disaster. Thomas Malthus (1766–1834), for example, feared that population was increasing faster than the ability of the land to support so many people. His predictions turned out to be wrong, because the land became more productive than he had foreseen. The Club of Rome, to take another example, was founded in 1968 and is known particularly for its 1972 report, *The Limits to Growth*. This report made predictions which, again, have not come about.

The history of false doomsayers should certainly make us cautious in our predictions. So far in this book I have tried to avoid them, preferring to focus on the present situation – with a look at the past in order to see how we got here and what it might teach us.

However, the purpose of this book is to encourage us to think about the future, to care about the future, so I summarise below what I think the future might hold for the threats presented in Part 1:

- In the long term, I don't believe we shall run out of energy, though in the short to medium term there is reason to fear that the burning of fossil fuels will cause air pollution in cities and the release of CO_2 into the atmosphere, with the possibility of long-term consequences for the planet.

- We can avoid running out of metals by reusing them.

- It is likely to be extremely costly to replenish exhausted resources of groundwater and phosphorus.

- There is reason to hope that the world population may stabilise at 10 to 12 billion.

- It is possible that we may be able to use less land to produce more food, but if I am wrong about this and about the global population levelling off there will be serious pressure on soil quality, wilderness, ecosystems and biodiversity.

- Ancient forests and other ecosystems, once destroyed, can be re-established, but this may take longer than a few human lifetimes.

- The long-term consequences of dispersing man-made substances in soil, groundwater, rivers, oceans and atmosphere are unknown and unpredictable. Past experience gives us little cause for complacency. We avoided the disaster that would have followed destruction of the ozone layer – but it was a narrow escape. Another time we may not be so lucky: by the time we become aware of the danger it may be too late.

- Whether we take a path leading to disaster or take steps to avert it depends on decisions made by countless people. Throughout this book I try to be an optimist rather than a doom-monger, emphasising the human capacity to learn from our mistakes, change the way we look at things and change the way we live. But I could be wrong.

Human capabilities

'You can't change human nature'
This is discussed in chapter 8.

'All this talk about morality is baloney. Science has proved that morality is bunk. Humans are just after their own ends. The selfish gene and all that'
This is discussed in chapter 6.

'I know we ought to change, but...'
We know that we *ought* to change our ways and live planet-friendly lifestyles. We don't argue with that. But somehow we don't actually seem to do much about it. That's just how we are.

J B Priestley understood that. One of his 'Delights'[12] was 'Fiddling while Rome burns'. After reading an advance copy of William Vogt's 1948 *Road to Survival* (see page 101), with its dire warnings of overpopulation, environmental degradation, wars, famine and death, and writing to the publisher to commend it, he discovered some old pianola rolls in a shop and describes his thirty minutes of pure delight as he played them: 'Our daft species was hell-bent for starvation and ruin. Never had the future looked worse. And I knew, I knew. But there I was ... a sound progressive man in his middle fifties, not giving – for thirty minutes or so – a damn.'

The primatologist Jane Goodall asks: 'If we really are the most intellectually gifted animal on the planet, how come we are destroying the place where we live? We, more than any other animals, can plan. Why aren't we doing so?'[13]

Of all the objections discussed in this chapter, this is perhaps the most powerful. The failure to live up to our ideals is something we all have to contend with. That is the human condition. Realism forces us to acknowledge that this is so; idealism leads us to keep trying.

Some general points

'Caring for the environment is a luxury we cannot afford'

There is so much human need. We must do everything we can to alleviate poverty and suffering. We cannot afford to divert money and effort to the luxury of looking after the environment.

On the contrary, we cannot afford not to look after the Earth. The economic cost of dealing with problems arising in the future (not to mention the human costs) will be much greater than that of dealing with them today: 'Technological solutions to environmental problems are routinely far more expensive than preventive measures to avoid creating the problem in the first place. ... All of our current problems are unintended consequences of our existing technology.'[14]

Today we have unparalleled wealth. We tell ourselves that we are going through hard times, but the vast majority of us in Britain have comforts and luxuries unimaginable to past generations and far beyond the reach of most people on the planet (not all of us: I shall discuss the issues of poverty and inequality in chapter 14). In spite of this, we have managed to build up a national debt of staggering proportions. This is our financial bequest to future generations. How can we dare to bequeath to them also the environmental problems of our own making, on the highly speculative grounds that they will be richer than we are?

The longer we continue to disperse pollutants, destroy forests and wildlife, degrade soils and exhaust non-renewable resources, the harder it will be to recover. The longer we continue to increase the human population of the planet, the longer we indulge our consumerist lifestyles, the more difficult we shall make it for future generations.

'But I can make no difference'

It is easy to point to the scale of the problem and say that my own contribution is so tiny that there is no point in me doing anything. I can't make a difference. Even the contribution of the United Kingdom is small, when we look at the global picture.

We may be convinced by the arguments set out in Part 1, we may agree that the world's consumption needs to be reduced, but feel that each of us individually can have no impact. We can make no significant difference. My holiday abroad makes a huge difference to me, and it makes no difference to the environment since the plane is going there anyway.

Edmund Burke, the eighteenth-century statesman who is much quoted as a political thinker, had a simple answer to this: 'No one made a greater mistake than he who did nothing because he could do so little.'

There are plenty of situations where we act in the public interest, even when we know that our personal contribution makes little difference to the global picture and that it might be in our interests to act differently. Individually, we gain nothing from making a certain sacrifice, but we do gain if everyone else makes the same sacrifice. We can take heart from observing that most people are not deterred from doing the right thing by the consideration that their contribution, or their sacrifice, is so small that it makes no difference. We are quite used to acting in the public interest.

Common resources such as grazing, forest, irrigation water or fisheries only work if each person refrains from over-exploitation of the resource. Provided that appropriate management structures are in place, such communities do succeed in operating successfully to the good of all (see page 136).

To take a few everyday examples, if I want to pick a few flowers in the park, I can take them home and enjoy them. It makes no noticeable difference to the display in the park – as long as I'm the only one to pick them. If, however, taking flowers from the park was accepted as normal behaviour, there would be no flowers left there. In practice, each of us leaves the flowers, trusting others to do the same. As individuals, we act in the public interest.

Voting is a waste of time.[15] One vote makes no difference, and your time would be better spent doing something else. But lots of people still turn out to vote, and many regard the right to vote as so important that they have campaigned vigorously, sometimes at great sacrifice, to win that right.

This is where virtue ethics comes in (see page 82). Virtue ethics means that we try to do the right thing even when other people do not, even when the consequences seem insignificant in the grand scheme of things, because that is the kind of person that we want to be. Virtue ethics has an important part to play in caring for the Earth.

We may not be able to influence the way that others behave, but each of us is responsible for our own individual decisions and behaviour. We are responsible to our own consciences, our own sense of who we are and the kind of person we would like to be; and we are responsible to other people, now and in the future. To say that it doesn't matter because everyone else is doing it is a very poor justification for unthinking, unsocial, irresponsible or damaging behaviour.

If we chuckle at the quip 'What did posterity ever do for me?', that is because we know that our responsibilities extend beyond helping people who help us; we know that it is in our nature to care about the future.

Notes

1. Tucker, John A, 2003, Japanese views of Nature and the Environment', 161–163 in Selin, Helaine (editor), 2003, *Nature across Cultures: Views of Nature and the Environment in Non-Western Cultures*, Springer
2. Eg Lawson, Nigel, 2008, *An Appeal to Reason*, Duckworth Overlook; Booker, Christopher, 2009, *The Real Global Warming Disaster*, Continuum; Delingpole, James, 2012, *Watermelons*, Biteback (revised edition); Ridley, Matt, columns in *The Times*; Paterson, Owen, I'm proud of standing up to the green lobby, *Sunday Telegraph*, 20 July 2014 – an article in which he coined the term 'the Green Blob'
3. Sachs, Jeffrey, 2005, *The End of Poverty: How We Can Make it Happen in Our Lifetime*, Penguin; Sachs, Jeffrey, 2009, *Common Wealth: Economics for a Crowded Planet*, Penguin
4. Collier, Paul, 2008, *The Bottom Billion: Why the Poorest Countries are Failing and What Can Be Done About It*, Oxford University Press; Collier, Paul, 2010, *The Plundered Planet: How to Reconcile Prosperity With Nature*, Allen Lane
5. *The Lancet* Commission on Pollution and Health, October 2017
6. Eg Ridley, Matt, 2017, The Poor are carrying the Cost of Today's Climate Policy, 201–215 in Marohasy Jennifer, (editor), 2017, *Climate Change: The Facts*, Connor Court Publishing
7. Ridley, Matt, 2010, *The Rational Optimist: how prosperity evolves*, Fourth Estate,
8. Sheikh Yamani (Saudi Oil Minister 1962–1986), *The Observer*, Sunday 14 January 2001
9. Eg Booker, 2009; Delingpole, 2012; Matt Ridley, columns in *The Times*; Owen Paterson, 2014
10. Delingpole, 2012, 16
11. Paterson, 2014
12. Priestley, J B, 1949, *Delight*

13. Quoted in *The Times*, 10 December, 2011
14. Diamond, Jared, 2011, *Collapse*, Penguin, 505
15. Levitt, Steven D and Dubner, Stephen J, 2005, *Freakonomics*, Allen Lane, 222f

Part 3

Human Potential and the Natural World

Parts 1 and 2 of the book have been about the past and the present: we should be looking after our planet better, and we have the capability to do so. Part 3 is different: it contains predictions and recommendations. All predictions are unreliable, and all recommendations are open to debate. I can only hope that the following pages will stimulate thought.

Part 3 attempts to chart a way forward, towards lives that are in harmony with the Earth. I look at personal lifestyle, at the role of government, at food and land-use, and at how technological innovation can help. Finally, I bring these strands together to sketch out what a functioning economy might look like in a society that values the environment.

There are four points to be made by way of introduction. First, I am not trying to take away everything that makes life worth living. I am not against people enjoying life. On the contrary, I argue that lives that are in harmony with nature are more fulfilling and satisfying.

Second, I am not against business, industry, the economy or technology. We, in Britain, have got used to a government that spends an enormous amount of money on our behalf (health and social care, education, infrastructure, police, defence etc; even food is subsidised). It can only do this if there is a thriving economy with a great deal of taxable activity. What is important for the environment is that this activity should be Earth-sustaining, not Earth-destroying. In order to achieve this, we need business, we need industry, we need science and technology and we need inventors.

Third, Britain is not a poor country (see pages 41–43). Our responsibility to deal with poverty should not be used as an excuse not to care for the environment. Indeed, if we allow large areas of the planet to become less congenial as places to live and thrive, it is the poorest people who will suffer most: they always do, when things go wrong.

Fourth, as well as being increasingly affluent, life in Britain (as in many other countries) since 1950 has been, by historical standards, extraordinarily steady, secure and peaceful. We have got so used to there being no major disruptions to our national life that we take it for granted. This contrasts strongly, for example, with the previous half-century, in which there were two world wars and the Great Depression of the 1930s. It would be a mistake to assume that future generations will find life so easy. Martin Rees, President of the Royal Society (2005– 2010) and Astronomer Royal, has written that unless the human race puts its house in order, 'the odds are no better than fifty-fifty that our present civilisation will survive to the end of the present century without a serious setback'.[1] Some of the threats that Rees describes – such as cosmic collisions and new, natural deadly viruses (the flu epidemic of 1918–19 infected 500 million people and killed about 50 million – 3 per cent of the world's population at that time. Imagine another such epidemic ten or a hundred times more virulent) are not of our making, but most of them, from global climate change and chemical pollution to terrorism and the threat from chemical, biological and nuclear weapons, are the direct result of human activity. Even if we are spared such major catastrophes, we cannot expect the trend of increasing productivity and gross domestic product to continue indefinitely. We cannot be justified in leaving our environmental problems to future generations on the assumption that they will have the wealth to deal with them. On the contrary, if present trends continue we shall leave future generations with massive debt to pay for our own self-indulgent lifestyles.[2]

The situations and issues described in this book mostly relate to the United Kingdom and other Western nations. People all over the world, however, aspire to Western lifestyles, along with the environmental impact that accompanies them. It is important that ways should be found for non-Western cultures to embrace much that is good in Western lifestyles while avoiding the environment-destroying practices. Is it possible for these cultures to find routes from their traditional ways of living into the lifestyles described below, missing out the destructive consumerism described in chapter 3?

Notes

1. Rees, Martin, 2004, *Our Final Century?: Will the human race survive the twenty-first century?*, Arrow Books
2. Eg Willetts, David, 2011, *The Pinch: How the baby boomers took their children's future – and why they should give it back*, Atlantic Books

Chapter 10
Lives that Remember the Future

It is not material wealth but non-material assets, such as strong relationships, active engagement, and thriving communities, that enrich our personal and social well-being.

Teresa Belton[1]

Human societies have been able to survive by observing the world around them and adapting to changed circumstances. Uniquely, we humans can think about the future, we can plan for the future, we can live for the future, many have given their lives in war for the sake of the future. We have a sense that there are right and wrong ways to live. We can change. We can make choices. Increasingly, we are learning to understand how we make these choices. The time has now come for us to draw on these powerful capabilities to ensure that the world that we hand on to future generations is as good as the one we have inherited.

There is a great deal of good advice about what we, as individuals, could do that would benefit the environment. Most of us have read leaflets and magazine articles, and maybe books, with suggestions.[2] Trying to live in harmony with nature doesn't mean taking away all that makes life worth living. Good lives don't have to cost the Earth.[3]

As individuals, we can decide how to live our own lives, we can decide which shops, businesses and industries to patronise, and we can decide which political and social movements to support. Here are two pieces of advice which place the emphasis differently.

David MacKay, author of *Sustainable Energy – without the hot air*[4] and Chief Scientific Advisor of the Department of Energy and Climate Change (2009–14), advised: 'make sure you are doing the things that will really make a difference – for example, turn your thermostat down, read your energy meters, stop flying, drive less, walk and cycle more, change to low energy light bulbs, don't buy clutter, avoid packaging, don't replace your old gadgets early and eat vegetarian six days a week.'[5]

131

Lester Brown, founder of the Worldwatch Institute and founder and former president of the Earth Policy Institute, put a different emphasis. The question most often put to him was 'What can I do?'.People expected him to say 'Change your light bulbs, recycle newspaper', but in fact he told them that we must restructure the world economy. To do this they must become politically active.[6]

The environmental impact of everything

My own response to the question 'What should I do to help the environment?' would be: 'Take into account the environmental impact of every action and decision you make'. Every human life has an impact on the environment. In the modern world we cannot reduce our impact to zero. I am not suggesting that we give up everything that makes life worth living. Quite the reverse. The point is that a life lived in harmony with nature is more satisfying than spending time chasing consumer products.

When we make decisions, large or small, we commonly consider the financial implications ('What will it cost?' or 'How much will I make?') and perhaps we think about how our decision might affect our family, friends or anyone else involved. I would suggest that we should also ask what effect our decision might have on the environment.

There is a parallel with the world of business. The term 'the bottom line' makes the point that, whatever else can be said or reported about a business, what really matters is the profit or loss. In 1994 John Elkington coined the term 'triple bottom line' to suggest that it is not just money that counts: social and environmental impact are also important.

Some general principles

It is for each of us to work out how we can keep our impact as low as possible, in the knowledge of our own personal circumstances. We don't all have to adopt the same lifestyle.

An environment-friendly lifestyle is not just a matter of not spending money. The question is how we spend it and how we earn it. Generally speaking, if our economic activities centre round services and experiences they do less environmental damage than if we are making and buying goods. Money spent on the arts, sport and other experiences, for example, generally does less environmental damage than money spent on manufactured goods. Modern information technology provides opportunities to earn and spend money though the internet, with very little environmental impact.

The contrast between goods and experiences is important, but it should not be overemphasised. Experiences may depend on manufactured goods. Travel is amongst the most enjoyable of experiences, but many modes of transport use fossil fuels and there is an environmental impact in the manufacture of a car, say, or a cruise liner.

It is human nature to acquire possessions and to enjoy them. What sets the consumer society apart is the amount of stuff we acquire that we either dispose of or hide away – stuff that we don't actually enjoy. Look critically at everything you buy or acquire, but look especially critically at everything that you store out of sight and at everything that leaves your house. Why did it come into the house in the first place? Did you really need it, if you now want to get rid of it? Now that you are getting rid of it, are you disposing of it in the most environmentally sensible way (see below)? Does it have a use to anybody else? If so, use one of the channels of the sharing economy.

Keep up with the latest information, and be willing to question. The environment-friendly choice may not be the one you think it is. A few years ago, diesel vehicles were encouraged because of their low carbon-dioxide emissions; now they are discouraged because of their nitrogen-oxide and particulate emissions. Transporting food for long distances consumes fossil fuels – but producing it locally in heated greenhouses or storing it for long periods until it is needed may consume more.

Decide on what kind of behaviour you admire in other people. Do you admire conspicuous consumption, or do you admire people who try to live sustainably? Who are your role models? What kind of role model do you wish to be?

Reduce, reuse/redistribute, repair, recycle

What do we do with stuff we no longer need and want to throw away? We may take a lot of time and trouble in sorting out all our unwanted things for recycling. This is excellent: recycling is much better than sending all our rubbish to landfill, but we should remember that recycling is the last on the list, to be done only after we have considered opportunities to reduce, reuse, redistribute or repair.

Reduce

First we should cut down on the number of things we get – especially things that we intend to throw away. Acquiring more stuff doesn't bring happiness. As we have seen, there are many other things we can do that are more likely to make us happy and fulfilled.

However, it is part of human nature to want to acquire things. Some people like to make and look after a collection. For others, it is the act of acquiring something new that counts; once they have got it they lose interest and move on to the next object of interest.

We all like to have nice things about us, things that are beautiful in themselves or that remind us of people, places and times in our lives. We can choose objects that will last, that do little damage to the environment, and that have brought pleasure to the person – artist or craftsman – who has made them; not just factory-produced stuff that we shall soon want to throw away. We can avoid acquiring stuff that we know that we shall dispose of; or, if we enjoy temporary ownership, we can make sure that we acquire things that will find another home through the sharing economy (see below).

We like to give presents to family and friends, and we can apply the environment-impact test to presents just as much as to what we spend on ourselves.

'Reduce' can be applied particularly to energy and transport. Using less energy saves us money as well as reducing carbon emissions. Examples include home insulation, lowering the temperature on the central heating, especially in rooms that are not being used, and using energy-efficient stand-by systems or turning off appliances when they are not in use. For transport, we can reduce the amount that we travel and for each journey we can choose the most environmentally friendly way of getting there.

We can try to reduce the amount of plastic we use, particularly avoiding plastic items and containers that we throw away as soon as we have used them.

Reuse and redistribute: the sharing economy

Second, before disposing of anything we should ask ourselves if it can be reused, either by us or by someone else. This is not the same as recycling: I take my empty honey jars to a bee-keeper and my empty jam jars to the local Country Markets, for reuse as honey jars and jam jars; my empty wine bottles go for recycling.

'Buying stuff? That's so last century.'[7] There are two aspects of the sharing economy. The first is to own something for a while (clothing, pictures etc), using it and enjoying it, and then selling it on or giving it to someone else. The other is for goods to be owned communally or by a hire company, and we borrow or rent them as required.

Sharing is a great way of satisfying our material wants while reducing the burden on the environment. Rachel Botsman and Roo Rogers in *What's Mine is Yours: How Collaborative Consumption is Changing the Way We Live*[8] describe numerous examples of sharing (their list of websites for UK examples is five pages long), which they organise into three categories:

- Product service systems (paying for the benefit of using a product without needing to own it). Examples include hire cars (this is probably the future for driverless cars; see chapter 13), bikes, toys, clothes, tools, launderettes and services such as catering and entertainment.
- Redistribution markets. Examples include charity shops, second-hand and antique furniture, book and bric-a-brac stores – and numerous websites.
- Collaborative lifestyles (people with similar interests banding together to share and exchange assets such as time, space, skills and money).

Botsman and Rogers coin the term 'collaborative consumption' for this way of living. By offering us the opportunity to use goods when we want them without the need to store them, look after them or throw them away when we are not using them, it offers us a way of satisfying our

135

consumerist instincts in a way that places less pressure on resources.

Using a spare room to provide a home for a lodger is a long-established custom, but other possibilities are to rent out storage space, garden (as an allotment, perhaps) or car-parking space.[9]

We may hear about situations where shared resources are not managed well (the so-called 'tragedy of the commons'[10]), but common property can be, and often is, managed to the benefit of all. The 2009 Nobel Memorial Prize in Economic Sciences was awarded to Elinor Ostrom for work in which she 'challenged the conventional wisdom by demonstrating how local property can be successfully managed by local commons without any regulation by central authorities or privatisation'.[11] Communities all round the world succeed in operating common resources such as grazing, forest or irrigation water for the good of all.

Repair

Third, before throwing something away we should ask if its useful life could be prolonged by repair. In a future in which many existing jobs will become automated, repairing could be a growing opportunity.

The American writer Matthew Crawford wrote *The Case for Working with Your Hands, or Why Office Work is Bad for Us and Fixing Things Feels Good*[12] to demonstrate 'the potential for human flourishing in the manual trades – their rich cognitive challenges and psychic nourishment'.[13] Crawford gave up a well-paid job as director of a think tank (a job which included making arguments about global warming that just happened to coincide with the positions taken by the oil companies that funded the think tank – an example of policy-based evidence; see page 29)[14] to set up in business repairing old and special motorcycles. He found this deeply satisfying, with the opportunity it offered for creative thought. In an age when so many jobs, in manufacturing or in the office, have become routine (and are therefore in danger of being carried out by computer or robot), there is satisfaction to be found in repairing things.

136

Recycle

Only after opportunities for repair and reuse/redistribution have been exhausted should recycling be considered. Recycling consumes energy, both in the processing itself and in transporting the stuff to where it can be processed – sometimes in distant countries. However, recycling is much to be preferred to dumping all our rubbish in landfill – and is especially important for toxic materials which pollute groundwater if dumped in land-fill sites and for metals and other reusable but non-renewable resources. As we shall see in chapter 13, the concepts of cradle-to-cradle and the circular economy are the way of the future, and they depend on all of us, householders and businesses, carefully sorting our unwanted items for recycling.

The proximity principle

The term 'proximity principle' is used by the Campaign to Protect Rural England for 'the idea that compact cities, towns and villages produce the best social, economic and environmental outcomes'.[15] The term has been used by Julian Rose for the economic relationship that follows from such communities, based on a 'reciprocal supply and demand chain' around population centres, making local populations, as far as possible, mutually dependent for goods and services.[16] It has also been applied in social psychology for the social outcome: the tendency of people to form closer relationships with those who are nearby.

From the environmental point of view, building up local social and economic relationships reduces transport and travel costs. I don't wish to deny the value of trade (page 210) and social contact (page 153) with other countries for establishing and maintaining global peace and harmony, but for most people most of the time it is social and economic relationships in the neighbourhood that can provide the greatest happiness and fulfilment.

The proximity principle helps to build local communities. Roger Scruton places the love of home ('oikophilia') at the heart of caring for the environment.[17] He says that successful attempts to reverse the tide of ecological destruction have come from local or national schemes to protect territory

137

known as 'ours', from the shared love of a shared place. He emphasises the importance of small civic associations and argues that it is through oikophilia and these small associations, leading to targeted action, that we shall preserve our environment.

But whence comes public spirit? It comes from patriotism, from love of country, from a sense of belonging and of a shared and inherited home. It comes from believing that this problem is *our* problem, and therefore *my* problem, as a member of the group. That belief disappears when anonymous bureaucracies confiscate our risks and pretend that they can regulate them to extinction.

Roger Scruton[18]

John Papworth presents an argument for devolving democratic decision-making to the lowest level: the village.[19] The English parish council, as an institution, has been flourishing in recent years,[20] and in cities many of life's problems can be solved more effectively by the mayor than by the national government.[21] Local democracy gives us a greater sense of influence over our own lives. Involvement in local affairs – politics, religious communities, sport, entertainment, voluntary work – helps to give us a sense of belonging, a sense of significance. We may still be outvoted, but we have a greater chance of ensuring that our minority view is heard. Watching television can give us the impression that everything that matters takes place at the national or international level, leaving us overwhelmed by the sense of our own powerlessness and insignificance. In fact, we can all contribute to changing things on the larger scale, if our view is widely shared (see below), but it is on the local scale that an individual is more likely to be able to make a difference.

To be attached to the subdivision, to love the little platoon we belong to in society, is the first principle (the germ, as it were) of public affections. It is the first link in the series by which we proceed towards a love to our country, and to mankind.

Edmund Burke[22]

Small independent local shops are becoming popular again, offering good customer service and a knowledge of the local community.[23] The Transition Town movement is about communities facing the big challenges they face by starting local.[24] Led by its city council, Preston, in the north of England, has set about keeping wealth in the local economy.[25] There have been other initiatives in recent years to enable people to eat food that has been produced locally: farm shops, farmers' markets, incredible edible (growing food in public spaces all over the town – an amazing project pioneered in Todmorden in the north of England)[26] – and the continuation of the long tradition of allotments. Locally produced food is fresh when it reaches the table, and you avoid the cost of storage and transport.

Colin Tudge points out that if food is produced under a system based on economic competitiveness, farmers will be undercut by other farmers in other countries working in quite different conditions against a quite different historical and economic background. This leads to farmers being put out of business, productive land left uncultivated, and people going hungry. He calls for biological reality and moral reality: biology tells us what we *can* do, and morality tells us what we *ought* to do.[27] All over the world, people should grow food for local consumption; trade should be an addition to local food, not a substitute for it. This balance will help food security as well as reducing pollution from transport.

People power

As customers, as voters and as campaigners, a great deal of power resides with the people. If enough of us support a certain shop or business, for example, it will do well; if enough of us boycott it, it will fail. We are often told that the economy is controlled by big business, that we are just pawns in their hands. The truth is, however, that, unless there is a monopoly or cartel, the real power, lies with the customers. It is customers who decide whether a business thrives or fails. If we buy products and services with a low environmental impact, that is what businesses will provide.[28]

Reflect on the power of the multitude. How multitudes change the world. Multitudes stopped going to Woolworths so it closed. Multitudes have left newspaper-buying alone, so newspapers close. Shops in high streets close because the multitude has spoken. Tesco and Sainsbury's and Walmart grow into behemoths because the multitude have spoken.

John Bird[29]

As voters, we may have to choose between candidates with little concern for environmental issues, but as citizens we can let our Members of Parliament know what is important to us. As individuals or as members of campaign or pressure groups, we can urge them to consider the environment at all times. Many politicians, manufacturers, retailers and others who influence the way we live take environmental issues seriously. They are encouraged by evidence of support from voters and customers. Whatever their personal views, they are more likely to act on environmental issues if they know that there is public support. We can all let them know that we support them.

A poll in 2016 found that almost 90 per cent of people between the ages of 16 and 34 think it is important for politicians to take care of wildlife and the environment.[30]

Social media add a new dimension. They enable us to make our views widely known. If we wish to support or boycott some shop, business, political candidate or pressure group, we can use social media to test if our opinion is widely shared. If it is, that's people power.

What does a greener life look like?

In *Happier People Healthier Planet*, Teresa Belton tells how she sent out a questionnaire to people, most of whom she contacted via an advertisement in *The Big Issue*, who had chosen to live a life of modest material consumption – and who said they were happy with it.[31] Of the 94 people who completed the questionnaire, 50 said that their modest lifestyle was partly due to financial circumstances and partly to choice. For 42 it was purely a matter of choice. Belton then went on to interview 37 of the participants in order to gain further insights. Her book describes in detail the lives of these 94 'modest consumers' and why they chose to live as they did.

Some of these modest consumers did without a washing machine, television or mobile phone. Many were enthusiastic reusers, repairers and recyclers. Most engaged in the sharing economy. Many had a particular dislike of waste. They were people who thought about their values. Many of them were motivated by a concern for the environment or social justice. Many of them were involved in voluntary work or community activities and making ethical purchases, like fair trade. They found pleasure in being engaged in challenging and absorbing activities. They were very much aware of the importance of the non-material aspects of life and the contribution they make to our well-being – like friendships, spirituality, creativity, playfulness and closeness to nature. They were active physically, culturally and socially. Their most frequent non-essential purchases included books, CDs, DVDs, theatre and music, and good food, wine and beer.

They differed a great deal in the choices they made – but all were proactive, forging their own ways of doing things. Some had been brought up to be modest consumers; for others it was a decision made at some point in adult life. Interestingly, none of them allowed their chosen lifestyles to jeopardise close family relationships. Avoiding conventional consumption patterns doesn't have to cut you off from other people.

Most of the modest consumers had low incomes and low expenditure, but an environmentally friendly lifestyle doesn't have to be like that. Belton points out that you could spend a fortune buying antiques, commissioning works of art, planting trees and donating to charity – and this would do far less damage to the environment than a smaller amount of money spent on clothes, novelty items, cheap flights or other popular items of expenditure.

James Wallman, in *Stuffocation*, also writes about people who have changed their lifestyle, but without necessarily giving up their well-paid jobs.[32] Wallman is a trend forecaster, and he could see that there were cracks appearing in the consumer society and the materialist values that underlie it. People were being suffocated by an excess of stuff and the pursuit of stuff. He describes the trend in the way people spend their money, away from stuff and towards experiences. The people whose life-changes he describes are motivated more by the search for personal happiness and fulfilment than by any desire to act for the good of nature or the environment. Some of them continue to have well-paid jobs – unlike most of Belton's subjects – but they spend their money differently, on experiences rather than stuff. For Wallman, the way ahead is not necessarily minimalism or simple living, which can sound rather negative, but experientialism, which sounds more exciting and allows for ambition, for making money and spending it.

These are two books, from different perspectives, both describing a trend away from materialist, consumerist, stuff-dominated lifestyles towards something different. The people described have a variety of motives for change – not all of them are motivated by a wish to care for the environment – but they illustrate a growing dissatisfaction with Earth-destroying lifestyles and the deeper attraction of Earth-friendly lives.

Notes

1. Belton, Teresa, 2014, *Happier People Healthier Planet*, Silverwood Books, 13

2. One such book – MacBride, Peter, 2008, *Teach Yourself Ethical Living*, Hodder Education – has chapters on energy, electrical appliances, in the home, food and drink, shopping, money and travel

3. Simms, Andrew and Smith, Joe (editors), 2008, *Do Good Lives have to Cost the Earth?*, Constable

4. www.withouthotair.com

5. *Cambridge Alumni Magazine*, Issue 58, Michaelmas 2009, 17

6. *New Scientist*, 5 February 2011

7. Headline, *Sunday Times*, 15 October 2017

8. Botsman, Rachel and Rogers, Roo, 2011, *What's Mine is Yours: How Collaborative Consumption is Changing the Way We Live*, HarperCollins

9. *The Times*, 4 July, 2016

10. Hardin, G, 1968, The Tragedy of the Commons, *Science*, 162 (3859), 1243–1248

11. www.nobelprize.org/nobel_prizes/economics/laureates/2009/ostrom.html

12. Crawford, Matthew, 2010, *The Case for Working with Your Hands, or Why Office Work is Bad for Us and Fixing Things Feels Good*, Penguin, 2010

13. Crawford, 2010, 32

14. Crawford, 2010, 108–109

15. www.cpre.org.uk/resources/housing-and-planning/housing/item/1939

16. Eg Rose, Julian, 2009, The proximity principle, *Fourth World Review*, No 150, Aug/Sept 2009, 23–25

17. Scruton, Roger, 2012, *Green Philosophy: How to Think Seriously about the Planet*, Atlantic Books

18. Scruton, 2012, 171

19. Papworth, John, 2006, *Village Democracy*, Imprint Academic

20. Girling, Richard, Love your parish council: that's where real power is wielded, *Sunday Times*, 27 April 2014

21. Eg Barber, Benjamin, 2014, *If Mayors Ruled the World*, Yale University Press; for specific applications in environmental politics, see Dobson, Andrew, 2016, *Environmental Politics: A Very Short Introduction*, Oxford University Press, 99–106

22. Burke, Edmund, 1790, *Reflections on the Revolution in France*
23. *The Times*, 24 November 2013
24. https://transitionnetwork.org
25. Thomson, Alice, *The Times*, 1 November 2017; *The Times*, 29 October 2017
26. http://incredibleediblenetwork.org.uk
27. Tudge, Colin, 2009, The age of biology, *Fourth World Review*, No 151, Nov/Dec 2009
28. Eg Paterson, Tony, 1989, *The Green Conservative: A Manifesto for the Environment*, Bow Publications: Chapter 13, The Green Consumer
29. Bird, John, *The Big Issue*, June 6–12, 2016
30. *The Times*, 25 July 2016
31. Belton, 2014
32. Wallman, James, 2015, *Stuffocation*, Penguin

Chapter 11
Beyond Democracy

His system of government, with a strong man dominating the state but not entirely able to ignore senate or people, lasted for centuries.

Robert Harris, writing about Augustus[1]

The well-ordered society

In a well-ordered society, members of society will generally, in pursuing their own ends, benefit other members of society at the same time. As the Roman philosopher and politician Marcus Tullius Cicero put it, 'It ought to be the chief end of man to make the interest of each individual and of the whole body politic identical.'[2]

We should recognise that, much of the time, we all act out of self-interest (not all the time, as we have seen – our motives can be altruistic and they can be very complex). Our social structures, laws and institutions should take account of this. They should be so ordered that society as a whole benefits from our self-interested endeavours.

A simple example of the well-ordered society is the free exchange of goods and services (the fundamental building block of the market economy, before it becomes cluttered with complications): if A wants to obtain something and B can sell it at a price that is acceptable to them both, A and B have both achieved what they wanted and have benefited each other as well; and if the transaction is taxable, the wider community benefits too. Another everyday example is that the people who acquire the most money for themselves and spend the most on themselves should also contribute the most in taxes.

In a well-ordered society, the interests of the various participants in a business enterprise are aligned: good management gives priority to satisfied customers and a satisfied and motivated workforce, leading to a profit for the shareholders and fair remuneration for the senior management and decision makers. The interests of businessmen and traders who make decisions will be aligned with the interests of those whose jobs and capital are at risk. One of our troubles recently is that some of our major enterprises have been structured in such a way that decision-makers have been able to benefit from courses of action that have had damaging consequences for shareholders, staff, customers, and even tax-payers; decisions that have important consequences for shareholders, staff and customers have been made by people who have no 'skin in the game'.[3]

If we accept this idea of a well-ordered society, we should recognise that those who benefit from exploiting nature and the natural environment should enable others to share the benefit. There will be structures and institutions, backed by the rule of law, to prevent individuals or governments furthering their own ends at the expense of future generations, or at the expense of the environment.

Although much of what I have said in the preceding paragraphs is well understood, this final point is not. We have seen governments and individuals inflicting damage on the environment in order to further their own interests, at the same time as piling up huge financial debts for the future. There is a need for institutions, political structures and social conventions so that, for decent law-abiding people, stealing from the future becomes as unthinkable as stealing from our neighbours.

Some natural resources, like agricultural land, managed woodland, fish, river water and groundwater, can, if we choose, be treated as renewable resources, managed for our own benefit in such a way that they continue to be available for future use. Similarly, natural and managed landscape, ecosystems and biodiversity can be looked after so they can be enjoyed by future generations. If the Earth's store of non-renewable resources is depleted, however, if we allow our soils to be eroded and degraded and if we pollute our soils, water and atmosphere with man-made substances and waste, we irreversibly deprive future generations of the opportunity to make use of these resources, and we should find some way to compensate them by setting aside a set of assets at least as valuable as the ones we have inherited and failed to pass on.

Natural capital

This leads us to the concept of 'natural capital'. When E F Schumacher coined the term in his book *Small is Beautiful*,[4] he was thinking particularly of the way that the Earth's capital store of fossil fuels was being used up as if it were income and of the loss of the natural environment as a consequence of pollution, but modern understanding of the concept extends to rocks, soil, water, air and all living things.

Dieter Helm, in *Natural Capital: Valuing the Planet*, states a simple rule: 'the aggregate level of natural capital should not decline'.[5] His book shows that 'there is a perfectly plausible and economically efficient way to protect and enhance our natural capital in order to achieve sustainable growth'. Finance can be raised from compensation payments and pollution taxes (following the principle of 'the polluter pays': a carbon tax, for example) to compensate for damage to natural capital, and from a share of the profits from the exploitation of non-renewable resources. This is how a well-ordered society should work: we who are benefiting from damaging or depleting natural capital should make sure that future generations have a share of the benefit.

Many countries do not do this. They have exploited their natural capital without leaving any benefit for the future. There are several countries, however, that have established capital funds of this kind. The largest is Norway's, which has accumulated a sovereign wealth fund worth more than $1 trillion – for a country with a population of about 5 million.

A substantial fund like this could be spent, at least in part, on enhancing natural capital: protecting ecosystems and biodiversity, cleaning up pollution, restoring groundwater resources, research into greener technologies … the list of opportunities is endless.

The downside, of course, is that if some of the profit from exploiting natural capital is creamed off into a sovereign wealth fund, that will mean higher prices in the shops. This will only be tolerated if there is general acceptance by society as a whole that it is the right thing to do – and if we wean ourselves off the values of the consumer society. Individuals, clubs and charities can all have a part to play in helping to maintain natural capital. The raising of a sovereign wealth fund is a task for government, but it is one that they can only carry out if they have the support of the electorate.

The trouble with democracy

Many of us would agree with Churchill's well-known sentiment:

Many forms of Government have been tried and will be tried in this world of sin and woe. No one pretends that democracy is perfect or all-wise. Indeed, it has been said that democracy is the worst form of government except all those other forms that have been tried from time to time.

Winston Churchill[6]

Democracy, by definition, favours the wishes of the majority, so minority groups may lose out. It is well designed for situations where there are two dominant political parties that differ in ideology or political philosophy, because voters can reasonably change their opinions and their support, and where there are at least two parties with enough support to be able to form a government from time to time, either as a single-party administration or in coalition with smaller parties. It is less suitable in situations where the parties represent different ethnic groups or other distinctive social groups, where the smaller communities may perpetually find that they are powerless.

Democratic politics is adversarial. Political parties set out to win votes by feeding a sense of grievance, telling people how badly off they are. Thus in the last few years, when most people are immensely better off than they were a generation or two ago, the talk is all of austerity – and this encourages consumerist values. We don't hear politicians in a democracy telling us how wealthy we are (or not since Harold Macmillan and 'You've never had it so good') and that this is our opportunity to use our wealth to do something for the future.

Edmund Burke described society as 'a partnership not only between those who are living, but between those who are living, those who are dead, and those who are to be born. Each contract of each particular state is but a clause in the great primeval contract of eternal society'.[7] Government and parliament have a greater duty of leadership than simply to follow their voters.

The trouble with democracy as it operates today is that it concentrates too much on those who are living, because only the living have votes. We too easily forget how fortunate we are to have inherited so much from past generations. We forget how much we owe to them. More important, we seldom stop to think what we are leaving behind for the future: 'All democracies tend to steal from the unborn since they can't vote.'[8]

The dangers of democratic government have been apparent for a long time. John Micklethwait and Adrian Wooldridge, in *The Fourth Revolution*, find that history has 'demonstrated the truth of Plato's two great criticisms of democracy: that voters would put short-term satisfaction above long-term prudence and that politicians would try to bribe their way to power – as they have done by promising entitlements that future generations will have to pay for'.[9] For Walter Bagehot and John Stuart Mill, 'the one great issue in British politics in the 1860s was how to prevent the party politicians, for purely opportunist reasons, making concessions to democracy which would substitute government by ignorance and brute numbers for government by discussion.'[10] A more recent (2007) quotation is that of Jean-Paul Juncker, 'We all know what to do, we just don't know how to get re-elected after we've done it'. Recalling his days as an MP, Roy Hattersley has written, 'How often was I told: "Say that and you will lose the Home Counties"'.[11]

All of this points to a gulf of understanding between politicians and the electorate: a belief that politicians know what is best for the country but voters are unable to understand or unwilling to support it, because they are motivated by their own selfish concerns – particularly money – and politicians have to follow the electorate. We may ask if this is really so. At the same time, politicians are held in low esteem by the electorate. They are believed to be only out for their own selfish interests. Again, we may ask if this is really so.

A few years ago I thought that this gulf between the electors and the elected was very relevant to the environment:

The future has no vote

The democratic system is the best;
We know it's so much better than the rest.
It means that we must hear what people say.
If we do that, the votes will come our way.

We strive to please the voters all the time
We watch the polls to see our ratings climb.
We know the people want more stuff to buy –
And more and more; a truth we can't deny.

You tell me we are damaging the Earth:
We're using up the oil for all we're worth,
Polluting air and water, land and sea,
Bequeathing desert to posterity.

You tell me that we ought to buy less stuff;
And use less oil and power: enough's enough.
For that's the only way to save the Earth
For generations yet to come to birth.

It may be as you say, I do concede;
I cannot argue with you when you plead
The cause of generations yet to come,
But we must march to the present voters' drum.

The voters need to have their cars, their planes,
Their every want: consumerism reigns.
It's economic growth that steers the boat,
It's not the future, for the future has no vote.

If voters tell us what they want is wealth,
It's not for us to seek the planet's health.
The future plight of Earth is too remote,
We must face facts: the future has no vote.

Now, in early 2018, I am more optimistic. There are so many encouraging signs (see pages 113–114). After Theresa May's speech on the environment in January 2018, there were few voices opposing her for adopting environment-friendly policies. Rather, she was criticised for being too weak, for not going far enough. It is beginning to look as if caring for the environment might be a vote-winner, not a vote-loser. The cynicism expressed in my verses is already looking out of date.

There is a very long way to go, of course, but there are signs that government and people are moving in the right direction. Perhaps we are all too cynical, unwilling to recognise the goodwill that is around us. Perhaps democracy would really come into its own if politicians had more faith in the goodwill, idealism – even selflessness – of the electorate and vice versa.

Right-wing or left-wing?

In the 1960s left-wing politicians tended to regard caring for the environment as a middle-class luxury, an example of the rich people extolling the simple life, pulling up the ladder behind them and telling the poor that they can't have the same lifestyle because if they did it would damage the environment. 'Looking after the environment for the sake of one's grandchildren is a rich man's preoccupation', wrote the economist Andrew Shonfield in *The Observer*.[12]

This is not the general view of the green movement today. We can now see that the problems of world poverty and the future of the planet are closely interconnected. As Nicholas Stern puts it, 'the problems of development and climate change cannot be decoupled, separated or ranked … We must be committed to both issues.'[13]

The pendulum has now swung so far that, in Roger Scruton's words, 'The environmental movement has recently been identified, both by its supporters and by many of its opponents, as in some way "on the left": a protest on behalf of the poor and powerless against big business, consumerism and the structures of social power.'[14] Margaret Thatcher, who, as Prime Minister, took seriously the warnings of climate change and approved the establishment of the Hadley Centre for Climate Research and Prediction, which she opened in 1990, later came to consider that the political movement was more powerful than the science could support, motivated by socialist, anti-capitalist ideology.[15]

Scruton goes on to reclaim the environmental movement for the right, arguing that care for the environment will rest on a love of place, a love of our home and its surroundings. Following Edmund Burke (page 138) and Adam Smith, he stresses the importance of the 'little platoon' that we belong to in society. Scruton's is a grass-roots approach to the issue.

To me, looking after the environment is an issue that transcends party politics. As Camilla Cavendish put it, 'adapting our way of life to live within the planet's limits is one of the greatest challenges of our age; and I don't believe that view should be the monopoly of any political party. I also believe that it is wrong to see green and growth as opposites: concern about the climate should not be the sole preserve of the anti-capitalists.'[16] Left and right can unite in seizing the opportunity to leave a legacy of which those of us who are alive today can be proud and for which those living in the future will be able to be grateful.

The role of government in caring for the environment

In the last chapter, I recommended that, as individuals, we should take into account the environmental impact of all our actions and decisions: the triple bottom line. How much more should this be true of governments. They make the laws that influence the way we live our lives, and they are responsible for the spending of around 40 per cent of the gross domestic product. Environmental considerations should be at the heart of all that they do, as emphasised in a 2017 publication by the Conservative Environment Network, *Thinking differently about our environment: a holistic approach to policy*.

Caring for the environment makes demands on the public purse. Illegal logging and wildlife trade must be prevented. Pollution standards must be established and enforced. Fly-tipping must be deterred. Precious ecosystems must be protected. Sustainable lifestyles and industrial processes must be based on sound research. Government can designate conservation areas – areas where human interference is banned altogether or strictly confined to activities that enable nature to flourish.

It is the role of government to pass laws to regulate business, industry and individuals. Many of the activities described in chapter 1 are, or can be, subject to government laws and regulations. Government can impose green taxes to discourage activities that damage the environment: 'If a proper cost is attached to pollution and waste, businesses will minimise both'.[17] Even the likelihood that a future government may impose new taxes or environmental standards can influence business decisions. Taxes on carbon emissions or on diesel vehicles – or even the fear that such taxes may be introduced – can be more powerful than the knowledge of the environmental risk in bringing about behavioural change.

The Behavioural Insights Team (the co-called 'Nudge Unit', pages 111–112)[18] could advise on ways to make it more attractive for us all to make environment-friendly decisions and more troublesome to make environment-damaging decisions.

As a general rule, the private sector can operate business and industry, but government can have a role in carrying out early-stage research and in subsidising and encouraging later-stage research and development. An example of this, in 2017, is the British government's announcement of an investment of £246 million to help British businesses progress the design, development and manufacture of batteries for the electrification of vehicles.

The UK Green Investment Bank, established by the government in 2012, was capitalised from general public funds, not specifically from green taxes, to invest in green projects on commercial terms and to mobilise other private-sector capital into the UK's green economy. It was such a success that the government sold it to the private sector in 2017 for a profit of £183 million.[19]

Some of the announcements by Michael Gove in his first few months as Environment Secretary help to illustrate the range of issues in which government can act: he announced plans to ban the sale of plastic microbeads (used in such products as cosmetics and shower gel), ivory and (from 2040) new petrol and diesel cars; he called for evidence concerning a deposit scheme for drinks bottles and cans, with a view to reducing the use of single-use plastics; he condemned farmers who drench their fields in chemicals and damage soil fertility; he announced import controls on plants, to protect our plants against imported diseases; he encouraged the installation of drinking fountains to reduce the number of single-use plastic containers that are thrown away; he announced plans to extend the UK's marine conservation zones; and he suggested that the UK aid budget could be used to help poorer countries to reduce plastic pollution.[20]

There is a great deal that government can do – but there is also a great deal that it can *not* do. It cannot reasonably control how we spend our money, how much stuff we buy only to throw it away; how much we travel; how much energy we use in the home. Only we, as individuals, can decide how we live our lives.

152

On the international stage

Each act of environmental destruction and damage takes place at a specific place and time – and the same is true of many acts of preservation, conservation, mitigation and restitution – but many of the causes and consequences of destruction are global. 'Think global, act local', as the saying goes. The high seas – outside coastal states' 200-mile exclusive economic zones – are a commons, where fishing and other exploitation are open to all. Winds in the atmosphere recognise no political boundaries. Even on land, pollution, habitat destruction and soil degradation in an overpopulated world and exhaustion of non-renewable resources have global implications. A great deal of the environmental damage in poorer countries is done to feed the consumerist appetites of rich countries. All this calls for concerted action by the nations of the world.

Many industries today are global, and there is a vital role for governments in collaborating to provide a worldwide system of regulations, incentives and disincentives, so that industry worldwide understands the regulatory and fiscal climate under which it operates. It doesn't help the planet if an industry finds that it is cheaper to operate in a country with lower pollution taxes or less strict pollution standards.

The governments of the world recognise the global nature of our environmental problems and real progress has been made in establishing international agreements and resolutions (eg the 1987 Montreal Protocol, the 2001 Stockholm Convention on Persistent Organic Pollutants (POPs) and the 2015 Paris Agreement on mitigation of greenhouse-gas emissions), and the United Nations is considering new international laws to govern the high seas, taking into account the three principal stresses in these waters: climate change, plastics and overfishing.[21] Business and industry need clear, internationally agreed regulatory frameworks for their operations.

One cause of damage to the natural world that I have scarcely mentioned is war: the environmental devastation and the colossal waste of resources. Protection of the planet may not be the main reason to prevent war, but it is certainly a powerful additional reason. Most countries feel the need to be protected by armed forces, but that alone is not enough. Both strong and weak nations can become involved in conflicts that are started by others. Neither the possession of nuclear and other weapons nor their renunciation can be guaranteed to prevent war. Peace depends on trust, understanding and goodwill between nations, and these are fostered by strong diplomatic ties between governments and by trade, professional and cultural exchanges (eg the British Council), young people studying and working abroad, the media (eg the BBC World Service) and a host of personal contacts and friendships between peoples.[22]

Throughout history, we humans have been aware of conflicts of interest between our own people and those of other tribes and nations. Now, more than ever before, we can see that our common interest in caring for our planet should outweigh our sense of difference.

Aid to developing countries
The value of aid to developing countries is much debated. In the second half of the twentieth century, trillions of dollars of aid was poured into African countries, and the way of life of most African peasants was very much the same at the end as it was at the beginning. That is not to say that the aid was wasted – very many people have had their lives enriched by aid projects – but real change comes when people buy goods and services from each other, supplying one another's needs. 'Countries have to lift themselves out of poverty', said Tidjane Thiam, an Ivorian businessman and former politician who at that time was CEO of Prudential, during an interview on BBC Radio's 'Desert island discs'.[23]

From an environmental perspective, however, well-targeted aid can make a huge difference, and this has been recognised by the UK's Department for International Development. First, protecting the environment costs money. Rich countries can help poor countries with the expense of enforcing national and international laws on such matters as logging, wildlife trade and environmental pollution.[24]

Second, as we have seen in chapter 3, foreign aid can help to make contraceptives available to the 220 million women in the world who want to avoid pregnancy but don't have access to modern contraceptives. It can also support countries in opening up educational and employment opportunities for girls and young women – the other prerequisite for falling birth rates. Reducing population growth is a priority in the interests of the poorer countries and of the wider world.

Third, aid can help developing countries to develop in a planet-friendly way, avoiding the destructive phase of development adopted by Western countries. Many people in poorer countries live closer to nature than we do in the West, so they may find it easier to adapt to the planet-friendly lifestyles of the future if they are not first drawn into the destructive, polluting, consumerist ways described earlier in this book. Again, aid spent in this way brings benefit to the wider world as well as the recipient countries.

Aid can support the development of clean power generation and clean transport rather than expanding the health-destroying practice of burning fossil fuels or timber in power stations and in the home. Almost all world populations with no electricity live in areas with good potential for solar power. Solar power in these countries can be generated locally, distributed locally and used locally, reducing or eliminating the need for an expensive national grid.[25]

Microcredit, for which the Grameen Bank and its founder Muhammad Yunus were awarded the 2006 Nobel Peace Prize, makes possible the growth of the kind of small businesses that enable communities to raise their living standards without massive damage to the environment.

Research and dissemination

Research

The development of new technologies to satisfy our material wants without damaging the environment is an essential part of our future. Clean technologies have been developed in recent years, but more research is needed. 'The entire global research effort on all forms of non-carbon energy, including nuclear power, [in the decade to 2010] was only about double Microsoft's spending on repeatedly upgrading Windows and Office', wrote Anatole Kaletsky in 2010. 'By contrast to the $10 billion spent globally on alternative energy and nuclear research, $250 billion was spent annually, according to the Stern report, on subsidising the extraction and burning of fossil fuels.'[26]

It is not only energy generation that needs more research. In transport, food production, manufacturing – indeed, all human activities that affect the resources of the planet – we need to carry out research to find ways of satisfying our needs in a sustainable way (see chapters 12 and 13). A great deal of this research will have profitable applications so should be attractive for the private sector, but government needs to create a financial climate in which such research can flourish. Often, too, the government needs to fund the first stages of research.

How do we know who to believe?

The public are bombarded with conflicting information and advice about what they should do to help the environment. It is little wonder that even people who want to do their best often end up confused: whom can they trust?

It is an old saying that 'You can't believe everything you read in the papers'. The public don't trust the Government: it has got it wrong so many times. They don't trust big business. Even some universities may be suspect, now that they depend so much on funding from Government and big business. It helps to build public confidence if information and advice is free of financial motivation. The Royal Institute of International Affairs, for example, can claim that it 'benefits from a wide range of philanthropic, research-related and membership support. This diversity of support is critical to the independence of the institute'.[27] Others who wish to be trusted would do well to build such a diversity of support.

The Royal Society, the Royal Academy of Engineering and the Royal Institute of International Affairs are widely respected and speak with authority. Their websites carry reports on current environmental issues, but they tend to be aimed at government and industry rather than the general public – and even their reports can be examples of advocacy rather than detachment.

What the environment-concerned public needs is authoritative advice on questions like: what are the pros and cons of buying cod from the North Sea, or a fleece made in China? What are the pros and cons of different types of car? Does it make any difference who I buy my electricity from?

Leadership and democracy

Caring for the Earth calls for a partnership between leaders and led: leaders can only lead where people are willing to follow. The model of leadership attributed to Augustus in the quotation that introduced this chapter has much to commend it. Effective leadership means understanding the people, with their shared values, their sense of fair play, their sense of what is right. Such understanding is at an altogether deeper level than the cleverness, competitiveness and cynicism conveyed by electioneering and elections, by opinion polls, journalism and focus groups. We need all these debates. They are an essential part of a free and democratic society, but if too much importance is attached to them they can create a divided society, with strongly polarised opinions, leaving many people with a sense of being alienated, misunderstood and left behind. True leadership should seek to restore trust between leaders and led, recognising the values and qualities that we have in common.

Notes

1. Review of Adrian Goldacre's *Augustus, Sunday Times*, 10 August 2014
2. Cicero, Marcus Tullius, 44 BC, *De Officiis*, Book III, Chapter VI
3. Taleb, Nassim Nicholas, 2018, *Skin in the game: Asymmetries in Daily Life*, Allen Lane
4. Schumacher, E F, 1973, *Small is Beautiful: A Study of Economics as if People Mattered*
5. Helm, Dieter, *Natural Capital: Valuing the Planet*, Yale, 2015
6. Churchill, Winston S, Speech in House of Commons, 11 November 1947
7. Burke, Edmund, 1790, *Reflections on the Revolution in France*
8. Scruton, Roger, *New Scientist* 7 January 2012
9. Micklethwait, John and Wooldridge, Adrian, 2014, *The Fourth Revolution: The Global Race to Reinvent the State*, Allen Lane, 264
10. Crossman, Richard, Introduction to Walter Bagehot's *The English Constitution*, 1963 edition, Fontana
11. Hattersley, Roy, *The Times*, 9 April 2010
12. Shonfield, Andrew, in *The Observer*, quoted by Taylor, John V, 1975, *Enough is Enough*, SCM Press
13. Stern, Nicholas, 2009, *A Blueprint for a Safer Planet: How to Manage Climate Change and Create a New Era of Progress and Prosperity*, Bodley Head
14. Scruton, Roger, 2012, *Green Philosophy: How to Think Seriously about the Planet*, Atlantic Books, opening words of Chapter 1
15. Thatcher, Margaret, 2002, *Statecraft: Strategies for a Changing World*, Harper Collins

157

16. Cavendish, Camilla, 'Green energy will boost growth, not stall it', *The Times*, 27 September 2012

17. Goldsmith, Zac, 2009, *The Constant Economy*, Atlantic Books, 3

18. www.behaviouralinsights.co.uk

19. Aldrick, Philip, *The Times*, 18 November 2017

20. *The Times*, 26 October 2017; 2 December 2017; 3 December 2017; 12 December 2017; more issues are covered in *A Green Future: Our 25 Year Plan to Improve the Environment*, issued in early 2018, www.gov.uk/government/publications/25-year-environment-plan

21. For a brief history of attempts at international agreement, see Dobson, Andrew, 2016, *Environmental Politics: A Very Short Introduction*, Oxford University Press, 78–99

22. Haslam, Henry, 1983, Disarmament – or peace? *Crossbow*, October 1983, 11–12

23. Thiam, Tidjane, 'Desert Island discs', BBC Radio 4, 4 November 2012

24. In February 2018 it was announced that British troops would be deployed to Malawi to boost efforts to put a stop to wildlife crime

25. Goodall, Chris, 2016, *The Switch: How Solar, Storage and new Tech Means Cheap Power for All*, Profile Books, 5,61

26. Kaletsky, Anatole, *The Times*, 16 June 2010

27. www.chathamhouse.org/funding

Chapter 12
Land and Food

Farming that is expressly designed to provide everyone everywhere with food of the highest quality, for ever, without wrecking the rest of the world.
The aim of enlightened agriculture, as expressed by the Campaign for Real Farming[1]

Approximately 71 per cent of the Earth's surface is covered by ocean, 3 per cent by permanent ice and around 8 per cent by desert. The remaining 18 per cent (approximately) has sufficient soil and water to enable terrestrial plants, animals and fungi to grow. This 18 per cent is very precious. Not only does it host most of the planet's life, but, when undisturbed by humans, it is a huge store of carbon, in peat, soil, trees and other plants. Nearly all the food for the world's population is derived from this 18 per cent. Apart from the small proportion that is used for development (homes, industry, transport etc), this hospitable zone is required for (1) production of food and other human demands (about 7 per cent of the Earth's surface is pasture, and 3 per cent is under crops) and (2) allowing space for nature to flourish (about 8 per cent of the Earth's surface is forest).[2]

Food production and nature conservation

When we consider how to use the 18 per cent of the Earth's surface where conditions are favourable for plant and animal life to flourish, there are choices to be made – and where there are choices, there is controversy. Our choices are dictated by two demands: the requirement to produce food and industrial raw materials for an ever-growing population; and the wish to allow nature to flourish, established ecosystems to survive and biodiversity to be maintained.

Nurturing nature

The priority should be to stop destroying natural habitats. Once an ancient ecosystem has been destroyed, it takes hundreds – even thousands – of years to re-establish itself.

159

In addition to natural ecosystems that have escaped human interference, there are other habitats that are man-made and have developed their own ecology over the years. Most, if not all, of Britain's ecosystems are products of human activity, habitats that have had hundreds or thousands of years to develop their own biodiversity. Examples include wetlands, wild-flower meadows, field-and-hedgerow patterns, blanket bog, heather moorland (periodically burnt to stop the plants growing tall) and grazed upland grassland. This last is attacked by George Monbiot,[3] who would have it returned to natural forest, with reintroduction of lynx and other species. Proposals to reintroduce lynx into the Kielder forest in northern England, however, have been opposed by sheep farmers. Attempts are being made in the Scottish Highlands to return some areas of moorland to native woodland.

Rich countries are expanding their forests – as, too, are China and India. Britain has twice the area of woodland it had a century ago.[4] Planting trees removes carbon from the atmosphere. Burning trees and replanting continues this process, if carbon-capture-and-storage technology (see pages 178–179) is available. Carbon is also removed from the atmosphere by increasing the organic content of soils and allowing peat deposits to grow. Trees and other plants, including water plants, have a valuable role in extracting pollutants from air and water.

Modern agriculture

Centuries of selective breeding (culminating in the so-called 'Green Revolution' of the twentieth century, for which Norman Borlaug was awarded the 1970 Nobel Peace Prize) have developed high-yielding strains of agricultural crops, particularly of grains such as wheat, rice and maize. Aided by the use of irrigation (Green-Revolution crops are thirsty), artificial fertilisers and pesticides, these new strains have enabled the output per acre to increase enormously, saving millions of people worldwide from starvation. In Britain, wheat now averages 8 tonnes per hectare, about four times as much as 100 years ago.[5]

Traditional methods of selective breeding have recently been augmented by genetic modification (GM). The use of GM crops increased steadily since they were first grown in about 1996, and by 2010 they covered 10 per cent of the world's arable land. In the USA in 2014, more than 90 per cent of the planted area of soya, cotton and maize were GM varieties.[6] Many people are concerned about the possible harm that could be caused by GM, and indeed it is possible to imagine new strains that could do a great deal of harm. Scientists developing GM, however, recognise the need for testing and regulation to avoid the release of a strain that could cause damage. We should not be complacent – GM crops have not been around for very long – but on present evidence it looks as if the standards of testing and regulation have been more rigorous and successful than those applied in the chemicals industry in the past (see chapter 1). The debate continues about the environmental and economic merits and drawbacks of new strains, those produced by traditional plant-breeding techniques and those involving GM.

In spite of increasing crop yields, Britain's dependence on imported food increased from 22 per cent in 1984 to 40 per cent in 2013.[7] Kenneth Mellanby, in his 1975 book *Can Britain Feed Itself?*, gave the answer: yes, if we eat less meat. More recently, Simon Fairly and Colin Tudge have looked at various agricultural scenarios, and concluded that several of them would enable Britain to be self-reliant in food.[8]

Environmental impact of agriculture

All agriculture has an impact on the environment. The scale of the impact depends on the agricultural methods used.

First, food production uses a great deal of land, which therefore cannot be used for other purposes. Specifically, land devoted to industrial-scale farming is not hospitable to nature. It is said that there is often more wildlife and biodiversity in suburban gardens than in neighbouring farmland.

It is this banishment of nature from large areas of the Earth's surface that leads Edward O Wilson to plead for half the Earth to be set aside from human activity and devoted to natural ecosystems.[9]

Second, food production requires water. This is no problem in countries with high rainfall, but large areas of the USA and China, for example, have low rainfall and are far from the sea. Livestock husbandry requires much more water than raising crops.

161

Third, upland soils may be drained to make them suitable for agriculture. The aim is to get water off the land as quickly as possible. At times of heavy rainfall, this leads to flooding of farmland and built-up areas downstream.

Fourth, repeated ploughing leaves soil susceptible to erosion, carried away in rivers to the sea. Cultivation of maize, particularly on sloping ground, also makes soil susceptible to erosion.

Fifth, food production has a significant influence on the distribution of carbon. Deforestation – the clearing of forested land for agricultural use – accounts for about 20 per cent of global greenhouse-gas emissions caused by human activity.[10] Draining and ploughing of soil causes further release of carbon into the atmosphere, leaving the soil impoverished in organic matter. Continued soil degradation like this can lead to productive agricultural land becoming unproductive.[11] The livestock trade (including feed production, livestock rearing, slaughter, processing, transport and retail) produces nearly 15 per cent of human-driven greenhouse-gas emissions – as much as the world's vehicles;[12] two thirds of this can be attributed to cattle.[13]

Sixth, food production leaves the land impoverished in nutrients. In nature, the chemical elements of which plants and animals are composed are released back into the soil when the organism dies. In farmland, the plants and animals are taken away for food or for other purposes, leaving the soil depleted.

Seventh, chemical fertilisers (nitrogen, phosphorus, potassium) and organic fertilisers (manure, slurry) are added to the soil to make good the losses. Both kinds of fertiliser have hazardous properties.[14] The surplus escapes from the fields, resulting in polluted groundwater, nutrient-enriched soils and surface waters (promoting the growth of stronger plants at the expense of weaker species), and eutrophication of rivers, lakes and seas, when the excess of nutrients promotes excessive growth of vegetation which, on decay, leaves the water deprived of oxygen and kills fish and other animal life.

Eighth, pesticides are spread over farmland. They kill wildlife in the fields where they are applied, and the surplus is washed away, polluting watercourses and, eventually, the sea. Worldwide, there have been thousands of serious poisonings

162

and fatalities caused by pesticides.[15] British water companies spend over £100 million a year taking agricultural and other chemicals out of the water supply.[16]

Farmers are well aware of these impacts, of course, and find ways of reducing their effects, preserving soil health and biodiversity. Farmland can be managed in a way that provides havens for wildlife in hedges and small areas of woodland and in uncultivated margins around arable fields. Traditional pasture and meadow can sustain a rich flora and fauna.[17] Coppicing of British woodlands is sustainable. Drones and robots can help to ensure that chemicals are applied only where they are needed.

The upper part of river catchments can be managed to retain rainwater, by planting trees, retaining hedgerows, maintaining soil porosity, avoiding soil compaction (associated with high livestock density, heavy machinery or late-harvested crops such as maize) and slowing down field drainage and river flow (beaver populations, recently reintroduced in some parts of Britain, can help in this). Such measures can significantly reduce the risk of flooding downstream in small river catchments and with moderate rainfall; they have less impact in large catchments or in mitigating severe rainfall events.[18]

Integrated agriculture and biodiversity

The call to go further in reducing the impact of agriculture on nature is led by such organisations as the Campaign for Real Farming, the Countryside Restoration Trust, Compassion in World Farming, Friends of the Earth, the Permaculture Association, the Soil Association, the Sustainable Soil Alliance, the Sustainable Food Trust and the two-year Food, Farming and the Countryside Commission recently set up by the Royal Society for the Encouragement of Arts, Manufactures and Commerce.[19] These movements seek to minimise the degradation caused by conventional agriculture by combining food production with the maintenance of soil health.[20] Their methods encourage nature, including the use of natural pest-control, they reduce to a minimum the input of chemical fertilisers and pesticides, and they use the waste from one crop and animal as input into another (animal waste to feed the soil, plant waste to feed livestock). They commend small, mixed farms employing more people than present-day farming. Colin

163

Tudge writes: 'A hectare of cows on fertile land produces less food energy and protein than a well-grown hectare of wheat – but properly organised mixed farms with animals and crops are the most productive of all'.[21] In contrast to the mechanisation of industrial-scale farming, small, mixed farms, sensitive to the health of soil, plants and animals, are more labour intensive (Tudge recommends that 10 per cent of Britain's work force should be in farming), offering employment to people of a wide range of ability – including those who lack the intellectual bent for the high-tech economy of the future.

UK sales of organic goods exceeded £2 billion in 2016, 7.1 per cent higher than in 2015.[22] Recent research has shown that organic agriculture is good for biodiversity, soil and water quality, farm-worker health and nutritional value (though not all studies agree on this last). Some studies find that the yield per unit area is less than conventional agriculture, but the yield could be increased if crop varieties were bred specifically for organic farming; at present, organic farmers mostly use varieties bred for conventional farming.[23]

Diet, environment and health
Of the world's land that is used for food production, about three quarters is devoted to livestock for meat and dairy products; the rest for grain, fruit and vegetables. Annual world production of cereals is about 2.5 billion tonnes, of which some 45 per cent is for human consumption, 35 per cent is fed to cattle, pigs and chickens and 20 per cent is used for biofuels and industrial materials. Rice and wheat are mostly consumed by people, but most maize is fed to livestock. In the high-income countries of North America and Western Europe, only 4 per cent of the maize crop goes for human consumption.[24]

Growing crops to feed to animals which are then fed to people uses more land, water and fossil fuels than feeding the grain directly to humans.[25] It is a particularly inefficient use of land, and should be strongly discouraged. It may be noted, though, that rearing poultry and pigs uses less land, water and energy than cattle, and with less greenhouse-gas emissions. More than half the world's agricultural land is suitable for grazing but not for growing crops:[26] flood plains and upland grassland in Britain, for example, and semi-arid land in countries with low rainfall (where the risk of over-grazing must be recognised). Livestock should obtain most of their food by grazing, supplemented by waste from arable farming (and microalgae – see below).

How does this fit in with modern understanding of a healthy diet? People in Britain are increasingly concerned about diet and health. More than 40 per cent of us actively avoid certain ingredients in what we eat and drink.[27] The Western diet is now strongly based on animal products (meat and dairy) and refined carbohydrates (wheat and sugar), with chemical additives used at all stages of food production from agricultural pesticides and fertilisers to chemical dyes, flavouring agents and preservatives. A diet based on manufactured foods is likely to contain too much salt (salt is an essential nutrient, but too much is harmful), sugar and synthetic chemicals. The healthiest diets, such as the traditional diets of China and the Mediterranean countries of southern Europe, get most of their protein from plant sources. Most humans are well-adapted to eating grain (rice, wheat, maize, etc), but it is recommended that a healthy, balanced diet should include a wide variety of fruit and vegetables, together with herbs and spices. It should also include plenty of fish, but not so much meat and dairy; should cut down on foods containing white flour and sugar; and should avoid man-made chemicals.[28]

According to a 2015 report from the Royal Institute for International Affairs (Chatham House), the average person in an industrialised country eats about twice as much meat as is healthy. This is thought to contribute to the rise of obesity, cancer and type-2 diabetes,[29] so a significant reduction in grain-fed livestock would be good for health as well as good for the environment.

Farmed animals are not the only source of meat. They can be supplemented by wild animals. Wild deer in Britain, like kangaroos in Australia, provide leaner and healthier meat than farmed animals. British woodlands are overpopulated with deer, now that there are no natural predators, and so are the hills and moorlands of the Scottish Highlands in spite of regular culling. Reducing their numbers facilitates the growth of the natural flora: a dramatic deer cull in the Glenfeshie estate in the Scottish Highlands has enabled the native pine forest to double in ten years. Other sources of animal protein are described below (pages 168–170). The kangaroo population in Australia has doubled in the seven years to 2016, but so far only a small proportion of Australians eat them.[30]

Early humans, like other mammals, became unable to digest lactose shortly after weaning: milk, after all, is for infants, not adults. However, in the last 10,000 years several human cultures, independently, started to domesticate livestock and to drink their milk. This led to the evolutionary selection of mutations able to digest lactose – different mutations in different cultures.[31] There is abundant scientific research showing how the consumption of dairy products increases the risk of cancers, particularly breast cancer and prostate cancer, as well as other conditions, and this explains the very low incidence of these diseases in cultures that do not consume dairy products, like the traditional Chinese diet. The results of this research have been introduced to a wider public in a series of books by Jane Plant and her colleagues.[32] Adult humans, like other adult mammals, including herbivorous species like cattle and hippopotamuses, can obtain all their requirements of calcium and other nutrients from a healthy plant-rich diet.[33] There are therefore strong health reasons, as well as environmental reasons, for reducing (or even eliminating) dairy products from the diet. The dairy industry does not merit the level of subsidy that it has been receiving: when Tidjane Thiam was in government in the Ivory Coast in the 1990s, he liked to say that there were 21 million dairy cows in the OECD countries and the subsidy to the dairy industry was enough to fly each cow around the world in first class every year.[34]

Not only would a reduction in our dependence on farmed animals give us a healthier diet and be better for the environment, it would also be in tune with the growing concern about the way we treat other animals for our own purposes: support for the causes of animal welfare, animal rights, and vegetarian and vegan diets has been increasing. And our food would cost less, too: a win-win-win-win situation.

Looking further to the future, we may be able to obtain meat from the laboratory (page 169). This would have a lower environmental impact, as well as satisfying our growing distaste for killing animals for our own purposes: the psychologist and science writer Steven Pinker predicts that in two or three

166

generations' time we shall look back on meat-eating with horror.[35]

Use of land for non-food crops

Industrial crops include those used for building materials (eg hemp, wheat, bamboo, reed), fibre (eg cotton, flax, hemp, papyrus) and biofuels.

Growing crops to burn as fuel is recommended by some because it emits less CO_2 than fossil fuels. *Miscanthus* (sometimes known as elephant grass), which is grown in parts of England, grows by absorbing carbon from the atmosphere, which is then released when the dried crop is burnt. On an annual cycle, it is carbon neutral – apart from the energy needed to grow, harvest and transport the crop. Growing trees for the same purpose is less carbon-efficient: it takes many years for new trees to grow and absorb the CO_2 released from the burning of the last crop. The trouble with a biofuel like *Miscanthus* is that it uses good agricultural land, which would be better used for growing food and/or letting nature flourish.

Most of Britain's maize crop is grown for cattle feed, but about a quarter of it goes for anaerobic digestion, yielding biogas.

The seas

The sea, like the land, provides us with food and other materials. Like the land, it also contains fragile ecosystems which we need to preserve. Good management of the seas is vital if both these interests are to be served. Although the oceans are vast, covering more than 70 per cent of the Earth's surface, human activities have had, and continue to have, a very significant impact:[36]

- Overfishing in the high seas is a constant threat to fish stocks, the classic example being the Grand Banks cod fishery off the coast of Newfoundland. Fishing there continued at sustainable levels for 500 years, until 1950. Greatly increased catches in the 1950s and 1960s, however, led to declining stocks in the 1970s and eventual collapse. By 2015 there were signs of recovery, but the future remains uncertain.

167

- Shallower seas on continental shelves are threatened by fishing techniques that damage the sea-bed ecosystems on which the fish depend.
- High levels of pollutants from the land (including agricultural fertilisers, sewage effluent and livestock waste), rich in nitrogen and phosphorus, are washed into the sea. This nutrient-rich water enables algae to flourish, leading to eutrophication.

These impacts can be reduced or eliminated by establishing partnerships between research, fishing and conservation interests, and setting up marine protected areas.[37] International agreement is vital, for the management of seas outside territorial waters.

Fish, crustaceans and molluscs are good sources of animal protein in the diet. Oily fish (sardines, herring, anchovies, salmon, trout, tuna and mackerel) are especially recommended.

Alternative sources of food

There are several ways of producing food which have a low impact on the environment because they use less land, less energy and less water, and they emit less greenhouse gases. With further development, these could become important sources of food.[38]

Fish farming

In 1970, only about 5 per cent of food fish came from farms; today the figure is nearer 50 per cent. Of the world's top 15 farmed fish, all except one (Atlantic salmon) are freshwater species. In addition to fish, some water-living invertebrates are also farmed, such as prawns, lobsters and mussels. Mussel farming, unlike other agricultural processes, is better than carbon neutral, since the organisms remove carbon from the water to make their shells.

Environmental impacts of fish farming include diseases and parasites, which can flourish in the confined space of a fish farm and can then spread to wild fish. Antibiotics to control disease and other drugs to promote growth can also escape into the environment.[39] As long as care is taken to reduce or eliminate these impacts, fish farming can be an efficient form of food production.[40]

Meat from the laboratory

According to a recent report by the Waste and Resources Action Programme (WRAP), laboratory-grown meat has the potential to use 45 per cent less energy and 99 per cent less land than the average for farmed beef, and emit 96 per cent fewer greenhouse gases.[41]

Macroalgae (seaweed)

Seaweeds are used for food (they are rich in valuable nutrients, including protein levels up to 47 per cent), food supplements (including amino acids), organic fertilisers, pharmaceuticals, biofuels, and more. As a saltwater crop, they use no fresh water. China and Indonesia account for more than 25 per cent of world production. The UK, especially Scotland, has sustainable harvesting of wild seaweed, and there is the potential for large-scale cultivation.[42]

Hydroponics and vertical farming

Hydroponics is the process of growing plants without soil, using water with added nutrients. It is used for growing high-value crops such as tomatoes. It can be used to produce crops in multi-storey structures, with a controlled water supply, making it economical in land and water. It can be combined with fish farming (aquaponics),[43] in a system that enables the growth of crops and fish together in a recirculating system; nutrients derived from fish waste are fed to the plants. The ability to grow produce with a short shelf life, such as strawberries, spinach and lettuce, around the year and close to market (typically on brownfield urban sites – including in a complex of tunnels under London), makes it an attractive, sustainable proposition. Asia contains more than half of the world's population but only a fifth of its agricultural land, so vertical farming has a particular attraction there.

Insects

It is estimated that insects, including nearly 2000 species, form part of the traditional diets of at least 2 billion people worldwide. They are highly nutritious, containing fat, protein, vitamins, fibre and minerals. Production of insects has a very low land-use requirement – less than a tenth of that for cattle, for the same weight of protein. Wild or farmed insects are suitable for small-scale production. There is potential for harvesting insects, wild or farmed, as a source of food for human consumption and feed for livestock in developed and developing countries.[44] In the Netherlands, one hectare of land can yield 150 tons of insect protein for animal feed.[45]

Microalgae
Microalgae are regarded mainly as a substitute for maize in cattle feed, but they also have great potential as food for humans and fish and as fuel and fertiliser.[46]

Food waste

It is estimated that a third of the food produced for human consumption worldwide is lost or wasted. This loss and waste occurs at all stages of production, processing, transport, retail and consumption. Some can be put to alternative use as animal feed or biofuel or returned to the soil.

In the UK, it is estimated that 10 million tonnes of food and drink goes to waste each year (excluding any loss on the farm): 17 per cent of this is lost in manufacturing, 2 per cent in retail, and 9 per cent in the hospitality and food service industries; the remaining 71 per cent is household food waste. It is further estimated that 60 per cent of this waste could be avoided.[47] Britain's supermarkets and restaurants aim to increase the amount of surplus food they redistribute to charities for people in need – and there are people ready and willing to put such food to good use. Retailers could also make it easier for customers to buy perishable foods in small quantities; discounts for buying larger quantities of such foods encourage waste by giving customers an incentive to buy more than they can consume before the use-before date.

In 2015, food with a retail value of around £13 billion was thrown away by UK households rather than being eaten – an average of nearly £500 per household. This avoidable waste was associated with greenhouse-gas emissions equivalent to a quarter of the emissions generated by cars on UK roads.[48]

Summary

The adverse impact of food production on the environment can thus be reduced, in Britain, by (1) cutting down the amount of meat (especially beef) and dairy in the diet and, as far as possible, only keeping livestock that can be grazed or fed on farm waste, (2) converting more land from conventional farming to organic farming, (3) improving the techniques of conventional farming by reducing the quantity of agrochemicals used and introducing organic practices to maintain soil health,[49] (4) expanding the use of insects, algae etc in the diet, and (5) taking steps to cut food waste.

These measures will enable us to produce more food on less land, permitting more land to be returned to nature.

Notes

1. www.campaignforrealfarming.org/about
2. Some of these figures are approximate. In semi-arid scrubland, for example, the classification into desert, scrubby forest and rough grazing may be somewhat arbitrary
3. Monbiot, George, 2013, *Feral: Rewilding the Land, Sea and Human Life*, Allen Lane
4. Ridley, Matt, *The Times*, 31 October 2016
5. Tudge, Colin, 2016, *Six Steps Back to the Land*, Green Books, 103
6. Wikipedia
7. *The Times*, 24 February 2015
8. www.thelandmagazine.org.uk/articles/can-britain-feed-itself; Tudge, 2016
9. Wilson, Edward O, 2016, *Half-Earth: Our Planet's Fight for Life*, Liveright
10. Juniper, Tony, 2016, *What's really happening to our planet?*, Dorling Kindersley, 140
11. The important issue of soil health was debated in the UK parliament on 17 November 2016, https://hansard.parliament.uk/Commons/2016-11-17/debates/E8DD244E-4FDE-4F29-B06C-81BAD4EBE843/SoilHealth
12. Wellesley, Laura, Happer, Catherine and Froggatt, Antony, 2015, *Changing Climate, Changing Diets: Pathways to Lower Meat Consumption*, Chatham House, The Royal Institute of International Affairs
13. *The Times*, 20 October 2016
14. McKinlay, Rebecca, Dassyne, Jason, Djamgoz, Mustafa B A, Plant, Jane A and Voulvoulis, Nikolaus, 2012, Agricultural pesticides and chemical fertilisers, 181–206 in Plant, Jane A, Voulvoulis, Nikolaus and Ragnasdottir, K Vala, 2012, *Pollutants, Human Health and the Environment*, Wiley-Blackwell
15. McKinlay and others, 2012
16. HRH The Prince of Wales, interviewed by Leaf Arbuthnot, *Sunday Times*, 30 April 2017
17. Eg Harvey, Graham, 2008, *The Carbon Fields*, GrassRoots
18. Dadson, Simon J and others, A restatement of the natural science evidence concerning catchment-based 'natural' flood management in the UK, *Proceedings of the Royal Society A*, 15 March 2017

19. www.campaignforrealfarming.org; www.countrysiderestorationtrust.com; www.ciwf.org.uk; www.foe.co.uk; www.permaculture.org.uk; www.soilassociation.org; sustainablesoils.org; https:// sustainablefoodtrust.org; https://www.thersa.org. Books include Tudge, 2016; Harvey, 2008; Juniper, Tony, 2015, *What Nature Does for Britain*, Profile. *Healthy Harvests: The Benefits of Sustainable Agriculture in Africa and Asia* (Christian Aid, 2011) applies the principles of sustainable agriculture to poorer countries

20. Eg Juniper, 2015, 24–26

21. Tudge, 2016

22. Arbuthnot, Leaf, *Sunday Times*, 30 April 2017

23. Seufert, Verena and Ramankutty, Navin, 2017, Many shades of gray – The context-dependent performance of organic agriculture, *Science Advances*, 10 March 2017

24. Juniper, 2016, 64–65; McCann, James C, 2006, *Maize and Grace: Africa's encounter with a New World crop, 1500–2000*, Harvard University Press

25. Juniper, 2016, 65

26. Tudge, 2016

27. *The Times*, 22 December 2016

28. Eg Plant, Jane and Tidey, Gill, 2010, *Eating for Better Health*, Virgin Books

29. Wellesley and others, 2015

30. The kangaroo population was seriously depleted in 2017 as a result of a previously unknown illness; *The Times*, 29 December 2017

31. Holden, Clare and Mace, Ruth, 2009, Phylogenetic Analysis of the Evolution of Lactose Digestion in Adults, *Human Biology*, 81(5–6), 597–619; quoted in Wilson, David Sloan, 2015, *Does Altruism Exist? Culture, Genes and the Welfare of Others*, Yale UP and the Templeton Press

32. Plant, Jane, 2007, *Your Life in Your Hands*, Virgin Books (first edition 2000); Plant, Jane, and Tidey, Gill, 2004, *The Plant Programme*, Virgin Books (first edition 2001); Plant, Jane, 2007, *Prostate Cancer*, Virgin Books (first edition 2004); Plant, Jane and Stephenson, Janet, 2008, *Beating Stress, Anxiety and Depression*, Piatkus; Plant, Jane and Tidey, Gill, 2010, *Eating for Better Health*, Virgin Books (first edition 2005); Djamgoz, Mustafa and Plant, Jane, 2014, *Beat Cancer*, Vermilion

33. Plant, Jane and Tidey, Gill, *Osteoporosis*, Virgin Books, 2004; Plant, Jane and Tidey, Gill, 2010, *Eating for Better Health*, Virgin Books

34. *The Times, Supplement on The Times CEO Summit*, 22 June 2011

35. Quoted by Matt Ridley, *The Times*, 24 April 2017

36. Juniper, 2016

37. Juniper, 2015, 73

38. Eg *Food Futures: from business as usual to business unusual*, WRAP, 2015, www.wrap.org.uk/sites/files/wrap/Food_Futures_%20report_0.pdf

39. Juniper, 2015, 64; Juniper, 2016

40. http://grist.org/food/everything-you-always-wanted-to-know-about-fish-farming-but-were-afraid-to-ask

41. *Food Futures*, WRAP, 2015; see also Andy Coghlan, Meat without slaughter, *New Scientist*, 3 September 2011, 8–9; Tom Whipple, *The Times*, 16 September 2017

42. *Food Futures*, WRAP, 2015; *The Times*, 27 September 2016

43. *Food Futures*, WRAP, 2015;

44. Huis, Arnold van and others, 2013, *Edible insects: future prospects for food and feed security*, FAO Forestry Paper 171, www.fao.org/docrep/018/i3253e/i3253e.pdf; *Food Futures*, WRAP, 2015; *The Times*, 5 November 2015

45. This Tiny Country Feeds the World, *National Geographic*, September 2017; www.nationalgeographic.com/magazine/2017/09/holland-agriculture-sustainable-farming

46. Tremain, Ian, 2010, *Agricultural Commodities in a Changing World*, Nuffield Farming Scholarships Trust – An Oldacre Foundation Award; *Food Futures*, WRAP, 2015

47. *Food Waste in England*, a report by the Environment, Food and Rural Affairs Committee, 30 April 2017

48. *Household Food Waste in the UK*, 2015, WRAP

49. Seufert and Ramankutty, 2017

Chapter 13
Technologies to meet Human Needs without Damaging the Environment

Our way of life has been influenced by the way technology has developed. In future, it seems to me, we ought to try to reverse this and so develop our technology that it meets the needs of the sort of life we wish to lead.

HRH Prince Philip, Duke of Edinburgh[1]

The circular economy aims to redefine products and services to design waste out, while minimising negative impacts.

Ellen MacArthur Foundation[2]

Cheap solar changes everything.

Chris Goodall[3]

The products that win competition today, and will continue to do so indefinitely, are those that cost less to manufacture and advertise, need less frequent repair and replacement, and give the highest performance with the minimum of energy.

Edward O Wilson[4]

If we are to change the way we relate to nature, we need a whole new set of technologies to replace the destructive, polluting industries to which we became accustomed in the twentieth century. We need to explore technologies that will enable us to live happy, healthy lives without taking a toll on the environment: the triple bottom line. Fortunately, research and development for sustainable technologies are progressing at an ever-increasing pace – so much so that this chapter, more than any other in the book, is likely to be out of date by the time it reaches the reader.

The challenges for technological innovation are:
1. the reduction of energy consumption through increased energy efficiency etc – for so long as we are burning fossil fuels,
2. the preservation of the Earth's stock of metals and other mineral resources so that they can be reused (the circular economy),

174

3. the reduction, nearly to zero, of the world's dependence on the combustion of fossil fuels (for electricity generation, transport, industry, heating etc), and the continued development of renewable sources of energy to replace them,
4. the maintenance of supplies of fresh water for domestic, agricultural and industrial purposes,
5. the use of the Earth's resources of land and sea to produce food and other human requirements while enabling nature and natural ecosystems to flourish,
6. the development of practices that reduce the environmental impact of industry and construction, and
7. the elimination of pollution and clearing up existing pollution.

In the twentieth century we came to expect that whenever there was something to be done we should look to government; it was governments that had the money. Only a few years ago, it seemed that industry was slow to respond to the environmental challenges of the age, and that change could only come as a consequence of strong government action. Increasingly now, there are signs that it is industry that is leading the way; it is the private sector that has the money as well as the will to address environmental problems.

Technological innovations may start with government-funded research, then move on to government-subsidised development and application, before becoming sufficiently well established for the private sector to take them forward profitably by making products that are attractive to customers – and making a taxable profit into the bargain. The change to green technologies depends on government to set the regulatory and fiscal framework and incentives, on industry to provide products that satisfy customer demand and on a public that wants to move towards more sustainable living. Even the human impulse to buy the latest product, which did so much to fuel the consumer society, is now leading consumers to buy the latest green product.

As an example of the leading role played by the private sector, when US President Donald Trump announced his intention that his country should withdraw from the 2015 Paris Agreement on mitigation of greenhouse-gas emissions, some

900 American firms wrote an open letter to the UN pledging to help reduce the country's carbon emissions by 26 per cent by 2025.[5] In July 2017, Jerry Brown, Governor of California, and Michael Bloomberg, former mayor of New York City, announced 'America's Pledge', an initiative aimed at keeping greenhouse-gas emissions from US cities, states, and businesses consistent with the goals outlined in the Paris climate agreement.[6] Prior to that, a consortium led by Bill Gates had established a $1 billion fund to develop 'cheap and reliable clean energy to the world',[7] and Ben van Beurden, Shell chief executive, described the shift towards greener energy as 'unstoppable'.[8] In the UK, green technologies that a few years ago required government subsidy are now commercially viable without subsidy.

Information technology

Information technology and computing will enable transport, manufacturing and even domestic activities to be more energy efficient, and therefore more environment friendly. Provided that the component parts of the hardware are recovered for reuse or recycling, the cost to the environment of these new technologies is not great, and they can help us to move to more sustainable lifestyles. They already enable many human activities to be carried out in a more energy-efficient way than in the past (eg communication, accessing and processing of information, and entertainment), and this trend will continue, requiring less power and doing less harm to the environment. Smart systems will control processes, from domestic appliances and transport to manufacturing, construction and agriculture, conserving scarce resources such as energy and water.

Energy

We have only to look around us to see that vast amounts of energy are going to waste, from the sun, wind, tides, waves and rivers, and from the heat generated in the Earth. As much energy arrives at the Earth from the Sun in 90 minutes as we use in a whole year.[9] There is potential for obtaining all the energy we need from sustainable sources. A few years ago, most of the existing methods for exploiting renewable sources of energy had severe economic or environmental drawbacks, but advances are being made all the time.

In June 2017, Bloomberg New Energy Finance forecast that solar energy costs would drop by a further 66 per cent by 2040, onshore wind by 47 per cent and offshore wind by 71 per cent, and that renewables would undercut most existing fossil-fuel power stations by 2030. Global carbon-dioxide emissions were predicted to peak in 2026 and to be 4 per cent lower in 2040 than they were in 2016. BNEF's global forecast is for a massive rise in electricity generated by solar and wind (from 1,500 terrawatt hours in 2017 to 13,000 in 2040), though still remaining less than fossil fuel (down 15,800 to 15,200); this is accompanied by small increases in other renewables (5,000 to 6,400) and nuclear (2,400 to 3,600, after a peak at 3,800).[10] ExxonMobil, however, predicts that fossil fuels will continue to dominate, and that the contribution from renewables plus nuclear in 2040 will be no more than 25 per cent.[11] The potential for renewables is immense, but how far and how fast this potential will be realised depends on the relative costs, on how far we can mitigate their visual and environmental impact, and on how far we can overcome the problems associated with intermittency of most renewables. The switch to renewables would be speeded up if governments were to impose a carbon tax on fossil-fuel power stations. However, the time may come when renewables provide cheaper energy than fossil fuels but cannot yet provide enough capacity; it might then be necessary to turn the subsidies around and subsidise fossil fuels or nuclear to fill the gap.

So long as we remain dependent on fossil fuels and biofuels for energy, environmental considerations make us look for ways of reducing our consumption of energy. If we look to the long term, however – 100 years or less, perhaps – when nearly all our energy requirements are derived from renewable sources, supplemented, perhaps, by nuclear fusion or fission, there will then be no environmental reason to save energy.

Fossil fuels

The burning of fossil fuels to meet our energy needs (principally coal and natural gas) releases large quantities of CO_2 into the atmosphere and is therefore a principal driver of climate change. Coal combustion is the most damaging environmentally, as it emits more CO_2 than is emitted by natural gas and it also emits other atmospheric pollutants such as sulphur dioxide, nitrogen oxides and particulates.

Gas-fired power stations might have a use in the future to supplement renewables, on standby to provide power in times of peak demand when renewables cannot meet the demand.

There has recently been much debate in Britain about fracking (hydraulic fracturing of rock to release oil or gas), a technique that has led to a reduction in the use of coal in the USA and lower energy prices. The case for fracking in Britain is that gas emits less CO_2 than coal and would provide us with power while renewables are being developed. The domestic production of gas would reduce our exposure to interruptions in the supply of imported gas and to increases in international prices. Fracking is opposed by those who would like to see the end of all burning of fossil fuels. It is also essential that regulations are in place to meet environmental concerns (which are more significant than in America because of the higher population density in the target areas), principally the contamination of groundwater.[12]

A few years ago it used to be said that in China two new coal-fired power stations were coming into operation every week. Recent reports, however, tell of a massive slow-down. In 2016 there was a dramatic drop in the global amount of coal power capacity under development, mainly due to changes in China and India.[13] Since 2014, China has been burning less and less coal; in 2016 it installed more wind-power capacity than any other country. The Chinese-led Asian Infrastructure Investment Bank follows a 'Lean, Clean and Green' policy and supports the Paris Agreement.[14] It has promised to avoid financing coal mines and power stations.[15] In India, it has been reported that 40 per cent of the coal-fired plant capacity is lying idle and there are ambitious plans to increase the country's capacity of renewable energy.[16]

Carbon capture

Carbon capture and storage (CCS) is the process of capturing the CO_2 produced in a fossil-fuel or biofuel power station or a cement-manufacturing plant and burying it underground where it will not enter the atmosphere. Recent studies have shown that natural accumulations of CO_2 have remained trapped underground for 100,000 years, demonstrating that long-term underground storage is feasible,[17] but other problems remain to be resolved. Ideally, this could make such power stations carbon neutral – and if applied to biofuel power stations it could yield a net reduction of carbon in the atmosphere. Development has been going on for some years and a few plants are operational, but it is still not widely applied. It may be that, with fossil-fuel struggling to compete financially with renewables, there will be little incentive for the additional expense of installing CCS plant.

An alternative is carbon capture and utilisation. Instead of treating CO_2 as a waste product for underground disposal, it can be treated as a raw material for industry. One example is in the production of algal fuels (see below). Another is a plant in India which captures CO_2 and uses it to produce baking soda.[18]

Renewables

As indicated above, the future lies with renewable sources of energy. Only a few years ago, the outlook for such renewable energy did not look very promising. Recently, however, there has been a dramatic reduction in the cost of renewable technologies, particularly solar. In June 2017, the province of Qinghai in China ran for seven days on renewable energy alone; in the first half of 2017, solar and hydro generated 35 per cent of Germany's power.[19] These technologies continue to improve – and this is increasingly recognised by the big energy companies.

The manufacture of solar panels does, of course, require energy, but the time needed for a panel to produce as much energy as was involved in its creation has dropped from 20 years to two years or less.[20]

Chris Goodall, in *The Switch*,[21] sees solar power as the market leader, providing cheap electricity even in the less sunny climate of northern Europe. Its drawback, in a small, high-latitude, densely populated country like Britain, is the amount of space required: Goodall estimates that if solar were to supply all of the UK's energy needs, panels would have to cover 16 per cent of the land area (making a strong case for supplementing solar with other renewables). Even with the present capacity of 12 gigawatts, solar can contribute 25 per cent of UK power generation in favourable conditions.[22] In

179

sunnier areas, however, solar panels are more productive: it is estimated that less than 0.1 per cent of the world's land area would be sufficient to meet all the world's energy needs.[23]

It is not best use of high-quality agricultural land to cover it with solar panels. However, it is possible to space the panels so as to allow sunlight and rain to reach the ground, and to place them far enough above the ground to enable the land also to be used for agricultural purposes – for grazing by sheep or poultry, for example. There is no such drawback when panels are situated on domestic and industrial roofs – or when they are sited in deserts.

Wind turbines are cheaper than solar in places like the west coast of Scotland, but this may not be so in the future, if the cost of solar goes down faster than that of wind.[24] Onshore wind farms are cheaper to install than offshore, but they meet with objections that they are unsightly and noisy and are a danger to birds.

Large wind turbines rising above hilltops may be thought particularly unsightly. As any hillwalker knows, you don't have to get high above a hilltop or ridge to feel the force of the wind: the wind, there, blows strongly at ground level and could be exploited by a less-unsightly vertical-axis windmill, like that designed by Erasmus Darwin (Charles Darwin's grandfather – a doctor, poet and inventor): an octagonal tower, open on all sides to the wind, with louvres that direct the wind upwards to drive vertical-axis wind-sails.[25] Kite-driven generators may also be deemed less unsightly than large wind turbines.

Large hydroelectric schemes have been in operation for many years. Small-scale schemes are now being installed in Scotland and North Wales. Such schemes can alter the landscape, but the impact can be minimised.[26] Even in lowland areas, the energy of rivers can be harnessed. In 1300 there were more than 10,000 water mills in the south of England;[27] energy that was once used for grinding corn could now generate electricity.

Waves and tides have potential as sources of renewable energy. The Wave Hub test site off the coast of Cornwall is testing the potential of wave energy to generate electricity, and the first four turbines have been installed for the MeyGen project to harness the strong tidal currents in the Pentland

Firth off the north of Scotland. The world's first tidal power station, on the estuary of the River Rance in France, has been operational since 1966. Plans for a tidal lagoon at Swansea Bay are the most advanced of several sites on the British coast.

Recent experience is that the cost of generating electricity by solar panels and offshore wind turbines, like the cost of lithium-ion batteries (see below) has gone down dramatically. The same may, in the future, be the case for tidal-lagoon technology, for example, and sea-bed tidal turbines.

Biofuels

Cultivating plants to be burnt as a source of energy (eg trees, *Miscanthus*) uses land that could be better used for producing food or allowing nature to flourish. Moreover, wood emits more carbon per unit of energy than most fossil fuels.[28] The use of waste from other industries (eg forestry, sawmills), however, has more to commend it.

Anaerobic digestion is used to convert organic waste to produce fuels such as methane. Goodall describes the use of semi-arid land, unsuitable for food production, to grow cacti which can be harvested and placed in an anaerobic digester to generate methane.[29] The use of good agricultural land in Britain to grow maize for the same purpose has less to commend it.

Algal fuels are more promising (see also page 170). They use very little land, they grow fast (20 times as much biomass per day as soya) and, in addition to oil, they produce a carbon-rich residue that can be buried or otherwise protected from oxidation – making the whole process better than carbon neutral. On an industrial scale, the process will require fertiliser (nitrogen and phosphorus) and CO_2 (a pilot plant uses CO_2 from the smoke stack of a cement works).[30]

Nuclear fusion and nuclear fission

Nuclear fusion (the process by which two small atomic nuclei join to make one larger nucleus) is the energy source for the hydrogen bomb (and for the sun). Nuclear fission (in which one large nucleus – usually uranium – is split into smaller nuclei) is the energy source for the atomic bomb and for all nuclear power stations built to date.

Fusion power, if it could be developed, would have many advantages: the raw material (deuterium, a heavy isotope of hydrogen) can be obtained from the oceans with no danger of the supply running out, and the environmental and safety risks are low. At almost any time in the last 50 years, it has been predicted that it will take another 50 years to develop fusion technology to the point where it it is feasible at an industrial scale. Unfortunately, after 50 years of research – 50 years in which other areas of science and technology have advanced by leaps and bounds – significant problems remain to be solved before it will be possible to harness this energy for electricity generation on a commercial scale. Research is continuing, but it still looks as if it will be 50 years till there is a commercial plant.

Power stations employing nuclear fission have been in operation since the 1950s. They are a practical alternative to the use of fossil fuels, but the construction of large power stations takes longer and is more expensive than the development of solar. Moreover, the high-level radioactive waste must be securely stored for a very long time. A few years ago, when it looked as if it might take 50 years to develop technologies to exploit renewable energy sources and replace fossil fuels, nuclear fission seemed the best option to fill the gap. It now looks as if renewable technologies are being developed more quickly than anticipated, but there may still be a gap to fill before they are fully deployed to meet demand. If the time comes that renewables cannot yet satisfy all the demand but are so cheap that fossil fuels are no longer competitive, there may be a useful role for nuclear fission installations that still have some life in them.

Small-scale nuclear reactors are quicker and cheaper to build than large reactors, and they could have a role in the energy mix.

Distribution and storage of electricity

Sources of renewable energy may be situated far from where the bulk of the demand lies (eg wind power in the Outer Hebrides; solar in the Sahara desert), creating a need for long-distance transmission. China has been leading the way in the application of ultra-high-voltage direct-current lines, transmitting electric power over distances of thousands of kilometres.[31]

Some renewables, notably wind and solar, vary considerably in output over time, and this creates a need for storage.

Pump-storage schemes have been in operation for some time: in times of surplus power, water is pumped from a lower reservoir to a higher one; in times of excess demand the water generates electricity by flowing back to the lower reservoir.

If a solar farm is sited next to a hydro scheme, the latter could shut off while the solar is generating electricity, thus providing continuity of supply.[32]

Lithium-ion batteries seem at present to have the greatest potential for storage. Design has been improving rapidly, the cost has gone down, and mass-production is more than keeping pace with demand. The technology is highly versatile, with applications for electric cars, for householders who want to store the electricity they produce from solar or wind for later use, and, on the larger scale, for grid operators to smooth out imbalances of supply and demand.

Other types of battery are under development; graphene enhancement can lead to significant improvement in the performance of conventional battery electrode materials.[33]

In countries like Britain, at higher latitudes, where the solar energy of the summer needs to be stored for use during the winter, surplus energy can be used to produce hydrogen by electrolysis.[34] Alternatively, solar energy can be used directly to produce hydrogen from water by artificial photosynthesis, without the intermediate stage of generating electricity.[35] The hydrogen can be combined with CO_2 using a chemical or biological process, to form a fuel. This fuel can be stored in existing oil and gas storage and distribution infrastructure for subsequent combustion and conversion into electrical power.

It is also possible to manage short-term demand, using price flexibility to bring supply and demand into balance.[36]

Transport

Transport, particularly road transport, is responsible for a great deal of pollution – nitrogen oxides and particulates (from diesel), as well as CO_2. The future lies with electrically powered transport; in the UK and France, for example, the sale of new diesel and petrol cars and vans will be banned from 2040. In July 2017, Volvo announced that within two years all new models would be electric or hybrid. The manufacture of electric cars in increasing numbers has been accompanied by the development and improvement of lithium-ion batteries and a substantial decrease in their cost: the cost to manufacture a battery pack fell by 75 per cent between 2010 and 2016.[37] Goodall estimates that by 2020 the battery pack for a car with a 200 mile range might cost about £5000, making the price of an electric car competitive with petrol as well as being cheaper to run.[38] Other types of battery are also being developed for use in cars, as also are fuel cells.

The change to the use of electric vehicles would add to the national consumption of electricity (estimates range upwards from 10 per cent) and would reduce carbon emissions even if the electricity was produced by fossil-fuel power stations because of greater efficiency.[39] In the longer term, however, the future for road transport lies in computer-controlled vehicles. For reasons of insurance and legal liability, this may mean that vehicles will be owned and maintained, on a fleet basis, by a small number of large operators;[40] the user will call up the size and type of vehicle required on each occasion.

Initially there are problems because of the shortage of recharging points, the inconvenience of having to stop to recharge during a long journey, and the limited range of such vehicles before the battery needs recharging. These inconveniences could be avoided if a run-down battery could be exchanged for a fully charged one. The motorist would simply take the car to a service station (as we do now), where an electrically operated lifting device (the batteries are heavy) would remove the battery and replace it with a fully charged one. This would do away with the need to charge the battery in the car. A precondition would be standardised batteries and standardised fittings, and there would need to be a means of placing a monetary value on each battery at the moment of exchange.

Electrification of rail transport using overhead cables is already well established. However, new technologies such as battery, hybrid electric and diesel, or hydrogen may prove to be more efficient in the future.[41]

For sea transport, nuclear-reactor technology is available for large vessels. Other vessels can be powered by electricity stored in a battery or by a gaseous or liquid fuel, produced on land by electricity or artificial photosynthesis. There is potential to use wind to supplement electricity; modern weather forecasting enables the best use to be made of wind-patterns at the time.

Hybrid electric technology is being developed for small, short-haul passenger aircraft.[42] For larger and long-haul aircraft, however, it is possible that batteries of sufficient capacity will be too heavy and that some kind of liquid or gaseous fuel will be required, as for sea transport and heavy goods vehicles. Liquid fuels for aircraft and lorries are being developed, making use of waste materials.[43]

Fresh water

Food production and industry require large quantities of water. There is scope for more efficient management of the use of this resource, but the requirement will remain very large. Many of the areas of water shortage are close to the sea, enabling fresh water to be obtained by desalination, and most such areas have a sunny climate suitable for solar power; as solar becomes cheaper, this should enable the use of fossil fuels for desalination to be phased out. The standard method for desalination of sea water is reverse osmosis – an expensive way to provide water on the large scale required for agriculture. It is likely to be replaced in the future by a technology based on graphene, which will require a much lower energy input.[44] Graphene filtration powered by solar would be very much cheaper and less demanding of resources than reverse osmosis powered by combustion of fossil fuels.

For areas of human settlement that have low rainfall and are far from the sea (parts of the USA and China, for example) it may be necessary, when groundwater resources have all been extracted, to pump water over long distances, cut down on water-hungry agriculture and industry and even encourage emigration to reduce the population density.

Manufacturing and construction

The manufacturing industry and the construction and demolition of buildings have in the past been extremely

185

wasteful of raw materials and energy. Too many manufactured products and buildings have not been made to last. We expect to discard many of our purchases soon, replacing them with a product that is only superficially different. Too many modern buildings, similarly, have a short useful life before they are demolished. This is wasteful of the Earth's precious resources, as well as being wasteful of human effort. Looking to the future, clearly there are some things, like computers, where technology is advancing so fast that there is no point designing them to last – but for that reason they should be designed so that their component parts or constituents can be readily reused. On the other hand, many buildings and many household goods such as furniture can fulfil the same function for many years. We still use, value and enjoy homes and hotels, chairs and china that were made long ago.

As with our personal decisions, industrial decisions in the manufacturing and construction industries should take account of environmental impact. Although the manufacturing sector plays a much smaller part of the economy than it used to, it is still responsible for a great deal of environmental damage, by pollution, energy use and non-sustainable consumption of raw materials.

Manufacturing should be governed by a few simple principles:
1. Manufactured products should only end up in landfill when there is no use for their constituent parts or materials.
2. Manufactured goods should be designed so that the constituent materials can readily be reused or recycled wherever this is practicable. This applies particularly where the product contains non-renewable resources that are in short supply but can be used again (rare metals, for example).
3. The waste from one industrial process should become the raw material for another.
4. Plant and animal materials should be obtained from sustainable (renewable) sources of supply.
5. Just as new pharmaceuticals are subjected to stringent tests before they are approved for use, so new chemicals and materials should be tested for their impact on nature before they are approved for release into the environment.

6. The cost of end-of-life disposal (including 1 to 3 above) should be included in the selling price of the product. So should the cost of any pollution involved: the polluter pays.

Cradle to Cradle, by William McDonough and Michael Braungart shows how this can be put into practice.[45] The book calls for the transformation of human industry through ecologically intelligent design. The authors make the case that an industrial system that 'takes, makes and wastes' can, instead, become a creator of goods and services that generate ecological, social and economic value. The authors propose that industry should develop clean cycles that are built on natural processes whereby waste from one process is feed for another. Carbon dioxide captured from combustion processes might be converted into fuels by artificial photosynthesis. The outflow water from factories should be cleaner than the inflow. Key to the cradle-to-cradle concept is the idea that all manufactured products, whether aircraft or mobile phones, cars or computers, should be designed from the outset for recycling 'technical nutrients'.

This idea is being taken forward by the Ellen MacArthur Foundation, which works with business, government and academia to accelerate the transition to a circular economy.[46] In November 2017, for example, Ellen MacArthur and Stella McCartney launched a report, *A new textiles economy: Redesigning fashion's future*, aimed at reducing the pollution and waste associated with the clothing industry and establishing a new system based on circular-economy principles.[47] This initiative is timely: the clothing industry is said to be one of the most polluting industries, and the British fashion and textiles sector is currently enjoying a renaissance.

Plastics

Chris Mullin, author of three widely acclaimed memoirs about his years as a member of parliament, contributed an article in *Prospect* Magazine in their series 'If I ruled the World'. His three measures would appeal to anyone who cares about the environment: he would phase out the private motor car (replacing it with bicycles and a rail network), he would uninvent plastic (almost every bit of plastic ever made still exists somewhere) and he would abolish factory farming.[48] We have covered transport and farming elsewhere. I here emphasise the urgency of finding a solution to the problems posed by plastic.

There are two problems to be addressed. The first is to find ways of dealing with the plastic that already exists: destroying or burying it – or, better, reusing it or putting it to good use as an industrial feedstock. The second problem is to stop producing plastics as we know them today, and that means using other substances to serve the same purposes – substances that can be kept and reused so they don't have to be disposed of or else that decompose naturally soon after disposal into landfill or the oceans. A major use of plastics is for use-once-and-throw-away packaging. We should eliminate the use of all single-use plastic.[49] There are numerous calls for other substances to be used for these purposes and for plastic containers to be reused. The recent discovery that some organisms (bacteria, caterpillars) eat plastic points towards one line of research for the disposal of unwanted plastic.

In late 2017 there were several announcements, from the government, from industry and from others with proposals to put a stop to plastic pollution. The news that the British government was to ban plastic microbeads was accompanied by the news that a biodegradable alternative has been developed.[50] The Environmental Audit Committee called for the introduction of a UK-wide deposit return scheme for plastic bottles and a requirement to provide free drinking water in public premises and to make producers financially responsible for the plastic packaging they produce.[51]

The New Plastics Initiative, led by the Ellen MacArthur Foundation, is an ambitious, three-year project. To quote Ellen MacArthur, 'we must fundamentally rethink the way we make and use plastics. We need better materials, clever product designs and circular business models. That's why we are launching the New Plastics Economy Innovation Prize, calling for innovators, designers, scientists and entrepreneurs to help create a plastics system that works.'[52]

Notes

1. HRH The Duke of Edinburgh, 1984, *Men, Machines and Sacred Cows*, Hamish Hamilton; Prince Philip was instrumental in establishing the Royal Academy of Engineering in 1976, to bring together engineers from

the several institutions representing different sectors of the profession (www.raeng.org.uk; www.princephiliphouse.com)

2. www.ellenmacarthurfoundation.org

3. Goodall, Chris, 2016, *The Switch: How Solar, Storage and new Tech Means Cheap Power for All*, Profile Books

4. Wilson, Edward O, 2016, *Half-Earth: Our Planet's Fight for Life*, Liveright

5. *The Economist*, June 10, 2017

6. http://uk.businessinsider.com/americas-pledge-jerry-brown-michael-bloomberg-climate-change-2017-7

7. www.forbes.com/sites/kerryadolan/2016/12/12/bill-gates-launches-1-billion-breakthrough-energy-investment-fund/#2b1368805b7d; http://www.b-t.energy/news-room

8. *The Times*, 3 February 2017

9. Goodall, 2016

10. https://about.bnef.com/blog/global-wind-solar-costs-fall-even-faster-coal-fades-even-china-india

11. http://corporate.exxonmobil.com/en/energy/energy-outlook/highlights

12. Mair, Robert, 2012, *Shale gas extraction in the UK: A review of hydraulic fracturing*, The Royal Society and the Royal Academy of Engineering

13. http://endcoal.org/wp-content/uploads/2017/03/BoomBust2017-English-Final.pdf

14. www.aiib.org

15. *The Times*, January 21, 2017

16. *The Economist*, April 1, 2017

17. *GeoCam: Earth Sciences Alumni Magazine*, Spring 2017; http://www.cam.ac.uk/research/news/carbon-dioxide-can-be-stored-underground-for-ten-times-the-length-needed-to-avoid-climatic-impact

18. www.theguardian.com/environment/2017/jan/03/indian-firm-carbon-capture-breakthrough-carbonclean

19. *The Economist*, 15 July, 2017

20. *The Economist*, 10 December 2016

21. Goodall, 2016

22. *The Times*, 27 May 2017

23. Llewellyn Smith, Chris, quoted by Highfield, Roger, 2017, Can Oxford Save the World?, 36–41 in *Oxford Today*, Vol 27, no 2

24. Goodall, 2016, 123

25. Darwin, Erasmus, 1800, *Phytologia, or the Philosophy of Agriculture and Gardening*, reissued by Nabu Press, 2014, quoted by King-Hele, Desmond, 1977, *Doctor of Revolution: The Life and Genius of Erasmus Darwin*, Faber & Faber

26. *The Times*, 16 October 2016

27. Sandbrook, Dominic, review (in *Sunday Times*, July 16, 2017) of Winder, Robert, 2017, *The Last Wolf: The Hidden Springs of Englishness*, Little Brown

28. www.chathamhouse.org/expert/comment/wood-not-carbon-neutral-energy-source

29. Goodall, 2016, 134–145

30. Holmes, Bob, Less than Zero, *New Scientist*, 8 December 2012

31. *The Economist*, 14 January 2017

32. Goodall, 2016, 141

33. Eg www.graphene-info.com/graphene-batteries
34. Goodall, 2016, 212
35. *The Times*, 29 July 2016; *Financial Times*, 5 July 2017
36. Goodall, 2016, 147
37. https://about.bnef.com/blog/lithium-ion-battery-costs-squeezed-margins-new-business-models
38. Goodall, 2016, 178
39. www.carbonbrief.org/analysis-switch-to-electric-vehicles-would-add-just-10-per-cent-to-uk-power-demand
40. *The Economist*, 24 September 2016
41. *The Times*, 25 March 2017; 16 January 2018
42. http://zunum.aero; *The Times*, 29 November, 2017
43. *The Times*, 28 August 2017
44. http://www.nature.com/nnano/journal/v10/n5/full/nnano.2015.37.html?foxtrotcallback=true; http://www.bbc.co.uk/news/science-environment-39482342
45. McDonough, William and Braungart, Michael, 2009, *Cradle to Cradle*, Vintage
46. www.ellenmacarthurfoundation.org
47. www.ellenmacarthurfoundation.org/news/one-garbage-truck-of-textiles-wasted-every-second-report-creates-vision-for-change
48. *Prospect*, August 2012
49. Eg https://www.sas.org.uk; aplasticplanet.com
50. *The Times*, 8 June 2017
51. www.parliament.uk/business/committees/committees-a-z/commons-select/environmental-audit-committee/news-parliament-2017/plastic-bottles-publication-17-19
52. www.ellenmacarthurfoundation.org/news/ellen-macarthur-foundation-and-the-prince-of-waless-international-sustainability-unit-launch-2-million-innovation-prize-to-keep-plastics-out-the-ocean

Chapter 14
The Economy as if the Environment Matters

We cannot rebuild this economy on the same pile of sand. We must build our house upon a rock.

Barack Obama[1]

The economy is indivisible. In order to look at the environmental impact of economic activity, we need to look at the economy as a whole, at how it works and at how it sets out to achieve its other objectives too.

Once again, we should keep in mind the triple bottom line: money, social and environment. The economy exists for people, not the other way round. Likewise, the economy must serve nature, not the other way round. It follows that the economy, like a business, must be sound: a failed economy fails people and it fails nature.

In 2018, we are still living in the aftermath of the financial crisis of 2007–2008, with high levels of government debt and personal debt. Financially, as well as environmentally, we are living at the expense of the future.

A different kind of economy

The next few decades will see huge changes in the world's economies. We have looked at some of the technological changes that are taking place. The fourth industrial revolution, as it is called, includes the replacement of large numbers of human workers by robots or computers, making more people available for different kinds of work.[2] We saw in chapter 3 that a great deal of human effort is devoted to designing, making, advertising, selling, buying and disposing of things that none of us really needs or wants. If we can reduce this element of our expenditure, that, too, will make human effort available for other work.

Diane Coyle, in *The Economics of Enough*, presents a manifesto for a different kind of economy – an economy that is organised as if the future matters. She emphasises the importance of values in setting the direction and objectives of the economy, and gives due weight to happiness, nature, posterity, fairness and trust.[3]

In an earlier work, Coyle writes that, although the industrialised countries were about 20 times better off at the end of the twentieth century than 100 years before, 'the output of the developed economies weighs the same as the 20 times less valuable output of the same economies at the end of the nineteenth century'.[4] Purchase of bulky goods (food, clothes, cars, household goods) took a smaller proportion of our spending than it did. Physical goods had become lighter. Services made up a larger share of what we spent our money on – services such as child care, eating out, health, education and financial services: 'A third of the increase in global output during the past half-century has gone into health and education and a third into "leisure", broadly defined to include the media.' These trends are likely to continue in the years ahead.

We thus have a huge opportunity to reshape the way our economy works. As well as expanding the experience economy, the sharing economy, the circular economy and the development of clean technologies for energy generation, transport, manufacturing and construction, the areas in which we need more resources, at the time of writing, are health and social care, education and security (police; armed forces; diplomacy and other soft power). All these do less damage to the environment than producing stuff.

At the end of an interview with John Humphrys on BBC Radio's *Today* programme on 27 October 2009, the economist Nicholas Stern said 'We have the opportunity to act and to act strongly, and actually to create something that is much more attractive. It will be more energy secure, cleaner, quieter, more biodiverse, safer; and in the transition from here to there we are going to have one of the most dynamic periods of innovation and investment the world economy has seen'.

Before discussing this in more detail, I want to take a look at some of the basics in the way the economy works.

How the economy works

The building blocks of the economy

The basis of the economy is that we produce goods and services for one another, in exchange for money. If we wish to enjoy the goods and services that others have to offer and if we agree on the relative values of our products, then we shall enjoy productive work and growing prosperity. If we think that our own work is undervalued and the goods and services produced by other people are overvalued, we shall decide not to do the work, and not to buy the goods and services. One or other of these scenarios will predominate, and that is what determines the level of unemployment and the health of the economy.

We are apt to emphasise the competitive nature of economic activity, but we should not forget that at its heart the economy is a matter of cooperation for mutual advantage. We work for one another.[5] Workers and consumers are not two separate groups of people: we are all consumers and nearly all of us are, have been or will be workers.

The situation is more complicated in today's world, with employers, governments, middlemen etc, but the basic truth remains that people will work if the rewards are acceptable (after taking account of their circumstances and the other options available to them) and they will buy if the price is acceptable. A thriving economy is one where most of us think that it is worth making the effort to earn money and that there are goods and services that are worth spending it on.

We should note that both scenarios (to agree to work and buy, or to decide not to) are driven by self-interest. We cannot say that one scenario is greedy and the other is not. The difference is whether our perception of our own self-interest leads us into a win-win situation or a lose-lose situation. The key is how much we value the product of other people's work. A thriving economy depends on how much we value what other people have to offer.

What are the factors that might influence us towards making win-win decisions or lose-lose decisions, towards taking on a job or making a purchase? Anything that increases productivity reduces prices, making goods and services more attractive and encouraging economic activity: this can be achieved by better management, and better technologies. Thus, although new technologies (such as robots and artificial intelligence) destroy specific jobs, overall they promote economic activity, higher levels of employment and greater prosperity.

Taxation puts up prices and discourages activity, whereas subsidy encourages it. It is possible that the widespread payment of working tax credits in recent years encourages people to accept low-paid work, enabling businesses to keep prices down; this might help to explain why unemployment levels in recent years have remained low, to the surprise of economic commentators: a subsidy from the taxpayer enables low pay and low prices that would otherwise not be acceptable or viable.

Building blocks such as these are the basis of the free market, operating by freely made decisions. The market is not an ism, like socialism or communism, which only exist when a government sets them up. It is not a theory or an ideal (though it may become so): it is what happens when people make their own arrangements, with no interference from government.

Advocates of the free market base their case on wealth creation: the free market has enabled millions of people to lift themselves out of poverty. Critics of the free market (who are more likely to use the term 'capitalism') focus on the way that the risks and rewards are distributed between suppliers, customers, capital providers (equity and loan) and paid executives, managers and staff.

Business models

A successful business needs staff, raw materials, capital, management – and customers. In the capitalist system, the business is owned and controlled by the providers of equity capital – individuals, partners, families or, in large businesses, shareholders; these are people who put their capital at risk, enjoying the profits or suffering the losses, depending on the business's profitability. Other models also exist in a free market, providing similar goods and services: some of these are not for profit, others are owned by different stakeholders – staff or customers. Such models coexist with competing businesses owned by shareholders without being notably more or less successful in terms of customer satisfaction and

194

economic viability. Whatever the model, the owners and controllers can, if they wish, decide on the business's policy on social and environmental issues. Investors, job-seekers and customers can make up their own minds, if they wish, whether or not to participate in the activities of any business on the basis of its social and environmental policies – people power.

Who controls the economy?

There are three players in a simple economic transaction: a supplier, a customer and the government. The government is responsible for the legal and fiscal framework, providing incentives and disincentives; it can also act to prevent monopolies or cartels. Suppliers bring together entrepreneurial flair, the skills of their staff and the latest technology, to offer goods or services that customers want. We have seen that in the consumer society customers – consumers – are in fact pawns, manipulated by government and suppliers, supported by advertisers. They are under pressure to keep buying, to keep the economy going. They buy stuff they don't need – when what they actually want is something quite different, like access to better health care. In a market economy, it is customers who have the real power: businesses succeed or fail by whether customers decide to purchase the goods or services they have to offer. We are sometimes told today that customers are pawns in the hands of big business, but this is only so if big business has the power of a monopoly or a cartel or if the market is otherwise rigged.

Robert Reich, in *Saving Capitalism*, argues that in today's world the market is not as free as we might think.[6] It operates within laws or conventions regarding property (what can be owned, including intellectual property), monopoly, contract, bankruptcy and enforcement. He gives examples of ways in which these rules and conventions, in America, enable the market to operate in favour of large, rich and powerful corporations. These corporations may well have become large, rich and powerful by supplying goods and services that customers choose to purchase, but there may come a point when too much power resides with the corporation and it is the responsibility of government to ensure that sufficient power ('countervailing power', to use Reich's term) remains with other parties, such as customers and employees.

People power

In a free market, customers have the ultimate power: there is more power to the people in a free market than there is in democracy. To get rid of a government, voters have to wait till an election, but if customers desert a business they can close it down in months or weeks. Jared Diamond, in *Collapse*, gives an example of customer power. The US meat industry resisted for five years pressure from the Food and Drug Administration (the voice of government – the voice of the voter) to change their practices in response to mad-cow disease, but when McDonald's made the same demands following plummeting sales of their hamburgers (the voice of the customer), the meat industry complied within weeks.[7] In Britain, the public reactions to the horse-meat-adulteration scandal of December 2012 and early 2013 and the collapse of a garment factory in Bangladesh in 2013 showed that customers are willing to think about the kind of industry that they are supporting, think about consequences, and adapt their shopping accordingly.

Terry Leahy, chief executive of Tesco from 1997 to 2011, was reported in a 2009 interview: 'It is going to take a long time for countries to reduce their carbon emissions but consumers can do it overnight just by changing their behaviour. We need a second consumer revolution. ... You need to work with the grain of human nature. If you force people, they don't take on board the reason for the change and alter their behaviour. Take cars and petrol: there is a huge tax on it but it didn't change how much they drove. You have to get society to make low-carbon living desirable and cool. People used to see success as living in a mansion in America. Now it has to be a zero-carbon house and an electric sports car. ... I have solar panels, new boilers and a hybrid car. We do all our own recycling and compost and water recovery. ... The science is incontrovertible and the implications are terrible, so I do what an ordinary person does. ... All my business experience has taught me that people are pretty wise and know what is best for their lives.'[8]

Externalities

Sometimes an economic activity leads to consequences – beneficial or harmful – that are not part of the deal that caused that activity to take place. When we buy a stamp and post a letter, for example, we are not deliberately paying for the time the postman spends exchanging the few friendly words with a customer – 'the brief exchange of words that is the breath of life itself, sharing the air, shooting the breeze, enjoying the moment, taking a little time, before I pass on up the road and on my way.'[9] It is not just the postman. All through the economy there are valuable human contacts that are not part of any contract but oil the wheels and help society – and the economy – to function happily. If we over-emphasise money, the single bottom line, we may fail to appreciate the value of loyalty and human relationships. We can too easily destroy these human contacts by a blinkered over-emphasis on money; the consequences may be unpredictable, but may well include more loneliness, ill-health and deprivation of one kind and another: more work for the health and social services to pick up.

These are positive externalities. The damage that we do to the natural environment and its impact on future generations is a negative externality. Most of us don't deliberately set out to destroy the natural environment. Destruction is the inevitable consequence of our economic and lifestyle choices, but it is not the reason we make those choices. We may be unaware of the consequences, or we may just prefer not to think about them or take them into account.

Instead of being externalities, environmental damage should be recognised as part of the original deal. In other words, the purchaser of goods or services should pay, at the point of purchase, the cost of non-polluting recycling and/or disposal of the goods and the cost of any remedial work for environmental damage done during provision of the service: the principle of 'the polluter pays'.[10]

How economics went astray in the twentieth century

Adam Smith (1723–1790), often referred to as the father of modern economics, was professor of moral philosophy at the University of Glasgow. In other words, economics was all about human behaviour. Early in the twentieth century, the great economist Alfred Marshall wrote, 'Political Economy or Economics is a study of mankind in the ordinary business of life … a part of the study of man.'[11]

Subsequently, however, a movement arose, in which Paul Samuelson (1915–2009) was a leading figure, that sought to present economics as a science, resembling the physical sciences in that it was subject to laws that could be expressed as equations. When a donation from the Swedish National Bank enabled the establishment of a Nobel prize for economics, it was named the Nobel Memorial Prize in Economic Sciences; Samuelson was an early recipient (1970).

The economic journalist, Anatole Kaletsky, wrote in 2010, 'One reason why economics has progressed so little beyond the insights of its founding fathers has been the convention adopted since the 1960s that all serious economic ideas must be expressed as equations, not words. By this weird standard, the work of the genuine giants – Smith, Ricardo, Keynes, Schumpeter, Hayek – would be rejected by academic journals and would not be recognised as serious economics at all.'[12]

The economist Paul Ormerod had written similarly in *The Death of Economics*.[13] Another early critic was J K Galbraith: 'Once students were attracted by the seeming urgency of economic problems and by a sense of their mission to solve them. Now the best come to economics for the opportunity it provides to exercise arcane mathematical skills.'[14]

Economics thus rested on a myth that humans are rational creatures – a mechanistic view of the human mind in relation to economic choices, finding expression in the notion of the 'economic man', or '*Homo economicus*'. Daniel Kahneman, in *Thinking, Fast and Slow*,[15] quotes a 1970s essay which starts 'The agent of economic theory is rational, selfish, and his tastes do not change'. Kahneman, a psychologist, records his astonishment at what he saw as the profound difference between the intellectual worlds of psychology and economics. He continues: 'To a psychologist, it is self-evident that people are neither fully rational nor completely selfish, and that their tastes are anything but stable. Our two disciplines seemed to be studying different species, which the behavioural economist Richard Thaler later dubbed Econs and Humans.' A few years later, Kahneman, with Amos Tversky, published a groundbreaking paper, 'Judgment under uncertainty: heuristics and biases'[16] and his subsequent career followed a path that led, in 2002, to the award of the Nobel Prize in Economic

Sciences 'for having integrated insights from psychological research into economic science, especially concerning human judgement and decision-making under uncertainty.'

The fact is, of course, that human behaviour, in economic and financial matters as in other areas, is unpredictable. The people have the power to disprove any economic prediction: all we have to do is to decide to behave differently – to earn, spend or save our money in different ways. Each of us may follow the herd, or we may go our own way. When we follow the herd, we all buy – until we all decide to stop buying. We all have confidence in a bank or some other institution – until we all decide that our confidence is misplaced.

In the face of such uncertainty, the one branch of mathematics which could be extremely useful in economic predictions is that of probability and risk assessment. However, as Robert Peston put it, the banks and bankers, during the period leading up to the crisis of 2007–2008, 'systematically failed to do what they were handsomely remunerated to do, which was to assess properly the risks of all that lending.'[17] Even ten years on, we read about economic predictions; we do not read about various possible future scenarios and the writer's assessment of the probability attached to each one.

Economics and business ethics

For a long time, as in Adam Smith's day, economics was 'seen as something like a branch of ethics'.[18] For much of the twentieth century, however, it generally ignored the role of ethical considerations or any other kind of non-monetary value (see also chapter 6). Richard Layard recalls that his celebrated economics tutor was always warning him about the pitfalls of do-goodery.[19] Amartya Sen, winner (1998) of the Nobel Prize in Economic Sciences, draws attention to 'the contrast between the self-consciously "non-ethical" character of modern economics and the historical evolution of modern economics largely as an offshoot of ethics.'[20]

It was this separation of economics from ethics that led Michael Sandel to write that if he ruled the world he would rewrite the economics textbooks, reconnecting economics with its origins in moral and political philosophy.[21] Ethical and other values are now back on the agenda. This applies particularly in

199

relation to business, where the public have seen that much recent practice has been morally wrong. In the last few years business leaders have been talking openly about business ethics. It was an investment banker, Ken Costa, who wrote in the *Financial Times* in 2011: 'We all need to learn the grammar of morality, not in a judgmental way but by becoming more comfortable in thinking, writing and talking openly about values and ethics. For many this will be like learning an entirely new language.'[22] According to Richard Branson, 'Ethics aren't just important in business. They are the whole point of business.'[23] The journalist Dan Matthews writes: 'An ethical approach to business can not only be profitable, but is also a requirement of discerning customers eager to safeguard the planet and protect workers.'[24]

Measuring the success of the economy

Just as money is not a true measure of a person's happiness or well-being but is still a necessary part of our life, so the economy is not a true measure of the happiness or well-being of a community or nation but is still an important part of national life. Most of the really important things that money can buy are paid for, largely, by the government, from money raised through taxation: healthcare, education, social care, police and the armed forces – even food is subsidised to the extent that half the national farm income comes from the taxpayer. The National Health Service alone costs about £2000 for every man, woman and child in the UK. In order to fund all these important things we have to pay taxes, and that means earning and spending money on other, less important things. The important things in life are paid for by the unimportant. The essentials ride on the back of the luxuries. We depend on taxes; that, in turn, depends on having a thriving economy.

All economic activity has some environmental impact but, generally speaking, traditional manufacturing and construction have a greater impact than services and on-line activities. The trend in recent years has been towards such low-impact economic activities, and this trend will continue if that is how customers want to spend their money, if businesses continue to adapt to provide such goods and services and if governments facilitate this trend.

The people described by Teresa Belton (pages 140–141) who are living simpler, happier lives, with minimal environmental impact, may not be paying much tax, though they benefit from government expenditure. The challenge for all environmentalists is to find ways of living nature-friendly lives at the same time as participating in tax-generating economic activity.

There are many ways in which we can work for one another, earning money and paying taxes, doing much less damage to the environment than our present jobs. We can put greater emphasis on teaching, artistic creativity, scientific research, scholarship, writing, caring and other service industries, and participating in the circular economy and the sharing economy for goods. The strengthening of local communities can reduce the need for travel and transport.

Writing in 1930, in an essay entitled 'Economic Possibilities for our Grandchildren', the economist John Maynard Keynes predicted that once we had solved the economic problem of making sure that everyone had enough for their basic needs we would be 'free to return to some of the most sure and certain principles of religion and traditional virtue – that avarice is a vice, that ... the love of money is detestable'. He thought that we would flourish in the arts, in culture, and 'even perfect the ultimate refinements of beauty and friendship'.[25] Well, that's not the way it went then – but there are signs that we could move in that direction today. Germany's large trading surplus, for example, is explained by a general reluctance to buy stuff: workers would rather have extra days off than receive a pay rise; and they would rather save for retirement than spend today.[26]

We shall now look at some of the ways that the success of the economy can be measured, seeing how they relate to the environment.

Gross Domestic Product (GDP) and growth

The Gross Domestic Product is a measure of economic activity. It is the total value of everything (goods and services) produced in a country during one year. It doesn't include unpaid work, such as cleaning one's own home, but it does include any economic activity, however damaging it might be to human or planetary well-being. GDP has many weaknesses.

Diane Coyle, in particular, makes a strong case for improving the way we assess the success of the economy.[27]

GDP tells us the total *amount* of economic activity. It is not a measure of the economy's success at achieving any of its objectives – objectives such as low unemployment, elimination of poverty, adequate remuneration of people in work, high enough tax take to meet government expenditure, low inflation, a healthy balance of trade – and the general happiness and well-being of the population.

The statistic that is most often quoted is not the actual level of the GDP but the rate of growth over the past year. Growth is generally thought to be a good thing, but here again it is not actually a measure of the economy's success at meeting any of its objectives.

The figures for GDP and growth had more relevance to people's lives when manufacturing played a larger part in the economy. When we look at the changes that we envisage, towards an economy with less manufacturing and more services, experiences and computer-based and internet-based activities, it is possible to imagine that the economy could become more successful in achieving its objectives without any growth at all.

Following the Club of Rome and *Limits to Growth* (page 121), many people have realised that we cannot expect growth, as we know it, to continue indefinitely.[28] If growth means producing more and more stuff in factories, damaging the environment in the process, then there are indeed limits to growth. If, on the other hand, growth means enhancing all our lives through the application of human kindness and ingenuity, aided by ever-advancing computer and on-line capabilities, then there is scope for growth to continue for some years yet. The change from making, selling, buying and discarding stuff to a service and experience economy might result in GDP going up or it might go down. It doesn't really matter. What matters is that people get happier and the planet gets healthier, to quote from the title of Teresa Belton's book (page 140).

Employment

We work to earn money – but work is more than that. It gives us a sense of dignity, identity and pride, a sense that we are contributing to the common good and that our contribution is recognised and valued.[29] If we keep this obvious fact in mind, we shall regard working as preferable to unemployment on benefit, and we shall regard the use of the term 'compensation' to mean salary as a dreadful misrepresentation of what work is all about.

The trend that I envisage away from stuff and towards services and experiences will involve the loss of many of today's jobs, but many of these jobs are likely to go anyway in the massive upheaval of the fourth industrial revolution. A recent analysis suggests that up to 30 per cent of UK jobs are at high risk of automation by the early 2030s; particularly at risk are those in transport, storage, manufacturing, wholesale and retail.[30]

Faced with this situation, it will be asked whether we face a future in which high unemployment is inevitable. My response is that high unemployment will become inevitable when all human needs and desires that can be satisfied by human effort are being satisfied – a situation somewhat beyond the foreseeable future. Levels of unemployment, as we have seen, depend upon how we value the products of other people's work. Technological innovation makes some jobs disappear, but unemployment in the economy as a whole may go down: new technologies can make other jobs viable by bridging the gap between what the worker or businessman thinks their job or product is worth and what the customer thinks it is worth.

The jobs that will remain are mostly jobs with a low environmental impact; they are also likely to be more personally satisfying than many of the industrial jobs of the past. The jobs of the future include:

- jobs that depend on human interaction: health care, social care, teaching, leisure; as more and more of life is taken over by robots, we shall appreciate more than ever the opportunity to relate to and be served by a real person – the postman or the shop assistant who can pass the time of day, for example, or the person who makes sure that your holiday goes smoothly by taking the worry off your shoulders,

- jobs requiring human judgement and decision-making (managers, doctors, plumbers, electricians etc); let us see a reversal of the trend by which diktat from on high has

203

been replacing the informed judgement of the person on the spot,

- jobs involving creativity – in the arts, scholarship and innovation (science, technology, engineering, business), and
- jobs concerned with computing (designing, programming, operating and maintaining computers and robots).

There may also be more jobs than at present in farming, if we are to see greater integration of food production and care of nature.[31]

Inequality

Steven D Levitt and Stephen J Dubner, in *Freakonomics*, describe the working of a gang of drug dealers. The leader of this gang received a monthly salary of $8500, equivalent to an hourly wage of $66; his three officers received $7 an hour each; and the foot soldiers $3.30 an hour – less than the minimum wage. That is why Levitt and Dubner call this chapter of their book 'Why do drug dealers still live with their Moms?'.[32]

The point about this is that drug dealing is outside the law, so it shows how business works when there is no interference, regulation, taxation or subsidy from the government. Inequality and hierarchical structure come naturally to human societies. Since they are also characteristic of chimpanzee societies and other primates,[33] it is likely that this kind of social organisation is something that we inherited from our pre-human, primate ancestors: 'The roots of politics are older than humanity'.[34] If so, it would be deeply ingrained in us and difficult to overcome. It comes naturally to us and, particularly in the past, it has been taken for granted that the tough guy, the alpha male, the guy who walks to the front of the queue as of right is not only respected but admired. This dominance, in other species as well as in humans, depends on character, not just physical strength.[35]

This admiration for the rich and powerful has coexisted, without apparent conflict, with a sense that everybody has an obligation to help the poorest in society and those in need.

In recent years, however, opinion has been divided. As Diane Coyle points out, 'There is a contrast between the postwar era of convergence in incomes due to an emphasis on more equal social and economic outcomes and the early twenty-first-century pattern of more extreme inequality.'[36] We may still admire the rich and successful, but at the same time we feel that there is something wrong with a society in which great riches exist alongside deprivation.

Inequality and the environment

After a period when we have allowed the free market to flourish, it is notable that inequality and the environment are two areas of greatest concern. High income-inequality in a society is associated with poor social outcomes (eg physical and mental health, trust and other indicators of well-being)[37] and also with lower environmental quality (eg waste generation, loss of biodiversity).[38]

A free market works to the benefit of those who participate in it. Most of us participate as customers and/or workers, but the poor participate less and the future does not participate at all. Amartya Sen has pointed out that, although it has many strengths, a weakness of free-market capitalism is that it fails to deal with the issues of inequality and the environment.[39] If the economy is also to serve the interests of the poor, the future and the environment, those who participate in it must have a broader vision, taking these interests into account. People have power through the economy as well as through politics (pages 139–140, 195, 196). A more equal society is more likely to have that wider vision, with a shared sense of purpose, acting together for the poor and for the future.

The very poor, in poor countries, may, individually, do little damage to the environment through individual consumption, but we have seen that it is these countries that have the highest population growth. It is also in these countries that overpopulation is damaging the environment through soil degradation, desertification and loss of biodiversity.

Poor people in rich countries like the UK have more affluent lifestyles, and therefore greater environmental impact through pollution etc. Their poverty makes them unlikely to make environmentally friendly choices if such choices cost more than environmentally damaging options.

The very rich have the opportunity for extravagant consumption, and they may well yield to this. They also have the opportunity to invest in a sustainable future, a notable example being Bill Gates and the Bill and Melinda Gates Foundation.

It is reasonable to believe that the environment is in safer hands in societies that are more equal, where people can come together in a common cause and where most people have the money, time and opportunity to make environmentally friendly choices, helped by a healthy work-life balance.

Poverty

Governments and people have a responsibility to help those in need. This has been part of our thinking for a very long time. For the last seventy years society has possessed wealth on a scale undreamed of by past generations. We have also had governments that attached great importance to helping people out of poverty, and huge sums have been directed to dealing with this – but poverty still remains a serious issue in our society. If money was the answer, there would be no poverty today: helping people out of poverty needs fresh thinking. Barry Knight, in *Rethinking Poverty: What makes a good society?*, suggests that we should stop relying on government programmes 'driven from the top down, based on unevaluated theories of change, rather than being developed using the skills, knowledge and expertise of people in communities'.[40] He, like John Bird, founder of *The Big Issue*, says you should do things *with* the poor, to enable them to get out of poverty.[41]

Perhaps communities climb out of poverty when they work together, providing goods and services for each other, supplying one another's needs. Key to such development would be those people within deprived communities who have particular gifts of leadership and creativity, those with the ideas and the ability to make things happen. Perhaps the best thing government can do is to offer incentives for such people to make things happen in their own communities rather than creating new lives for themselves elsewhere.[42] In addition to government incentives, support can come from the business sector, from people with investment capital and business expertise to offer. Deprived communities impose a financial cost on the nation;[43] thriving communities pay taxes.

Many of the low-paid jobs in Britain are at the interface with customers: in social care, retail and catering, for example. If these people received enough to live on because their customers appreciated the value of what they were doing, they would not need to be subsidised by the taxpayer through tax credits.

Income inequality and the rich

Led by America, there has been a global trend since the 1980s of rising pay for senior executives. In the US, CEO pay rose by 937 per cent between 1978 and 2016. In the UK, FTSE executives were paid 330 percent more in 2015 than in 1998. American CEOs are now paid 335 times as much as the average worker; in the UK it is 140 times as much.[44] This increase has not been accompanied by any notable increase in performance – a situation that has given rise to much public concern and criticism.

Some writers say that the answer to high income-inequality is to tax the rich more heavily. There are three caveats here. The first is the Laffer principle: that raising the taxation rate above a certain critical level doesn't increase revenue, because taxpayers move abroad or find some other way to reduce their taxable income. Second, to depend on such a small number of people could make revenues unpredictable and risky. Third, if the intention is to reduce inequality, it is self-defeating: the more we depend upon the very rich to keep the exchequer afloat, the more firmly entrenched this inequality becomes. We dare not reduce inequality because we need the high earnings of the very rich so that the rest of can live off their taxes: the top 1 per cent in the UK pay 27 per cent of all income tax (compared with 11 per cent in 1978).[45]

If we want to reduce income inequality, we should tackle the causes of the high salaries – recognising them as a failure of the market, which 'can be effectively reduced only by tackling inequality in the market place'.[46] In a free market, competition drives down costs – and that should include the cost of employing a senior executive. The argument that talent is scarce may apply to a very small number of people, but if talent is normally distributed there must be many senior executives who are no more gifted than the numerous people who would be glad to do their job for lower pay. This market failure is an example of Robert Reich's point (page 206) that markets operate within laws and rules, which tend to favour the rich and powerful. If the rules and procedures under which executive salaries are determined can be identified, they can be changed so as to allow the free market to operate.

Taxes

The first responsibility of government is security: to defend their people from enemies abroad and criminal activity at home. In the UK in recent years, the diplomatic, defence and police budgets (with a combined budget of about a tenth of government expenditure) have been under severe pressure.

The second call on government expenditure, which, for more than a century, has taken up an ever-increasing proportion of the budget, is to provide a wide range of services to enable everyone (in theory) to maintain a reasonable standard of living: healthcare, education, social protection, pensions etc. This eats up about two thirds of government spending, and there is always pressure to increase the amount.

Third, government has responsibilities for protecting the environment (chapter 11), but at present this takes up a very small proportion of government spending.

The money for this government spending is raised by taxing economic activity, so, in the transition to a more service-based and experience-based economy, there is a need to maintain a high level of economic activity.

In recent years the government has been spending much more than it raises in taxes, so, as well as a damaged planet, we are bequeathing to the future a massive financial debt.

Can we reduce government spending? The obvious target is social protection: benefits, tax credits etc. Welfare spending is much higher in Europe than in the rest of the world. Europe has 7 per cent of the world's population, 23 per cent of the world's economy, and 50 per cent of the world's welfare spending;[47] it is suggested that the equivalent figures for the UK are 1 per cent, 4 per cent and 7 per cent. Very little of this largesse goes to the people who need it most. The world's largest economies, those of the USA and China, spend much less on welfare. This enables them to take less tax, as a proportion of GDP, and to spend more on other things (even so, the USA has a huge, and increasing, national debt).

Many people would regard the European rate as unsustainable. If more people were paid enough to live on, a

208

great deal of government expenditure would be unnecessary. It has been estimated that in 1485 the average English peasant needed to work 15 weeks in the year to earn the money needed to survive for the year. In 1564 it was 40 weeks.[48] More recently, most families expected to live on the earnings of one breadwinner. Now, many families need two salaries, two people in full-time employment, and some of them also receive government support. If we, as customers, placed a greater value on the work that people do, government spending could be reduced.

Can we increase government revenue? The 2017 Social Attitudes Survey showed that 48 per cent of the UK population would like to see more taxation and spending (but then 44 per cent of adults don't pay income tax at all).[49] In 1997, when Kenneth Clarke was Chancellor of the Exchequer, the basic rate of income tax was 23 per cent and the economy was unusually healthy, so there might be scope for increasing tax rates. There is also a case for taxing environment-damaging activities more heavily.

Productivity

Productivity is the output per worker. It can be increased by improvement in technology and management. Spread over the economy as a whole, productivity is the total output per hour worked. We should be cautious in using productivity as a measure of the success of an economy that is increasingly dominated by services: 'Productivity is a concept appropriate in industries producing products, but not for many of those delivering services.'[50] 'What would it mean for a teacher or a management consultant to be more productive?'[51]

In a green economy we shall produce better quality goods that last longer; does productivity go up or down? Similarly in some service industries (repair and maintenance, for example) in a green economy we shall do a job that lasts longer than a slipshod job that has to be repeated soon; which represents the higher productivity?

Productivity, like GDP, is a useful measure of the success of an economy based on manufacturing. It is less useful as a measure of the green economy of the future, based on experiences and services. They are useful measures when the trend is for more of the same; they are less useful when the trend is towards something different.

Trade

Trade has been going on for millennia. It is well-established that it can make for a higher standard of living. If crops are grown and goods are manufactured in the countries where they can be produced most cheaply or efficiently or to the highest standard or with the lowest environmental impact – and these factors outweigh the cost and environmental impact of transport to the customer – the customer benefits and so does the world economy. As with other economic transactions, trade should be led by customer demand.

Nevertheless, the importance of trade, like that of GDP growth and rising productivity, can be overstated. Producing for the local market and buying local products reduces the environmental impact of transport. It also helps to build community cohesiveness.

As inequality between nations decreases, there may no longer be an incentive to manufacture goods far from the market solely because of cheap labour. The UK fashion and textiles sector is expanding, for example. China has plans to rebalance its economy from external to domestic demand,[52] and in December 2017 it announced that it would cease importing UK plastic waste.

New manufacturing techniques, using robotics and 3D printing for example, may make it more attractive to produce goods in small quantities close to the customer.[53] In more general terms, it may be argued that under present-day globalisation, 'the previously iron-clad rule that all nations win from free trade is no longer a given'.[54]

The virtue of trade is that it is a win-win-win situation: the customer gets the desired product, the producer and trader get business, and, as with other economic transactions, the government gets its cut as well, in tax and/or duty. Trade loses its social value if there is a price to be paid by the community (in government subsidy) or by the environment. Government subsidy distorts the market. In Mali, for example, successful, tax-paying cotton-growers faced unfair competition when world prices were depressed by heavily subsidised cotton exported from the US and the EU.[55] Trade, like most economic transactions, should be led by customer demand, not by government subsidy.

Trade in animals and plants can have an environmental cost. International demand for ivory and rhino horn, for example, leads to the slaughter of endangered animals: the UK government in October 2017 proposed a ban on the sale and trade of almost all ivory items. Trade in plants leads to the importation of plant disease.[56] If imported species become too well established, this can lead to the disappearance of native species and the destruction of native ecosystems.

Inflation

It is one of the first responsibilities of government to maintain the value of the currency. In 1997 the UK government handed this responsibility over to the Bank of England. It can be argued that a low rate of inflation is preferable to zero inflation (the UK target is 2 per cent), but high inflation has harmful consequences:

- It destroys the value of people's savings, discouraging saving and hurting people who have saved for retirement.
- It causes interest rates to be raised, hurting those with domestic loans, mortgages or business loans.
- It generally destroys confidence, in consumers and businesses.
- It leads to rising unemployment: during the period from 1970 to 1997, each period of high inflation was followed, a year or two later, by rising unemployment; low inflation was followed by falling unemployment.[57] This may be because the uncertainty caused by high inflation can lead to unrealistic pay bargaining and higher pay settlements than can be afforded – and 'one man's pay rise may be another man's job'.[58]

A sound currency breeds confidence. For that reason alone, people are more likely to care about the environment and to take the long view if inflation is low.

The green economy

The aim, as argued by Kate Raworth in *Doughnut Economics*, should be for a level of economic activity that is strong enough to keep everyone out of poverty and deprivation but restrained enough to avoid critical planetary degradation.[59] It is not just about the size of the economy, though. What matters is its environmental impact.

Not so long ago, it was believed that a business could be profitable or sustainable, but not both. This myth still lingers on, despite our greater awareness of the harm done by unsustainable practices and the strong business case that can be presented for sustainability.[60]

China is the largest country in the world by population and it is likely soon to have the largest economy, so it is worth noting the direction in which it is heading. President Xi's goals include: 'shift the economy from manufacturing to services; shift from external to domestic demand; shift from a state-controlled to a market-based financial system; crack down on corruption'.[61]

The service economy – the experience economy – the sharing economy – the circular economy – leisure – health – education – information – communication: all these will continue to grow. These activities mostly have low environmental impact, and robotics and IT can be applied to reducing the impact still further. New technologies can also help to reduce the impact of the more environmentally damaging activities: agriculture, manufacturing, construction, energy generation and transport. Goods can be made to last, and the sharing economy can ensure that they can be enjoyed throughout their long life.

Notes

1. Speech, April 2009
2. Schwab, Klaus, 2017, *The Fourth Industrial Revolution*, Portfolio Penguin
3. Coyle, Diane, 2011, *The Economics of Enough: How to Run the Economy as if the Future Matters*, Princeton University Press
4. Coyle, Diane, 1997, *The Weightless World: Strategies for Managing the Digital Economy*, Capstone
5. Eg Layard, Richard, 2008, *Happiness: lessons from a new science*, Penguin; Haslam, Henry, 1985, Employment and unemployment, *Economic Research Council Occasional Paper* No. 43; Haslam, Henry, Unemployment – the irony the critics don't see, *Crossbow*, Summer 1985, 18–19; Tudge, Colin, 2013, *Why Genes are not Selfish and People are Nice*, Floris Books, 120
6. Reich, Robert, 2015, *Saving Capitalism: For the Many, Not the Few*, Knopf Publishing Group; see also Raworth, Kate, 2017, *Doughnut Economics*, Random House

7. Diamond, Jared, 2005, *Collapse*, Viking Press
8. *The Times*, 17 October 2009, Saturday Interview
9. Mayall, Roy, 2009, *Dear Granny Smith: A Letter from Your Postman*, Short Books. In Japan, too, with their respect for the elderly, 'posties are expected to keep an eye on the frail' – Alice Thomson, *The Times*, 30 August 2017
10. Eg Coyle, 2011, 228; Scruton, Roger, 2012, *Green Philosophy*, Atlantic Books, 382; Helm, Dieter, 2015, *Natural Capital: Valuing the Planet*, Yale, 160–164
11. Quoted by McGarvey, Robert, Things economists can't tell us and why, *Britain and Overseas*, Vol 40 no 2, Summer 2010
12. Kalestky, Anatole, *The Times*, 29 September 2010
13. Ormerod, Paul, 1994, *The Death of Economics*, Faber & Faber
14. Galbraith, J K, 1958, *The Affluent Society*, Hamish Hamilton
15. Kahneman, Daniel, 2012, *Thinking, Fast and Slow*, Penguin, 269
16. Tversky, Amos and Kahneman, Daniel, 1974, Judgment under uncertainty: heuristics and biases, *Science*, Vol 185, reproduced in Kahneman, 2012
17. *The Times*, 9 December 2008
18. Sen, Amartya, 1987, *On Ethics and Economics*, Blackwell
19. Layard, 2008, 141
20. Sen, 1987
21. *Prospect*, October 2012
22. Costa, Ken, *Financial Times*, October 2011
23. Quoted in Flannery, Tim, 2011, *Here on Earth*, Allen Lane, 217
24. Matthews, Dan, *Raconteur*, *The Times*, 29 November 2017
25. Written in 1930, and published in Keynes, John Maynard, 1963, *Essays in Persuasion*, W W Norton & Co, 358–373
26. *The Times*, 12 August 2017
27. Coyle, 2011; see also Goldsmith, Zac, 2009, *The Constant Economy*, Atlantic Books, 24; Scruton, 2012, 379; Jackson, Tim, 2009, *Prosperity without Growth*, Earthscan, 179–180; Gus O'Donnell in *The Times*, 1 November 2012 – and he quotes David Cameron
28. Eg Jackson, Tim, 2009, *Prosperity without Growth*, Earthscan
29. Quoting Sandel, Michael, 'The Public Philosopher', BBC Radio 4, 7 March 2017
30. Economic Research Council Chart of the Week, 30 March 2017
31. Tudge, Colin, 2016, *Six Steps Back to the Land*, Green Books
32. Levitt, Steven D and Dubner, Stephen J, 2005, *Freakonomics*, Allen Lane
33. Eg de Waal, Frans, 1982, *Chimpanzee Politics*, Harper & Row; Goodall, Jane, 1990, *Through a Window*, George Weidenfeld & Nicholson; Sapolski, Robert M, 2002, *A Primate's Memoir*, Vintage
34. de Waal, 1982, 211
35. Tudge, 2013, 120
36. Coyle, 2011, 5
37. Eg Wilkinson, Richard and Pickett, Kate, 2009, *The Spirit Level: Why Equality is better for everyone*, Allen Lane
38. Eg www.un.org/esa/desa/papers/2015/wp145_2015.pdf
39. Sen, Amartya, 1999, *Development as Freedom*, OUP paperback, 2001

213

40. Knight, Barry, 2017, *Rethinking Poverty: What makes a good society?*, Policy Press, 94

41. Bird, John, *The Big Issue*, 18–24 September 2017

42. Matthew Parris (*The Times*, 20 Jan 2018) is not alone in pointing out that deprived areas become still further impoverished if people with get-up-and-go have got up and gone

43. Knight, 2017, 124

44. Neicho, Josh, *Raconteur, The Times*, 29 November 2017

45. *The Times*, 27 April 2016

46. Atkinson, Anthony, 2015, *Inequality: What can be Done?* Harvard University Press, 113

47. Merkel, Angela, quoted in *Financial Times*, 16 December 2012

48. Boyle, David, 2008, We have been here before, in Simms, Andrew and Smith, Joe (editors), *Do Good Lives Have to Cost the Earth?*, Constable, 36,37

49. Aldrick, Philip, *The Times*, 18 March 2017

50. Coyle, 2011, 200

51. Coyle, Diane, Doing Less with More, *Prospect*, December 2017, 26–28

52. Ferguson, Niall, *Sunday Times*, 6 September 2015

53. Conway, Ed, *The Times*, 17 November 2017

54. Baldwin, Richard, 2016, *The Great Convergence*, Harvard University Press

55. Mitchell, Andrew, *The Times*, 25 January 2013

56. Eg Aslet, Clive, *The Times*, 24 October, 2016

57. Haslam, Henry, Inflation and unemployment, *Britain & Overseas*, Winter 1991, 29–30; Haslam, Henry, Inflation and unemployment, *Britain & Overseas*, Summer 1999, 21

58. Prior, James, *Hansard*, 18 July 1974

59. Raworth, 2017

60. Whelan, Tensie and Fink, Carly, The Comprehensive Business case for Sustainability, *Harvard Business Review*, October 21, 2016

61. Ferguson, Niall, *Sunday Times*, 6 September 2015

Epilogue

Man is a rational animal – so at least I have been told. Throughout a long life, I have looked diligently for evidence in favour of this statement, but so far I have not had the good fortune to come across it, though I have searched in many countries spread over three continents. On the contrary, I have seen the world plunging continually further into madness. I have seen great nations, formerly leaders of civilisation, led astray by preachers of bombastic nonsense.

Bertrand Russell[1]

The purpose of this book was twofold: to understand how our recent lifestyles have been damaging our planet, and to understand how we can change. We have seen that many changes are indeed taking place.

There is another theme that emerges from the foregoing chapters: the poor quality of thinking in the public arena throughout much of the twentieth century.

In chapter 1, we saw what risks we have been taking with our planet. The concepts of Health and Safety and of risk assessment pervade many areas of modern life and our business relationships with each other are constrained by acres of small print, but we have been conducting a gigantic experiment with the health of our planet with very little thought, understanding or concern about the risks involved.

In chapter 2, we looked at the difficulties standing in the way of serious debate about serious issues. We looked at the role of the media, with their preference for controversy rather than agreement, for presenting an even balance rather than discriminating intelligently between good sense and nonsense, for reporting human error rather than competence, and for scare, sensation, disaster and tragedy rather than plodding on OK. We saw that scientists who wished to have some public impact were influenced by the media in the way that they communicated with the public. We saw that, even in serious matters, protagonists are inclined to concentrate on point scoring rather than seeking a deeper understanding of issues of public concern.

In chapter 3, we saw how consumerism – which promises so much but fails to deliver what it has promised – was promoted by mistaken economic and psychological ideas.

In chapter 4, we saw that during the period when the world's population was growing at its fastest rate (it more than doubled from 3 billion in 1960 to 7 billion in 2011) there was a taboo against talking about – and addressing – the problem of population growth.

In chapter 6 we saw how it became fashionable to denigrate the idea of moral thinking – failing to recognise its potential as a powerful tool in the human character.

In chapter 7 we saw how a deep respect for nature pervades religious teaching and human spirituality – but in the twentieth century this was replaced by unthinking and uncaring emphasis on wealth at all costs. Humility was replaced by the desire for mastery: both Christendom and its atheistic offshoot were seduced by the belief that humans had the power to control the Earth.

In chapter 11, I suggested that progress in caring for the environment might have been held back by cynicism pervading the democratic system as we know it: politicians believing that voters are only interested in their own pockets, neither the electorate nor their leaders daring to challenge this orthodoxy.

In chapter 14 we saw how economics departed from its roots as a study of human behaviour and ethics, to embrace a mechanistic view of human behaviour and promote the concept of the economic man, a seriously distorted image of human nature.

Perhaps we should not be surprised at this failure of thinking. It is what we might expect of an organ, the human brain, which, as suggested in chapter 5, looks like work in progress, a long way from reaching its full potential. I started this epilogue with a quotation from Bertrand Russell's essay, 'An Outline of Intellectual Rubbish'. He goes on to say that when he studied the past he 'found, as Erasmus had found, that folly is perennial'.

Some of these misguided ideas represent a denial of what it is to be human, a denial of human potential. It became smart to be cynical about human nature. Monetary values became a substitute for human values.

However, we also saw in chapter 5 evidence that human thinking is capable of improvement and in chapter 8 we noted the huge capacity that humans have for change and adaptation. We further saw in the last part of chapter 7 that the environmental movement has not been lacking in visionary thinkers. Particularly interesting, though, is the evidence in Part 3 of new ideas from different quarters. Chapter 10 showed ordinary people, for a variety of reasons, choosing to live in greater harmony with nature. Chapters 12 and 13 showed that inventors, entrepreneurs and thinkers are producing ideas to reduce the environmental impact of food production, energy generation, transport and manufacturing. There is reason to hope that we shall put nature and the natural environment high on our list of priorities before it is too late.

Our world needs not just our goodwill but clarity of thinking. Humans have amazing potential. We have four key attributes that can help us as we seek the way ahead: adaptability (how to survive in changing circumstances), morality (urging us to understand what is right and to seek to do it), intelligence (enabling us to work it out) and self-control (the willpower to carry it through). Can these help us to overcome the thoughtlessness, laziness and ill-informed self-indulgent destructiveness that have led us to where we are now? We can choose how to think, and the way we think can influence the way we behave.

Note

1. Russell, Bertrand, 1950, An Outline of Intellectual Rubbish' in *Unpopular Essays*, George Allen & Unwin

Index